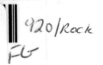

LEABHARLANNA CHONTAE FHINE GALL
FINGAL COUNTY LIBRARIES

Garristown Library
Ph: 8355020

Items should be returned on or before the last date shown below. Items may be renewed by personal application, writing, telephone or by accessing the online Catalogue Service on Fingal Libraries' website. To renew give date due, borrower ticket number and PIN number if using online catalogue. Fines are charged on overdue items and will include postage incurred in recovery. Damage to, or loss of items will be charged to the borrower.

Date Due	Date Due	Date Due
11 MAR 10.		
11. MAR 10		

Always Me

Tony McCullagh is a Dublin based journalist and author. He co-wrote the Number 1 Bestseller, 'They Never Came Home – the Stardust Story', which was later adapted for the IFTA award winning RTÉ drama, 'Stardust'. In 2003 he co-authored 'Danger to Society – Elaine Moore's Story', a true account of how a former Irish model was accused of serious terrorism offences in the UK and had to cope with life in prison before the charges against her were dropped. This is Tony's third book with Merlin Publishing.

Always Me

Dickie Rock

MERLIN
PUBLISHING

First published in 2007 by
Merlin Publishing
Newmarket Hall, St Luke's Avenue,
Cork Street, Dublin 8, Ireland
Tel: +353 1 4535866
Fax: +353 1 4535930
publishing@merlin.ie
www.merlinwolfhound.com

13-Digit ISBN 978-1-903582-74-9

A CIP catalogue record for this book is available from the British Library.

10 9 8 7 6 5 4 3 2 1

Typeset by Gough Typesetting
Cover Design by Graham Thew Design
Printed and bound by WS Bookwell Ltd, Finland

To Judy and my children — Joseph, Jason, John, Richard, Sarah and Peter. Also to my adorable grandson, Benjamin.

Acknowledgements

Writing this book has allowed me to reflect on the people who matter most to me. I would like to acknowledge the love and support I have received from all my friends down through the years. Within the entertainment business, I have enjoyed the friendships and support of great people including Larry Gogan, Tommy Carey and Billy Hughes, an old neighbour of mine from Cabra West. Another great friend of my family is Dale King, the man I credit with being the first to introduce cabaret to Dublin – and possibly Ireland. Dale used to run great shows out in the Drake Inn in Finglas and I have many great memories of playing there. Lynne Hamilton is a great fan of mine in the North and I'm very grateful that she keeps me informed about everything that is going on up there. In Spain, I would like to pay tribute to Pearce Webb, who works at the Sunset Beach resort and has invited me to get up and perform a few songs there over the years. And in keeping with all things Spanish, a special thanks also to the Podge and J B Burkes in Fuengirola.

Outside the world of showbusiness, we have enjoyed many valued friendships, with great people like Sam Campbell and his wife, Maeve, from Rathgar. Also my cousin Michael Rock and his wife Eileen Rock have been great friends to us for years. Similarly, I would like to mention another lovely couple, Margaret and Tony Robinson, from Donnybrook. These are all wonderful people who have helped us at different stages of our life.

To Judy and the children – Joseph, Jason, John, Richard, Sarah and Peter – my heartfelt thanks for all your love and support over the years.

I would like to thank everyone at Merlin Publishing for giving me the opportunity to tell my story, particularly managing director Chenile Keogh and editorial director Aoife Barrett. Thanks to Kieran

Kelly for his legal advice. To Tony McCullagh for helping me put it all into words and to his wife Kathryn, for the loan of her husband. A word of thanks also to Rosaleen Rogers of Aideen's Secretarial Services for her efficiency.

I've had the great privilege of working with some top class musicians over the years and I would like to pay tribute to their talent and professionalism. To my showbusiness contemporaries, you have my ongoing respect and admiration. I am grateful to those in the broadcast and print media who supported me in the past and have treated me fairly through good and bad times.

I also want to thank Tom Moran from Morans Hotel for being so kind to Judy and I when she was incapacitated after an operation and for putting us up in his hotel for five weeks.

A special word of thanks to my manager Jackie Johnston and to everyone who has managed me since my career began.

I would also like to recognise and pay tribute to the friendships I've made but later lost through misunderstandings on both sides. Sadly, these things sometimes happen in life but I would like to say I regret all of that.

As well as telling my life story, this book is intended as a tribute to the many people who supported me throughout my career and helped make me who I am today. Even if I have inadvertently neglected to mention you by name – you all know who you are.

Dickie Rock,
2007

Contents

Prologue

December 1965

The 'full house' signs have been up for hours. It still hasn't deterred the few hundred or so diehard fans waiting outside in the rain. Earlier, the queue had snaked around the entire perimeter of the grim-looking building. Our wagon pulls up outside and the tranquillity of the evening is instantly shattered. There is chaos as the crowd surrounds the bus, with eager young faces pressed flat against the windows. I can actually feel it start to shake.

"Looks like we're going nowhere for a while yet, lads," says Brendan, our driver.

I glance over at the others and they're loving every minute of the siege. They're well used to it by now. This sort of thing happens all the time. There's Murty, Clem, Dennis, Martin, Tommy, Tony and Joe. They're all just ordinary guys who, like me, could well have ended up in ordinary jobs. But when you put us all together as The Miami Showband something extraordinary happens. We take to the stage and there's an instant chemistry, a musical alchemy that has a strange effect on people – particularly the girls! They scream, they faint, they cry and – most importantly – they laugh.

We kick off with an Elvis number to get the crowd going – not that they need much coaxing to take to the dance floor. There's hardly room to stand down there, let alone dance. The young girls packed tightly up against the stage have no interest in dancing. They stare at us, transfixed, with arms outstretched.

As lead singer I seem to be the centre of attention but not all eyes are on me. There are a few heartbreakers in this band. Martin, our sax player, is a big hit with the ladies. So is Tony, although he's usually obscured by his drum kit. They're good-looking blokes, all right. Can't understand what the women see in me, though. Not that I'm complaining.

There's mild panic as the crowd surges forward, overwhelming those closest to the stage. "I can't breathe, I can't breathe!" a teenage girl screams.

From what I can see she's not in any real danger but she's dramatically plucked from the scene within seconds. Those first aid boys are going to be busy, for sure.

There will be plenty of Rock 'n' Roll here tonight. That's the type of music that got me into the business in the first place. There'll be romance, too. We set the mood with 'There's Always Me', one of our best loved ballads and our first hit record. We'd a Number One hit with it for six weeks the year before. Even The Beatles couldn't dislodge it from the top spot. We follow it with another slow number, 'From the Candy Store on the Corner' and then, of course, one from the master himself, Frank Sinatra.

The dance floor is filled with young couples. Some have met here before and are now officially an 'item'. It could lead to something, you know. It's hard to believe it all starts with one simple line: "Are ye dancin'?"

Not every request is met. "Sorry, I'm too tired – ask me friend" is an all-too familiar response from the ladies. Some rejections are even blunter: "Will ye get away from me, I'm trying to listen to Dickie."

I wouldn't say I'm too popular with the boyfriends.

Outside the ballroom, the rain is turning to sleet but it feels like a furnace in here. The smell of sweat competes with the aroma of sweet perfume and tobacco. The mineral bar is doing a roaring trade tonight. I wave up to those lucky enough to get up to the balcony – the best seats in the house.

It's non-stop work on stage. We'll be up here for over three hours but the minutes seem like seconds. Before we know it, it's all over.

We're completely drenched in sweat as we try to make our way back to the wagon. We're mobbed as soon as the stage door opens. There are numerous requests for autographs. One girl tells me I looked great on Telefís Éireann's *Showband Show* last week. "My mother loves you as well," she adds.

It will be another few hours before we load our gear into the wagon and hit the road for Dublin. We'll do it all again tomorrow night. We're in the Seapoint Ballroom in Galway, I think. Or is it Jetland in Limerick? It's hard to keep track these days. Before the year is out, we'll have played in front of 500,000 people. They just can't seem to get enough of us.

As the saying goes: "There's No Date Like A Miami Date."

ONE

The Cabra Choirboy

Towards the end of my father's life – I think he would have been 81 years old at the time – I sat down to write him a letter. I'm sure he knew that I loved him but I wanted him to know how I *really* felt about him. I wrote that people probably considered me to be a success because of the hit records, the packed out concerts, the television appearances and all of that. But I told my father that he was a complete success – and he had the kind of success that mattered most. I had done well from all the singing and had earned a few bob all right but here was an ordinary guy from Dublin who had succeeded as a man, succeeded as a husband and succeeded as a father. I ended the letter with the line:

> 'Dad, I don't think I have ever told you this, but at the end of my days and when I'm your age, if I could have the respect and the love of my children that you have had from your children and your wife, only then will I say that I am a success.'

I still feel that way today. All the fame and fortune derived from almost 50 years in the music business means nothing if you are not deemed to have been a good father by your children. It remains my overriding ambition in life. My father later asked me why I had written the letter. I replied that there are some things that can't be expressed verbally and I wanted him to know how I felt.

Perhaps that's why I'm writing this book now. Much has been written about me and my family over the years – some of it positive, some of it inaccurate, some of it hurtful. Now, in my own words, I would like to take this opportunity to debunk the myths, while sharing some of my precious, most intimate memories with you. I have experienced some extreme highs and some unbearable lows over the years but have been able to count on the support of my family and friends throughout it all.

* * * *

My story begins in the working-class Northside suburb of Cabra West in Dublin. I was the eldest child of Joseph and Julia Rock, born in Dublin's Rotunda Hospital. I won't reveal what year I was born – I think it's better to have a certain mystique about your age. RTÉ's Ronan Collins recently wished me a happy birthday on his radio show and people were ringing in to find out how old I was. Ronan knows well how old I am as he used to play the drums in my band and we go back a long way. But I see my age as one of the secrets of my trade and was glad that Ronan didn't spill the beans on me. When I tell you, however, that I'm now in my fifth decade as a performer, you can draw your own conclusions.

Some people you talk to will romanticise about having a happy childhood but I genuinely remember it that way. Number 66 Dingle Road, an old Dublin Corporation house, is where it all happened for me and my two brothers and two sisters. After me there was Lillian, followed by Margery, Brian and Joseph.

Growing up, I was probably closest to Brian. I was around eight-years-old when he was born. I distinctly remember the day when my mother went into the hospital to have him. My aunt was in the house at the time and my mother suddenly went into labour. We had no car back then and she had to get the bus into town to have the baby. I have very vivid memories of her leaving the house that day.

Life was particularly tough for working-class Dublin women back in those days, although my mother was one of the lucky ones in that she had married a man who was a complete husband to her in every way. My father was a real ordinary Dubliner and had been reared in Donnycarney. For him nothing existed other than his family. We were the most important things in his life. And because there was so much love in my father's heart, it made life so much easier for my mother.

It also helped that my father had a good trade – he was a blacksmith with the Board of Works. He was also an amateur boxer and had represented Ireland in competitions, fighting in prestigious venues such as the National Stadium in Dublin and the Ulster Hall in Belfast. By all accounts, my father was something of a wild child when he was growing up and was always getting into harmless fights – certainly nothing like the vicious carry-on you see these days. He had a reputation for being well able to handle himself and was known locally in Donnycarney as "King of the Kids". From what I've been told by my relatives, my grandparents were a bit concerned about all the trouble my father was getting into and they made him join a boxing club so he could channel his energies in a more positive way. He became a member of St Andrew's Boxing Club on York Street and used to cycle across to the south side of the city a number of times a week to train.

Boxing quickly became my father's number one passion in life and he was soon marked out as a rising star by the club's trainers. Needless to say, it was a tremendous source of pride to have an Irish amateur featherweight champion in the family. Even though my father was an accomplished boxer, he was not a violent man in any way. Boxing seemed to give him a strong sense of discipline and succeeded in taming his wild ways. Of course, he would have been well able to look after himself if and when the need arose but he never went looking for trouble.

My memories my father are just wonderful. We used to walk everywhere together and he was incredibly generous with his time. He'd bring me to the Phoenix Park where we'd spend hours collecting chestnuts. He'd regularly take me to watch the football matches in Dalymount or Tolka Park. They'd let young kids in for nothing back then and my father would lift me over the turnstiles when we'd arrive at the football grounds. He was still doing it when I was around 14-years-old, although by then the match officials would be challenging him about my age.

"Will ye get out of that, sure he's only a child," my Dad would snap back at them in a typical Dublin way, as he ushered me through the entrance.

My father came from a family of steel-working tradesmen and most of them would have been employed as welders, fitters and riveters down in the Liffey dockyard. There were six children in the family, three boys and three girls. The Rock bloodline can be traced back to Germany. My great-grandfather was German and first came to Ireland when he was 19. He was living in digs on Henrietta Street in Dublin's north inner-city when he met my great-grandmother. After they fell in love and got married, my great-grandfather decided to settle in Dublin, where he worked as a clockmaker.

I was named Richard after my grandfather on my father's side. I have stronger memories of my father's family than my mother's. My Uncle Victor, who died only a few years ago at the age of 73, would later become a great fan of mine. He was actually a very good singer in his own right. My success in later life was a great source of pride to my father's family. I was very close to my grandfather and grandmother. As a young child I used to visit them regularly. My Dad would put me on the crossbar of his bike and cycle over from Cabra to their house in Donnycarney. I was the first grandchild so naturally my father's family would always make a big fuss of me. My grandmother used to sit on her chair in the corner of the room and beckon me over to her with her finger. Then she'd take me by the hand, lead me into the kitchen and give me sixpence. She'd always put her finger up to her lips and say "sssshhh", as if it was a big secret between us.

I loved visiting my grandparents and cherished all the time I got to spend with them. It was great that they were alive to see me become famous. When I started to have some success I used to pick my grandfather up in the Rolls Royce I had bought and drive him around in it – he used to love that. He'd sit in the front passenger seat with a big smile on his face, joking about being chauffeured around in style. "Did you ever think we'd see the likes of this?" he'd always say to me.

I used to bring my father around in the Rolls as well, which must have seemed a world away from his working-class upbringing. Even though he was proud of my success, he had always advised me to have a trade to fall back on. I'm sure he sometimes worried about my future because of the fickle nature of the entertainment business. My father was a very unsophisticated man but I mean that in the best possible way. Unlike a lot of men, he wasn't a big drinker and he only smoked five cigarettes a day. He'd meet his brothers for a pint in Hanlon's Corner on the North Circular Road every Saturday evening. They really got on great and there was always a real closeness in the Rock family.

I only have vague memories of my grandmother on my Ma's side.

My mother came from a more fragmented family. Her two brothers went off to work in England when they were just 16 or 17 and my mother stayed in Dublin. Her father had died soon after fighting in the First World War – he was only around 27-years-old at the time. I believe his death was as a result of something that happened to him during the war. My mother was only five at the time and would have been considered semi-orphaned. She spent a few years being looked after by the nuns in the Poor Clares' in Harold's Cross. This resulted in her getting a better education than my father did and she would have progressed a little bit further than him academically.

She was around 19 when she met my father. Looking back at old photographs, they made an extremely good-looking couple. There was a strong attraction between them, even though she thought he was a little bit rough when she met him first. At one stage, however, the relationship looked doomed to failure. My mother was having some sort of trouble at home – I was never privy to the full details of what happened – and things weren't going well for her. By that stage her own mother had met somebody else. Whatever happened, the situation at home deteriorated to such an extent that my mother decided to go to England and stay with relatives. My poor father knew nothing about this as he waited for her on O'Connell Bridge for a date that night. My mother never showed up. Instead, she sent a friend to break the news to him that she had taken the boat to Liverpool. The friend also wanted to hand him back the joint savings book that my parents had held together. My father would later tell me that my mother had left him standing on a bridge. All he had by way of explanation was a short note from her.

My father went back to Donnycarney that night, heartbroken – he would have been only 21 at the time. When she saw his gloomy face his mother immediately knew that something was wrong. He explained that Julia had left him for a new life in England because of difficulties at home.

"How do you feel about her – do you love her?" his mother asked.

"Yes, I love her. I'm mad about her," my father responded.

"In that case," she said, "you get yourself on that boat to Liverpool tomorrow night and go after her – you don't get second chances in life."

And that's exactly what he did. After hastily arranging to take a couple of days off work, my father packed an overnight bag and made his way to the docks. He must have felt mixed emotions as he boarded the mailboat. I'm sure he felt nervous about the type of reaction he would get from my mother but he had resolved that he wouldn't return to Dublin without her.

He arrived in Liverpool at around six in the morning and went straight to the house where my mother was staying with her cousins. One of them answered the door and my father asked if Julia was there. Of course they wanted to know who this strange young man was and, as my mother came down the stairs, she heard my father say: "I'm Joe Rock."

She couldn't believe it when she saw him standing there.

"Joe, what are you doing here?" she gasped.

My father got straight to the point and asked her if she loved him. When she replied that she did, he told her he would be bringing her back home to Dublin that night.

"I'm here for you because I love you too – now get your coat," he said decisively.

My mother was stunned by the lengths he had gone to find her and went back inside in a daze. She thanked her relatives for their hospitality but told them there had been a change of plan. She would be catching the next boat back to Dublin with Joe and needed to get packed in a hurry.

After saying her goodbyes to her cousins, she took my father by the hand and they made their way to Liverpool port. I imagine that they must have been talking excitedly about their future together as the ferry set sail for Dublin.

They got married pretty soon after that. I mean this was a case of a girl breaking up with a fella and leaving him to go and live in another country. For my father to go over after her and lay his feelings on the line was a big thing for a man to do. Any woman would have realised that this was a man, not only telling her that he loved her, but showing her that he did too. It was an incredibly beautiful thing to do.

My father was a very romantic man and was completely devoted to my mother. He'd say to me regularly: "Richard, your mother is a wonderful woman." After cycling home from work, he'd open the door and say "Hi sweetheart" to my mother – that's what he always called her.

He'd go straight to the sink and wash his hands and as soon as he was finished he'd turn around and his dinner would be put on the table. That probably goes against the modern way of thinking today but that's how it was back then. He was the worker, going out each day and bringing home the bacon; she was there for him at home, as a wife and as a mother. He used to tell me that my mother was far more important than him. He just had to earn the few bob. My mother, on the other hand, had to look after the home, bring me to school, be there for me when I came home and take care of me if I was sick. She was a constant presence throughout my childhood. I remember one time getting a cyst on my chin and having to go into the Mater Hospital to have it removed. After the operation I woke up to find her sitting there, holding my hand. She leaned over and gave me a kiss on the cheek. It was a simple gesture but I was struck by the amount of affection I felt from it.

My father had a lot of respect for the role of the mother in the home, which was probably unique for men in Ireland at that time. His attitude towards my mother had a major influence on me. Seeing my mother and father so much in love gave me a strong sense of security as a child. That's not to say that there wasn't any discipline in the house. My father would give me the occasional wallop – but nothing more serious than that – when it was called for. I remember hiding under the bed as he took swipes at me with his belt. My mother never laid a finger on me, although she'd often threaten to tell my father on me when I did something that annoyed her.

My parents hardly ever exchanged a cross word. I only remember one occasion when they had an argument and it sticks in my mind only because it was such a rare occurrence. It was only a mild row but it upset me deeply because I had never witnessed it happening before – or since. I must have been only around six or seven at the time. I started crying and my mother said to my father: "Now look, you've got little Richard all upset." They were sitting at the table and I went up and put my arms around both of them, probably in an attempt to stop them fighting. Then my mother got very emotional.

I never heard them argue ever again.

My parents' love and devotion for each other continued for the remainder of their lives. There's one particular memory that springs to mind when we were all over in Spain to celebrate my father's 70th birthday. He was sitting beside my mother in a restaurant at the top of the table and I was reminded of the words of that song that goes "the look of love is in your eyes …". The conversation was flowing and everyone was having a great time but my father seemed detached from all the banter and was just staring over at my mother. Then he reached over and touched her hair.

"There's a bit of grey there, love," he gently teased her.

"Sure what do you expect, Josey?" she quipped back at him. "I'm 70 years of age."

But that was the whole point. He didn't see her as a 70-year-old woman – he still saw her as the beautiful young woman he fell in love with all those years earlier. It was a lovely thing to witness – that look of love. After all that time together, he still adored her; he was still besotted. I think my parents' rock solid marriage brought out the romantic side of me in later life. I love soppy films on television and in the movies with happy endings, although I know well that not everything in life goes like that.

While my father was emotional when it came to my mother he was also a very practical man. As soon as he got married he gave up the boxing. He was aware of the responsibilities that marriage brought with it and wasn't willing to take any chances. Then, when I was around six, he was asked to make a comeback in the ring. He hadn't boxed since before I was born and hadn't trained or anything. The bout was to be held in the National Stadium and my father was asked to stand in at short notice because the organisers of the match were stuck for a fighter. At first he was reluctant but after much persuading he caved in to the pressure and agreed to fight, for that one occasion only.

All his friends and family went along to the fight to cheer him on but my mother stayed at home. I'm not sure how she felt about my father's return to the ring but I suspect that she wasn't too pleased about it. I remember staying awake until he got home that night, dying to find out if he'd won.

"I was beaten, son," he told me, as he knelt by my bed. "But sure I expected it – I wasn't fit enough."

And that was the end of my father's fighting days. It's incredible to think that he was past his prime as a boxer, even though he would only have been around 29 at the time. It never bothered him, though – all that really mattered to him were his wife and children.

There's one particular memory I have of him that sums up his devotion as a father. Back in those days there was no such thing as central heating in places like Cabra West. An open fire in the living room was as good as it got. Every night, my father used to go upstairs and lie on each of our beds for 10 minutes or so to heat them up for us. My mother would say: "You'd better go to bed now, your father's upstairs." As soon as we'd enter the room my father would get up off the body-warmed bed. It was a lovely thing to do.

We wouldn't have been well-off financially by any means. My father was certainly a good provider but he was the only earner in the house. He had to look after five kids and his wages were eaten up by rent, medication, hospital bills and food – all the basics in life. There were seven of us living in a modest three-bedroomed house, with a living room and a separate kitchen. We were lucky because some of the smaller parlour houses in places like Cabra only had two bedrooms. There was a family of 15 living in one of these houses not far from us. We were well off compared to them but they were well off compared to people who had as many children and were living in single rooms in Dublin's tenements. Life for many working-class families in places like Cabra West was certainly a step up from the tenements but was still tough by today's standards.

Can you imagine what it must have been like for those poor mothers? Unless they were married to someone decent like my father, they had a terrible life raising all those children on their own. Many of them had to cope while their husbands drank all the money. I'm not saying all the men were like that, but some of them certainly would have been. On top of all that, there was no contraception allowed or anything back then. And these women were having up to 15 children – it doesn't bear thinking about. They simply had no life.

I'm sure money was often tight for my parents but I don't remember any poverty when we were growing up. I always say that my mother and father made me the person I am today. While my father would have been the one to take me places, I credit my mother with giving me a love of music. One of my earliest memories is of her singing 'Only God Can Make a Tree', which was her party piece at family get-togethers. From the moment I started school she tried to get me to learn a musical instrument. She didn't play one herself but she had a beautiful voice and would have received a bit of training from the nuns. First she tried to get me to learn the piano but I just couldn't stick it. Then she bought me a clarinet on George's Street. It must have been a lot of money to spend at the time because she had to pay for it by the week. When that failed, she encouraged me to join the choir in the Church of the Precious Blood in Cabra. She used to say to me: "Make sure to open your mouth wide when you sing to get everything out."

My mother also taught me to be proud of my working-class background and I think this is something that has stood me in good stead. Some people will say that Dubliners will never let you forget where you came from, no matter how successful you become. But I don't think it's just a Dublin thing. I know a lot of country guys who would have started out as carpenters, bricklayers, firemen – whatever – and they became extremely wealthy builders. But to this day they still have a down-to-earth, working-class way about them. I still consider myself to be working-class because it's the background I come from. Maybe it's that working-class people recognise the value of what they have because they didn't have much starting out. On the other side of the coin you have the comfortably rich. They're the type who let the wealth go to their heads and are inclined to forget where they came from. At the end of the day it's all down to your upbringing. I believe that if you are taught basic values by your parents such as honesty, hard work and respect for others, then you have an automatic head start in life.

My mother and father certainly gave me that. I definitely learned more about life from them than I ever would at school. I was soon to discover that I wasn't really cut out for formal education.

Two

Heartbreak Hotel

I don't have good memories of school, to be honest. I went to the Dominican Convent in Cabra West first and I was only there for a couple of years. I used to hold my mother's hand as she walked me to school each day. It must have been a mile and a half walk for her, there and back to Dingle Road, but it didn't seem to bother her, even during the harsh winter months when we'd get soaked to our skins. I can't remember what we used to talk about to pass the time on the journey but we certainly enjoyed each other's company and chatted a lot.

From there I went to primary school in St Finbar's in Cabra. I was glad my mother had got me to join the choir around this time as it took my mind off school, which I didn't enjoy at all. I don't have any recollections of cruelty or anything like that but I do remember that conditions at the school were appalling. People might give out about overcrowded classrooms these days but back then there were 60 of us in each class. We had the same teacher for all my school years. We used to call him Hitler because he had this little moustache and it wouldn't have been too long after the Second World War had ended. I can't remember if he was a good teacher or not but I know that I wasn't a great pupil – I was too fidgety and distracted. I'm a little bit like that still. In fairness, it's hard to shine academically when you are in a class with 59 other boys. It was a real case of survival of the fittest. The bright ones got all the attention but anyone who was just average – like me – found school very difficult.

Apart from singing in the choir, sport was another outlet for my frustrations with school life. I used to play hurling for St Finbar's and I loved it. I remember going to the Phoenix Park to play a match, only to be taken off the team at the last minute. I was gutted by the decision and couldn't understand the reason for it. The school coach explained that he couldn't let me on the hurling team because word had got out that I had also been playing soccer with the street leagues. The street leagues were great and we used to play on a big green in Cabra West, with all the different roads competing against each other. The reason I was given for being excluded from the hurling team probably seems harsh by today's standards but not even kids were allowed to play the 'foreign game' in those days and it meant I was automatically banned from GAA sports. Back then, the very notion of soccer or rugby being played at Croke Park would have been unthinkable – how times have changed.

Another vivid memory of my schooldays is the time I was supposed to make my first Holy Communion. I say "supposed to" because it didn't quite turn out as planned. My mother had dressed me in all my finery for the big day and we walked together in the rain up to the convent. By the time we arrived I was thirsty so I took a drink of water out of one of the taps. I looked up to see a deaf mute girl wildly gesturing towards me. These poor people used to live within the convent system and do work for the nuns. I wasn't sure what she was on about, to be honest, and I went down to join my classmates to make my Holy Communion.

Meanwhile in the church, my mother waited with all the parents, expecting me to arrive in with all the other kids. But when everyone walked in there was no sign of me. I had been removed from the line because the deaf mute had informed the nuns that I'd taken a drink of water. You were meant to fast beforehand and even water – the "oil of the body" – wasn't allowed. There used to be a great, big breakfast held after the ceremony and everyone would look forward to that because they'd be starving after all that fasting. My mother wasn't annoyed at me because she knew I had taken the water out of innocence. I had to wait until the following week before I could make my Communion. I didn't mind too much – I got to eat another breakfast the second week, as well.

That incident gives a pretty good indication of what life was like in Catholic Ireland during the 1950s. My mother and father would have been very religious, right up to the time they died. They not only believed in the Catholic Church but in Christianity, too. They never missed an opportunity to go to Mass. I considered my father to be a very holy man, particularly as he advanced in years. He never had a bad word to say about anyone and only saw the good in people. On one occasion I called down to see them and my mother told me that my father had gone to Mass in St Peter's in Phibsboro. By the time I got there the service was over and the church was virtually empty, except for a few people. I saw my father – who would have been about 60 at the time – sitting alone near the altar and I walked quietly towards him. I sat close to him but he didn't see me. I could see that his lips were moving in silent prayer. Then he got up, genuflected, blessed himself and turned to leave. He didn't seem too surprised when he saw me sitting there.

"I saw your mouth moving, what were you saying?" I asked him, as we walked out of the church together.

"Sure I was praying for you all," he replied.

I loved going to Mass as a young boy but for a different reason to my parents. By the age of eight I was known as "Richard Rock, boy soprano", having made a name for myself locally by singing in the school choir. I didn't get a hard time off any of the lads in school for being in a choir. In fact, there was an element of prestige attached to it. I sang every Sunday at Mass and sometimes during the week, too, when it was called for. The Church of the Precious Blood in Cabra was just a tin hut at the time, with a corrugated roof. It was eventually replaced with the fine church that stands there today. Our choir once entered a Feis Cheoil in the Fr Matthew Hall and we won it, which was a fantastic experience. I genuinely don't think that I stood out as a special talent from the other kids. Maybe others thought that but I certainly didn't.

By the time I'd reached my teens my mother had accepted that I was never going to master a musical instrument. I didn't have the patience to learn the guitar or anything – I just wanted to sing. I had started to realise that my voice was going to be my instrument. You can't just go out and pick up an instrument and play it proficiently for the first time – it takes dedicated practice over a prolonged period of time, not to mention talent. But you can either sing or you can't sing – it's as simple as that. Back in pre-RTÉ Ireland, we'd gather together in the evening and listen to the radio. One of the first songs I ever remember hearing was 'The Roving Kind', sung by Guy Mitchell. That song really sticks in my mind.

I used to sing it as a boy soprano and later when I joined a variety group called the Casino Players. They were a wonderful group of people who used to go around hospitals and nursing homes to perform for the sick and elderly. I was only a kid when I joined, probably around 13 years of age, and I loved the whole experience of travelling around with the group and getting to sing to a whole different audience. I still remained with the choir but performing with the Casino Players opened up my eyes and ears to new musical experiences and possibilities.

I was still in the Players when I left Finbar's at the age of 14 and enrolled in the local tech. I was happy to leave school and was looking forward to getting a job and earning a few bob. Tech suited people like me who were not very academic. It offered a taste of the trades such as carpentry and metal work – there was a bit of everything taught there, really. It kind of made sense for me to go in that direction. After all, I came from a background of tradesmen – my father, my uncles, my grandfather all had trades. The sole ambition of working-class people like myself was to get a trade – it was the holy grail, if you like. The thing is people who lived in places like Rathgar or Terenure would have had ambitions to go to senior school and later on to college. They would become part of the professional class of doctors and lawyers. But if you came from a working-class area and your father was a tradesman, that's what you aspired to. The top trade at the time would have been an electrician and it was almost impossible to get into. I personally think that carpentry is probably still one of the best trades you can have. And even by today's standards, if you have a young lad who isn't academic, as a parent you couldn't go wrong by encouraging him to learn a trade. That's certainly the direction my parents pushed me in. I didn't know anything about the Leaving Cert or anything like that – I'd never even heard of it. Our ambition was to go to school, leave school at 14 or 15 and get a trade. It's how we were conditioned.

Of all the trades taught at tech, welding was something I seemed to have a natural aptitude for. The educational environment was not for me, however, and I only stayed in the tech for about a year. I left at the age of 15 and got my first job at Edward's Jewellers on Talbot Street.

The position was advertised in the paper with the promise of "great prospects". I believed at the time that this opportunity could possibly lead to me getting something better than a trade. I even thought that

I could follow in the footsteps of my great-grandfather and become a watchmaker. I remember going for the interview in my short trousers. I was very small for my age, a little, skinny, pale-faced fella. Even though I was a healthy kid, people used to think I was sick because I was so puny looking. Much to my delight I got the job.

The first day was fine and I just had to polish the jewellery and clean the glass cases. But it all went wrong just three days into the job. One of the assistant managers approached me with a mop and ordered me to clean the toilets. I did what I was told and as I mopped, the same manager stood over me and remarked, sarcastically: "Oh, you've great prospects alright." He was obviously referring to the ad in the paper and was probably just poking fun at me but I took it badly. One thing about me – back then and even now – is that I get hurt very easily. I was an extremely sensitive child, naive even. People mightn't realise that about me as I can put a brave face on it sometimes. But that manager – Paddy was his name – had hurt my feelings and I went home from work that evening extremely upset.

I told my mother what had happened and she took the bus into town with me the next day and accompanied me to work. I'll never forget how she gave that poor manager a piece of her mind.

"I'm Julia Rock, Richard's mother," she announced. "You made a very insensitive remark to my son yesterday about him having great prospects while he was cleaning the toilets – it was a stupid thing to say to a young boy."

Paddy was naturally mortified and immediately apologised, trying to explain that it was simply a flippant remark. But my mother made sure he said sorry to me, too. The incident had a lasting impact on me. To this day I try to be sensitive to people's feelings, particularly if I don't know them. I try not to say anything that could ever be seen as hurtful in any way to anybody – be they a friend of mine or a stranger working in a restaurant. I was glad my mother came to work with me that day to defend my dignity. Some lads my age might have felt embarrassed bringing their Ma in to fight their battles but I didn't. Looking back on it, I think this was because I was pretty immature for my age. When I was 15, other lads my age were talking about finding girlfriends and things like that. But I was around two years behind them in that way of thinking. I was a bit of a loner, to be honest. I was always happy in my own company and still am. I was never one to succumb to peer pressure. If a bunch of lads were egging me on to do something with them and I didn't want to, I'd simply go home. Even by 1950s' standards I was a late starter, sexually. People may find this difficult to believe – particularly because of all that's happened to me since – but I didn't even kiss a girl until I was 21. And it wasn't even a proper kiss – it happened during a game of spin the bottle.

I stayed working in the jeweller's for around a year and there were no further incidents with Paddy thanks to my mother's intervention. It's funny, because I still see him around occasionally. In fact, many years later I saw him in the audience at one of my concerts. I looked over at him from the stage and said: "Hiya Paddy, great prospects, eh?"

* * * *

As it turned out, the prospects at Edward's weren't that great after all. By the time I'd worked there for about a year I realised that I was going nowhere. I handed in my notice and immediately found a job down in the Liffey dockyard, where my grandfather and uncles worked. This was my first step towards starting an apprenticeship as a welder and it seemed likely that I was going to become part of the family tradition of getting a trade down in the docks. It was great to have my relatives there and I knew that my uncles, Victor and Dick, would be looking out for me. I remember one day in particular when my grandfather, who was a riveter, was working on a ship that was in dry dock for repairs. I was delighted when he asked me to join him on board during our lunch break and we sat and chatted about work. The time we spent together that day is one of the most precious memories I have of him.

Music was the one constant throughout my teenage years as I tried a few different jobs. Even when my days as a choirboy were well and truly over I was still singing with the Casino Players. Apart from my mother, the first person to see my potential as a singer was a man by the name of Kevin Raythorn. He was a senior member of the Casino Players and I used to think he was really old, although he would only have been in his 20s at the time. I remember him singing 'Walking My Baby Back Home' during the many concerts we gave. Kevin really took an interest in me and was extremely encouraging. I think he must have seen something special in me that I didn't see myself. He played an important role in building my confidence as a singer by telling me how good I was and giving me prominent roles in the group's various productions.

Outside of music, it was a time of great change in my life. I didn't stay working for long at the Liffey dockyard and after a few months I left and got a job with a company called Milners in Santry, who made gates. I had been doing a bit of everything down in the docks but the new job presented me with a fantastic opportunity to concentrate purely on welding. They were great employers, real working-class people who had started up a factory and were doing very well for themselves. I became friendly with a couple of young lads there who were working as welders. They told me they were going over to work for a company in Manchester and asked if I wanted to join them. I was open to the idea as I had relatives over there who I used to visit during the holidays. After discussing it with my parents, I decided to go to England, hoping that the experience would advance my career prospects. I enjoyed my time at Milners but because they only specialised in gates there was only so much I could learn working there. I felt that by moving to a larger company in England, I would improve my welding skills in a shorter space of time. Besides, from what I had heard from the other lads, there was more money to be made in Manchester, even for someone at my level.

My mother and father saw me off at the North Wall where I caught the boat for Liverpool. Being their eldest child, it was only natural that they'd miss me but they didn't get visibly upset as I walked up the gangway. I suppose they were comforted by the fact that I would be staying with one of my mother's brothers and only planned to be away for one year. Even though I was extremely close to my parents, I didn't cry as I hugged them goodbye and boarded the boat. I considered the whole thing one big adventure.

When we arrived in the UK, I took the train to Manchester where I was met by my relatives. Even though I was living with my uncle and aunt and my three cousins, I was extremely homesick from the beginning. I got a job in the same factory as the lads I had worked with in Santry but it didn't seem to make life any easier. There was nothing bleaker than Manchester on a miserable winter's morning and it was a lot for an innocent 16-year-old like myself to take.

Every morning I'd get up at six and walk down the lane to the bus stop. It always seemed to be dark and raining. The job itself was fine, it has to be said, and I was serving an apprenticeship that I knew would set me up for life. The company manufactured big, metal, pressurised tanks and they were fabulous employers but I just felt lonely all the time.

As I welded, I used to sing inside these giant tanks to try to pass the time. The acoustics in those things were amazing and I obviously made quite an impression – after a while my fellow workers even started to request songs. At first I thought they were just joking but soon realised that they were actually enjoying my singing.

The first time I ever heard Elvis was while working there. I was in the canteen and I heard this incredible voice booming from the radio, singing: "Since my baby left me …". I thought to myself: "Elvis Presley, that's a terrible name." But the sound he generated certainly resonated with me. It was like nothing I had heard before – I thought it was fantastic. Before Elvis, it had been the likes of Sinatra, Bing Crosby, Guy Mitchell, Frankie Lane; they were all brilliant singers but very different from what Elvis was doing. His influences seemed to be drawn from Gospel, rhythm and blues and country, creating an exciting new sound in popular music. Rock 'n' Roll had barely started at the time. Hearing 'Heartbreak Hotel' for the first time had a profound effect on me – I'll always remember how exciting and different it sounded. I found out later that Elvis had started his singing career with the legendary Sun Records label in 1954. I was hugely impressed that it only took him two years to become an international sensation. It's amazing to think that he ended up starring in 33 films and I read somewhere that he sold over one billion records. In the end, of course, he tragically paid the ultimate price for his success. I prefer to remember him as the exciting new voice I heard booming out of the radio in Manchester that day. I sensed that Elvis marked the arrival of an exciting new era for music. He opened up endless new possibilities for budding singers like myself.

Hearing 'Heartbreak Hotel' for the first time is one of the few happy memories I have of that time in Manchester. To put it mildly, I was miserable there. I used to go up to the foreman looking for as much overtime as possible. Apart from earning the extra few bob, I just wanted the whole day to go as fast as it could so I go back home. I knew that I needed to serve at least one full year as an apprentice welder in Manchester to get any real benefit from the experience but time just dragged. The quicker each day passed, I reasoned, the sooner I would be heading home to Dublin. Some days I'd be in work from half seven in the morning and I wouldn't get back home until eight at night. I didn't drink, I didn't smoke, I didn't socialise – my whole life there was just sleep, work and sleep. My relatives were great people but I missed my parents and family terribly. I was chronically homesick and incredibly lonely. I saved almost every penny I earned and used to send money home all the time. I always got great pleasure from doing that, being the eldest in the family and all that. Even when I had worked at the jeweller's I brought my first pay packet home to my mother and handed it to her, unopened. At first she didn't want to take it but I insisted. She used to give me back whatever she thought I needed and put the rest in a savings account for me, even though she probably could have done with the extra few bob herself.

On days when I'd be feeling particularly lonely in England I used to go to the airport in Manchester and listen out for the public address system announcing the departure of the evening flight to Dublin. I'd close my eyes and fantasise that I was about to board the plane home to Ireland and imagine what it would be like. Those daydreams used to keep me going when I was at my lowest point. I would be standing at the airport, crying, wishing it was time to go back home. Hearing the flight to Dublin being announced somehow gave me a connection to my native city, however tenuous. Again, it just shows how unbelievably immature I was for my age. Other lads would have been out drinking and smoking and all that goes with it, but that lifestyle was never for me. It wasn't even that I had grown up in an overprotected family or anything like that – it was just in my nature.

Finally after 12 painfully long months, the time came for me to leave England and return home. I decided to live out my airport fantasy by booking a flight home with some of the money I had saved. This would have been long before the days of Ryanair and flying was expensive and considered quite a luxury. I had never been on a plane before so it was an incredible way to mark my homecoming. This fella sat beside me and we chatted during the short flight to Dublin. For some reason he looked familiar to me. Suddenly I recognised him – I had seen him on my aunt and uncle's telly the previous week and remembered the commentator remarking that he was a great player. His name was Liam Whelan and he played football for Manchester United. He was known as "Billy" and was one of the legendary "Busby's Babes" who would later tragically perish in that dreadful plane crash in Munich in 1958. He was a lovely man to talk to and it's unbelievably sad what eventually happened to him.

My father met me at the airport in Dublin and couldn't believe how much I had grown – I was at least five inches taller than since he had last seen me. We went straight home to Cabra and I was thrilled to be finally reunited with my mother and brothers and sisters. The bouts of homesickness I had experienced in Manchester made me realise how much I had missed Dublin and it didn't take me long to settle back in. Now firmly convinced that working abroad was not for me, I was determined to find a job that would allow me to stay close to home.

THREE

The Melochords

Thanks mainly to the experience I had gained in Manchester, it didn't take me long to find a welding job in Dublin. I had saved most of the money I earned over there which meant I wasn't under any real financial pressure to get work straight away. As it happened, however, a job opportunity came my way almost immediately. My father had an old workmate who was a manager in a Finglas-based firm called Unidare and he put a word in for me, explaining that I had just returned from working for a large welding firm in the UK. I was delighted to be starting a new job so soon and was glad that my decision to better my prospects by going to Manchester appeared to be paying off. Little did I realise that it would also indirectly lead to a lifelong career in the world of entertainment. It's how I was 'discovered'.

The job at Unidare was in this small section of the factory where they made welding rods. While I hadn't fully served my time in Manchester, I had still gained a lot of practical experience. I was convinced that welding was going to be my career and I was lucky enough to be very good at it. The fact that there was a history of tradesmen on my father's side of the family probably explained my aptitude for that type of work. Welding was certainly a good trade and there was the potential to make a decent living from it. My parents were naturally pleased that I was well on my way to getting a solid trade and everyone expected that I would become a welder – even me.

I was working on my own most of the time, surrounded by a safety screen while I tested the rods. To pass the time I used to spend the day singing, completely oblivious to the fact that I was attracting a growing audience. Two of the women who worked on the assembly line – they were around 10 years older than me – used to come over all the time and say: "Richard, sing that song you sang the other day." It was probably a Sinatra number or something like that. Their interest gave me confidence and I started to realise that they obviously thought I could sing those songs really well.

One day a young lad called Gerry Hayes was sent up to me from another section of the floor to learn about welding. After hearing me sing, he asked if I had ever considered joining a band. I hadn't, to be honest, as I was just a very shy 19-year-old at that stage. He told me he had a band called The Melochords and they were looking for a singer. I was invited to a rehearsal at a little ballroom off Parnell Square called Connarchy's. I'd never even heard of the place and Gerry had to give me directions how to get there. I was reluctant at first but eventually decided to go along.

I was pretty nervous by the time I got there. It was one thing singing with a choir, or even the variety group, but performing with a band was completely alien to me. It was an entirely new experience and I really didn't know what to expect. The musicians in the band were all set up and ready to go when I arrived. I could sing hundreds of songs but I wasn't sure what they wanted to hear. I asked them if they knew 'Bernadine', which was a popular Pat Boone song, and they said they did. I started singing and it was incredible to experience the power of a band behind me for the first time. The drummer was really getting into it as the chorus kicked in. Suddenly he stopped playing, put down his sticks, and said: "Jesus, Richard, do you want the job?"

I didn't need to think twice about their offer and agreed to join on the spot. I was told that I couldn't have turned up at a better time as far as the band was concerned. They'd just lost their singer, Butch Moore, who eventually went on to have great success with the Capitol Showband. In fact, a few years later, in 1965, Butch would be the first singer ever to represent Ireland in the Eurovison Song Contest. Needless to say, his departure came as a huge blow and they were delighted when I said I'd be his replacement. I remember feeling thrilled and excited at the prospect of being in a band. I simply couldn't believe the unlikely chain of events that had led to me getting the job.

It was 1959 and I was now officially the singer with The Melochords. It's funny how it happened because I never went out looking to join a band or anything like that – it just came to me. Strange as it sounded, all that singing in the Unidare factory had led to my first real break in showbusiness.

* * * *

In some ways I was an unlikely frontman for a band. I'm not trying to be modest or anything, but I never had any delusions about my looks. I was certainly an instantly recognisable individual but not necessarily for all the right reasons. I was a tall, skinny lad with sticky-out ears and definitely not good-looking in the traditional sense. Maybe it would be more accurate – or charitable – to say that I was ordinary looking, whatever that means. I've always been honest with myself about that.

One of the great things about joining The Melochords was that they were already pretty well established on the scene and had regular gigs booked. They were good musicians, too. Gerry, the fella who had convinced me to join, played the accordion and the piano. He was the band leader as well. We also had a great drummer, a good bass player and a talented guitarist. Musically The Melochords were very tight; a solid Rock 'n' Roll band with plenty of live experience. It was fantastic for me to be singing the exciting Elvis songs of the time with the powerful rhythm of a full band behind me. It was a fresh and invigorating experience and a world away from my days as a choirboy.

The Melochords opened my mind to a lot of the popular music of the time but I think I had an influence on them, too. Soon they were playing songs that I had introduced them to, by the likes of Nat King Cole and Frank Sinatra, and our set became a mix of ballads and Rock 'n' Roll. That made us unique because there were no other bands on the scene doing those slower, more romantic songs.

I was a bag of nerves by the time my first show with The Melochords arrived. Apart from having to meet the expectations of the rest of the band, I knew there would be friends and relatives in the audience that night as the gig was in the Finglas Hall, just walking distance from Cabra West. The place was packed and buzzing with energy as we took to the stage. I can't remember the first song we played that night but it was possibly an Elvis number. The feeling I got from performing in front of such an enthusiastic audience with a Rock 'n' Roll band was simply exhilarating. I was instantly addicted to it. I could have stayed on stage all night and probably would have if the owners of the ballroom had let me. I'll always associate Finglas Hall with a local fella called Barry Scully, who used to stand to the side of the stage to watch us any time we performed there. Barry, who played bass guitar, was a great fan and supporter of The Melochords and his father was a musician, too. It's funny how things turn out because these days Barry plays bass in my band.

The band's regular slots included Saturday nights at the Ritz in Ballyfermot, which is now a supermarket. Back then it seemed like a huge place although looking at it today it doesn't seem that big. I remember that the Ritz had a really high stage with the dressing-room for the bands to the right of it. It was managed by a fella called Eddie Downey, a very respected ex-boxer who used to know my father. The Carlton Hall in Marino was another great place to play. It wasn't a huge venue but they used to cram in around 800 dancers when we played there. One of the reasons I loved playing the Carlton Hall was that my father's family lived nearby in Donnycarney and all the relatives always came to see me when I performed there.

I used to cycle to all the shows. You could always tell if there was a big crowd inside by the number of bicycles parked outside a venue. I used to get 10 shillings for doing four hours on stage. It doesn't sound like much but it was good money at the time – probably the equivalent of getting €300 nowadays.

Even though I was a quiet individual, I loved getting up on stage to sing before a big crowd. During those early shows with the band I began to notice that I was getting a lot of attention from all the young ones – I honestly couldn't understand it. Here I was the centre of all this female attention and I'd never even kissed a bloody girl. They came from everywhere, including my native Cabra West, to see The Melochords. Our popularity grew quickly due to our word of mouth reputation for putting on a good show. As a singer I was starting to come into my own. I may not have been able to play a musical instrument but I was very rhythmic and would never lose time with the rest of the band.

Some venues we'd play once a month, others every week. But the band's ambition was to break into the big time. In Dublin in the late '50s and early '60s this meant playing the legendary Olympic Ballroom on Pleasant Street. Up to that point The Melochords had mainly played in smaller venues in the suburbs to local audiences but the Olympic was in a completely different league altogether. People would travel from all over the city to see big names such as The Royal Showband and The Clipper Carlton play there. Finally in early 1960, the call came through that we had landed the dream gig. Being asked to play the Olympic as the main band was a huge honour for The Melochords as it was a big ballroom to fill. Once you had played there to a capacity crowd, you knew you were on the road to success. We were really excited at the prospect of playing the Olympic, although it was little bit daunting, too. Taking to the stage of the Olympic that night, I could hardly believe that it was little over a year since I had joined the band. I remember every detail of that concert vividly. By that stage I had started to become really popular in my own right as a singer. The place was packed and I can still see all those faces looking up at me from the front of the stage. Eyes seemed to follow my every move – it was a tremendous feeling.

That night at the Olympic Ballroom was the first time I ever signed an autograph – it was on a girl's arm! She came from Cabra West and was a dedicated fan of The Melochords. In fact, she ended up marrying the band's guitarist, Brendan O'Connell. We used to slag Brendan for being from one of the posh, private houses in Phibsboro. As for me, the amount of girls interested in me seemed to be intensifying as the popularity of the band increased. I knew I was performing and singing well but I still couldn't understand why women responded differently to Richard Rock the singer, as opposed to Richard Rock the welder. It took me a while to get why all these beautiful young ones reacted to me in the way that they did – and still do today. I can only describe it as a kind of metamorphosis, which occurs every single time I perform. I often joke that it's a little bit like Dr David Banner turning into the Incredible Hulk. Once I hit the stage I'm different. Family and friends have said to me that I give out a completely different type of vibe. The person you see performing up there in the glare of the lights is not the same person that you'd meet on the streets, in the supermarket or wherever. Richard the performer and Richard the person were entirely contradictory characters. One was confident and extroverted – the other was a shy, introverted loner. Something just happens when I'm on stage and it's the same for me today as it was back in the early '60s. Mick Quinn, who would later become my manager, once said to me: "Richard, once you walk out onto the stage, even before you sing, people are reacting to you. Your very presence has created an expectation. You have a certain way about you; you have a swagger. Elvis has it, Sinatra has it and you definitely have it!" I certainly never considered myself to be in their league but I knew what Mick was getting at.

Despite my growing personal popularity, I never felt any resentment or jealousy from the other members of The Melochords. The lads in the band were very focused individuals and I think they recognised that I had given them an extra hook. The more popular I became, the bigger the gigs we got and the more money we pocketed. Shortly after our triumphant Olympic gig, most of the concerts were then billed as 'The Melochords featuring Richard Rock'. It was definitely a bit of a thrill to see my name on the posters for the first time. In a way, though, it put extra pressure on me. When you're unknown you've got nothing to prove but once you become a name you have to prove yourself every single night – to your band, your manager, the venue owner and – most importantly – to the audience who have parted with their hard-earned cash to come and see you. The upside of our success was that the money was great, although we were being paid a lot less than people would have believed. I loved being able to give my mother the type of money that she could only have dreamed of previously.

Back at the day job in Unidare, however, things were not going so great. I was on the verge of being sacked. Performing with The Melochords meant a lot of late nights. Sometimes we'd have to play down the country and wouldn't arrive back in Dublin until the early hours of the next morning. It was obvious that something was going to have to give. I had gotten to a point where I'd come in to do a day's welding and end up falling asleep behind the protective screen. My boss, who was a good friend and former workmate of my father's, couldn't take much more of these types of incidents. One day, out of sheer exasperation, he phoned my Dad.

"Joe, what am I going to do with Richard?" he asked. "I can't have him coming in here and falling asleep when he's supposed to be working."

"What are you ringing me up for?" my father responded. "If he's not doing his job you should sack him."

That was typical of my father – he was very black and white, a bit like I am now, I suppose. He called it the way he saw it and wanted me to stand on my own two feet. I'm the same with my own kids today. I might ask people I know in business to give my children jobs but I tell them that if it works out, then great; if it doesn't, well, there will be no hard feelings – I just ask them to give my kids the opportunity to prove themselves.

I didn't stick around at Unidare long enough to be sacked. I knew myself that it had come down to a simple choice – welding or singing. And let's face it, welding and sleeping on the job weren't exactly a safe combination. In the end it wasn't a difficult decision to make. There was no way I was going to give up singing and, besides, I was making more money from the band than I was at Unidare. Even at that stage I would have been earning more than my father was – and he was a skilled tradesman. But I was conscious all the time of how this success wasn't going to last. I hoped, optimistically, that I would get five years' good money out of it. I never could have imagined that I'd still be doing it 47 years later.

My parents were naturally worried when they learned about my plans. I suppose I would be the same if my own kids told me that they were leaving a solid career to go into the entertainment business or something equally unstable. My Dad, in particular, would have preferred at the time for me to finish learning my trade so I would have something to fall back on if the music thing didn't work out for me. To my mother's and father's credit, however, they respected my decision and never stood in my way. I handed in my notice at Unidare and left the company on extremely good terms with my colleagues and boss. I remember them all wishing me well on my last day and promising to come and see me perform.

From the moment I left Unidare I decided to approach music in a business-like fashion and was determined to make a proper career out of it. Performing was a job to me and I just wanted to get on with it. As soon as I came off stage, there was no hanging around – and I carry that tradition through to today. There has always been a perception that people in showbusiness lead promiscuous lives and are tempted by all the girls hanging around after a gig. That may be the case for some people but it wasn't like that for me. Sure, there were loads of women coming on to us after the shows and stuff, but I wanted to remain professional at all times. The rest of the lads in The Melochords were like that, too, although they might have had the occasional drink. There were plenty of opportunities to get caught up in a drinking scene when you were in a band but I was never tempted to go down that road. Alcohol simply held no fascination for me.

After the success of the Olympic gig we were busier than ever and the money was steadily rolling in. I was no longer cycling home after a show. I'd graduated to a motorbike thanks to the money I was earning. It wasn't too long before I had a crash, though. One night, a car came from nowhere out in front of me. I had to jam on the brakes to avoid it and I skidded across the road. I wasn't badly hurt or anything but I decided there and then that I would have to get rid of the bike. That's the practical side of my personality, I suppose. I saw the potential for more serious injury or even death and I wasn't willing to chance it. In 1960 I sold the bike and bought a car, a 1956 Ford Prefect. There was no heater or radio in it but that didn't matter – to me it was like driving a Rolls Royce. In Cabra, in the early '60s, it would have been highly unusual to see a lad my age driving a car – they were considered quite a luxury, even by the older generation.

A year later I bought a Skoda and then I really felt that I had died and gone to heaven. Things felt like they were really starting to happen for me. Although we played the occasional country gig, The Melochords' main fan base was in Dublin. We were booked solidly throughout 1961 and it seemed we could do no wrong with the fans and the venue owners.

But then, out of nowhere, it all went wrong. Without explanation, The Melochords suddenly folded and I was no longer making any money. It happened very quickly and I never really understood why the band split. It seemed to be that some of the lads just decided they wanted to leave and in the end we all went our separate ways. There was no big row or anything, just a simple discussion after one of our gigs. The fact was that some of the guys in the band saw the kind of money being made by the showbands and they wanted to go in that direction. The Melochords was considered to be a Rock 'n' Roll group and for the owners of some of the larger venues we weren't as bankable a proposition as the showbands.

After the split, most of the lads in the band went on to have great success with The Cadets. There was some talk of me joining the new showband but in the end they went with a female singer, the great Eileen Reid. I just had to accept their decision and move on.

The financial reality of The Melochords' split hit me like a sharp smack on the face. I had gone from being a key provider in my household to being a complete dependent again. My mother even had to keep up the repayments on my loan for the new Skoda. The only reason she could afford to do that was because my sisters had started working. It was a very bleak time for me because I had no job to fall back on. I became a gun for hire and did a bit of freelance singing here and there but nothing that provided me with a regular income.

From where I was standing, my initial hope of a five-year-long singing career with The Melochords, or anybody else, was looking decidedly overoptimistic.

Four

Cliff Richard and the Irish Dancers

Shortly after The Melochords went their separate ways I decided to put a new band together. Some people I knew had recommended a few local musicians who were available and in no time at all Richard Rock and The Echoes were formed. After just a couple of rehearsals we were ready to hit the road. The songs were similar to the ones I had performed with The Melochords so it was really just a case of me telling the lads in the new band which songs they needed to learn. Much to my frustration we were only able to get occasional bookings in relatively small venues, unlike the showbands who were playing huge places in front of thousands of people every night. It was becoming clear to me that ordinary Rock 'n' Roll bands like The Echoes simply couldn't compete with the ballroom scene. Things were looking so bleak at one stage that I even contemplated returning to welding. Then Cliff Richard came to Dublin and changed everything for me.

When it was announced that Cliff and The Shadows were billed to play at the National Stadium, Dublin in 1961, the excitement and hype it generated was the same as when U2 play Croke Park today. Back then Dublin certainly wasn't the Mecca it is these days in terms of the big names it attracts, although I remember that the Theatre Royal would have hosted stars such as Matt Monroe and Andy Williams. Cliff, though, was a different, story – this was Rock 'n' Roll.

Cliff was the self-styled king of pop and was the British equivalent of Elvis, although I think Elvis was in a different league. But people definitely thought Cliff was the biggest star of his generation in our part of the world. From what I'd heard he first tasted stardom in 1958 when he changed his name from Harry Webb and was signed by EMI. The Shadows were legends in their own right as well, fronted by the talented, bespectacled guitarist, Hank Marvin. They'd had chart success with instrumental hits such as 'Apache' which I always thought was a great tune.

As it got nearer the day I remember there was a real buzz about the concert. It was one of the most eagerly anticipated musical events ever. Everybody loved Cliff Richard and The Shadows hits, especially 'Move It' and 'Living Doll', which are still popular songs today. I was just as excited as everyone but little did I think when I was singing to the welding rods in Unidare just a few years earlier that I would be invited to play a part in the most talked about concert of the time. It turned out that through The Melochords I had earned a reputation as a good singer and this paid off when I was invited to support Cliff Richard. I immediately accepted of course – you don't get offers like that every day. It was funny because going on to perform before Cliff in such a big show should have been a big deal but I wasn't really fazed by it. I suppose the prestige of opening for such a major star didn't hit me at the time but by the night of the concert itself my nerves were pretty frayed.

I arrived at the National Stadium that afternoon to prepare for my performance and, as I stood on the stage and looked around the venue, my thoughts turned to my father who would have boxed there on many occasions as a young man. It's hard to believe by today's standards but I didn't even get to rehearse with the band I was playing with that night. All I had was just a quick chat with them before the show, telling them what songs I was going to sing and in what key. There wasn't even time for one dry run through the songs – nothing! Here I was, a young lad going out to perform an unrehearsed set in front of somebody else's audience. I was also well aware that these people were not my regular fans from places like Cabra or Ballyfermot. Many of them would have come from the more middle-class, affluent areas of Dublin and I wasn't sure how they'd respond to me. After all they were here to see Cliff Richard, the most exciting star of our time, not Richard Rock, former boy soprano.

It was a daunting prospect – even with a rehearsal!

As the time for my performance approached I shuffled anxiously backstage. The excited noise of the audience out front started getting really loud as people took their seats. The sense of anticipation from the crowd was almost unbearable and I started to wonder what I had let myself in for.

The MC on the night was a fantastic fella called Joe Cahill, who went on to become a great friend of mine. "Go out there and look the part," he said before introducing me to the crowd. I was feeling terrified as I heard my name announced. With a rush of adrenaline, I went out on stage and gave it everything I'd got.

First I did an Elvis thing to warm the audience up. Then I thought to myself: "To hell with this, I'm going to get this bunch going!" I sprang on to the piano – the poor piano player nearly died – and the crowd erupted. I later learned that even Cliff himself ran out to the side of the stage to see what all the commotion was about. Against the odds, I had taken on somebody else's audience and had managed to win them over. For many years afterwards, much to my amazement, people still came up to me to congratulate me on my performance that night. I had clearly made something of an impression with the media, too, with most newspaper reviews giving me a bit of praise the next day.

Cliff and The Shadows put on a fantastic show that night, although I have to admit that while I admired his success and professionalism, I wasn't a huge fan of his. I certainly wouldn't have put him in the same class as Frank Sinatra or Elvis. He was a really good-looking guy, though, with beautiful eyes and jet black hair. That said, he was a bit too much of a pretty boy for my liking. I felt that he was more style over substance, a case of 80 per cent image and 20 per cent talent. Even looking at Cliff performing today, there's nothing natural or spontaneous about him and everything is choreographed. I remember thinking that night that he wasn't a patch on Elvis. In fairness to him, though, his National Stadium show was slick. The Shadows, in particular, were amazing and produced a sound that was unique to them.

I got to talk to Cliff after the concert and he complimented me on my set. I wasn't starstruck or anything like that but I was delighted to meet him.

"You did well out there tonight," Cliff said to me.

"I had to," I replied. "Look who was coming on after me!"

I think Cliff was trying to give me a bit of encouragement when he went on to say: "Always give the audience more than they expect."

His words struck a chord with me as that's exactly how I felt about performing. It wasn't enough to give the audience what they wanted – you had to exceed their expectations every time.

Cliff's parting words to me were: "Make sure you only get your name in the papers for the good stuff." I agreed that this was fine, in principle, although even then I knew it was not something you could always have direct control over yourself.

That night, back in my dressing room, I was approached by Phil Solomon, who was a major player in the UK music scene. He told me to drop by and see him the next morning at the Gresham Hotel. I was hugely excited about this but I remember my mother telling me to be very careful before I set off to meet him. I suppose she didn't want me to have unrealistic expectations and was possibly concerned that I might be tempted to leave Ireland again.

I drove into town that morning and parked close to the city centre. I was naturally curious about what this music industry bigwig would have to say to me, but not wanting to appear too eager I tried my best to keep my cool as he greeted me in the foyer of the Gresham.

Mr Solomon got straight to the point – he'd been impressed by my performance the night before and wanted to make me a big star. He explained that it would mean I would have to leave Dublin to go and live in England. In his words, he was going to make me the next Cliff Richard. That sounded unbelievable to me: Cliff was a fabulous looking fella but I was a skinny little fecker with ears that stuck out.

I told him I would think his offer over but that was the end of that – I never took him up on it and nothing ever came of it. There are many who might feel that this was a wasted opportunity on my part. Perhaps it would have led to the successful international career that ultimately eluded me but I have no regrets – I've never believed in looking back. I think that this philosophy has served me well in life. At the time it probably looked like career suicide to be passing up such an opportunity but I would still stand by my decision today. It was difficult though as I still didn't have a regular singing gig. The reality was that my band, The Echoes, was going nowhere fast. We played a number of gigs and had some modest success but I don't think we were on the road to stardom or anything like that. The launch of Telefís Eireann that same year, however, presented us with a valuable opportunity to break into the big time.

The new station held a competition called *Search for a TV Star* and I was encouraged to enter it with the band. We were delighted to make it to the finals, which were held in the prestigious Theatre Royal on Hawkins Street. It was a big venue that was capable of holding around 5,000 people. The comedian Jack Cruise, who was a major star in Irish entertainment at the time, was synonymous with the theatre and used to run hugely popular variety shows there. On the night of the Telefís Eireann talent contest there were a number of different acts in the final shake-up. I took to the stage with The Echoes and the crowd went crazy – it seemed like half of Ballyfermot and Cabra had come out to cheer us on. If the competition had been judged on crowd reaction alone, then we would have won – no question about it.

To everyone's amazement, a bunch of Irish dancers were declared the overall winners. I'm sure they were good at what they did and all that, but they were hardly the faces of the future in the world of entertainment. Two Limerick comedians called Tom and Pascal came second and we took third prize. It was a bizarre decision, really. Here was Ireland about to enter into the exciting new age of television and the best that Telefís Eireann could come up with in their search for a star were some Irish dancers. I found it difficult to conceal my disappointment because I really felt we deserved to win and it would have been great for us. When you think about it, the judges must have been dinosaurs. Maybe some of them were priests who didn't approve of Rock 'n' Roll. People were coming up to us after the show telling us we had been robbed and that we should have won.

The decision to declare the Irish dancers the winners was typical of Irish television when it first started – it was crap, mainly because religion was so strong in this country at the time. The Catholic Church wielded extraordinary power in Ireland back in the '50s and '60s. As a result we were pretty sexually repressed as a nation and the Church's opposition to birth control led to large families and a lot of poverty. Even the showbands weren't safe from the iron grip of the Catholic hierarchy. Most of the ballrooms closed for the 40 days of Lent and this caused hardship for the less successful showbands on the circuit. Larger groups, such as the

Royal or the Capitol – and later The Miami Showband – were able to ply their trade in Britain and even America when the ballrooms temporarily shut their doors. For the smaller groups, however, Lent resulted in huge hardship because they couldn't work.

It was disgraceful, when you think about it. It was purely a religious thing. It wasn't as if there was a law forbidding ballrooms to open during Lent. Some of the larger, more commercial ballrooms in Dublin stayed open but most of them remained shut until Easter Sunday. One of the main culprits for enforcing this oppressive regime was the Archbishop of Dublin, John Charles McQuaid. I think the Irish Federation of Musicians even wrote to him to explain that hundreds of bands had no work during Lent. Not that it did any good. Archbishop McQuaid was extremely conservative and was determined to keep Ireland in the dark ages and he refused to back down on the issue.

The influence of the Church could be felt in every facet of Irish society, even within political circles. Years later, when we played in Northern Ireland, I remember seeing banners stretched across the roads that read: 'Home Rule is Rome Rule'. That didn't make any sense to me at the time but looking back on it I think that sentiment was correct – Irish society was effectively controlled by the Vatican and continued to be until recent times.

After the talent show debacle I started to feel a little despondent about continuing on with The Echoes. We were still doing these little gigs around the place but it wasn't really working out. One night I went to Dublin's Olympic Ballroom to see The Clipper Carlton Showband. They were considered to be the original of the showband species, having started out in the late '40s. Hailing from Strabane in Northern Ireland, the Clippers had the type of success that all the rest of us could only hope to emulate. Before the explosion of the scene in the late '50s, all the bands were simply expected to provide music for the dancers. I was too young to go to dances at that age but from what I've heard it wasn't unusual for the musicians to be seated on a stage in a parish hall or ballroom, obscured by their music stands and largely ignored by the audience. The Clipper Carlton changed all that in the early '50s. They switched the emphasis away from the dancing and onto the bands themselves. Suddenly it was all about the performance and singers like Fergus O'Hagan and later Dominic 'Dom' Shearer from the Clippers emerged from the shadows of anonymity to become the centre of attention. After they set the scene and established the winning formula, showbands – quite literally – were all about putting on a show. Some of the bands would dress up in costumes and impersonate the big stars of the day, such as Elvis, and there were sometimes even comedy routines between the songs.

While The Clipper Carlton Showband had been huge, I got a sense they were starting to fade a little by the time I saw them that night in the Olympic. I wasn't wrong – they broke up a few years later, only to reform again in the second half of the '60s.

During the show I met a fella there I knew from Cabra called Tony Bogan. He told me he was a drummer in a new band and they had been playing out in Palm Beach in Portmarnock, in north Dublin. He said they were called The Miami Showband and I remember thinking that it was a terribly corny name. Tony invited me out to see them play, promising to leave tickets for me at the door. I was glad to accept his offer as I hadn't got much money at the time.

I decided to check them out and made the trip out from Cabra the following Sunday night. Even though I considered myself a Rock 'n' Roller and had never been a big fan of the showbands, I was impressed by the Miami. The band leader was another Cabra man, Joe Tyrell, who played keyboards. They had a strong backbone of other talented musicians including Murty Quinn (trombone), Martin Phelan (saxophone), Tommy O'Rourke (trumpet), Clem Quinn (guitar) and Dennis Murray (bass guitar). More importantly, they seemed to be getting the best gigs at the biggest venues. In The Echoes we were still struggling and just playing small shows.

Shortly after the gig, I decided to pay a visit to Tom Doherty, whose company Topline Promotions managed The Miami Showband. I wanted to see if he would be interested in taking on Richard Rock and The Echoes as a client. I suppose my hope was that he would do for my band what he had done for the Miami. Tom, a really big, nice man from the country, ran major dances in the National Ballroom on Parnell Square and was well known in showband circles. His brother, Jim, was the manager of the hugely successful Capitol Showband. Much to my disappointment, Tom immediately turned me down. Before I could find out why, he asked if I would be interested in joining the Miami – he dropped the bombshell that their lead singer, Jimmy Harte, had left to go to America.

The question stopped me in my tracks. To join the Miami I knew I would have to change my whole way of thinking about the music I performed. I was into romantic ballads and Rock 'n' Roll whereas the Miami were cut straight from the showband cloth as far as I was concerned. To me, the showbands seemed a bit frivolous and gimmicky, with their fancy costumes and on-stage theatrics. Some showband performances were more like something you'd see at a variety show but, for me, entertaining was all about the songs and the quality of the music. I wasn't convinced I could make the transition from a Rock 'n' Roll singer to showband performer. In my innocence I thought I would be becoming something I couldn't respect.

I had other reservations, too. For me to even consider this offer, I felt that the Miami would have to be a full-time band. I wasn't happy to learn that two or three of the lads had other jobs. I said to Tom: "They are going to have to quit working and concentrate fully on the band. There's no point in them coming home from gigs at six in the morning and then going to work, bollixed, and still be expected to give their best again for that night's show. If I join, it has to be all or nothing. We've got to go for it 100 per cent from the beginning."

Tom replied that while it was true some of the musicians had jobs outside the band, they were planning to hand in their notice and dedicate themselves full-time to the Miami. I was delighted to hear him say that because it proved to me they were all committed to taking a serious shot at the big time.

Despite the fact that Tom had asked me to join the band, I was a bit perplexed to be told that I had to meet the rest of the Miami out in Palm Beach the following afternoon for an audition. Arriving there, I confronted Tony, the drummer, telling him: "You all know what I can do. Everybody knows that I can sing. Why do I have to go through this ritual?"

Tony simply responded: "That's just the way it is, Richard – it's how Tom wants it."

There's wasn't much I could say to that so I just got on with it.

The rehearsal got underway and was a carbon copy of the day I went to audition for The Melochords. I made an instant connection with the other members of the band. Sidney Rose, a Jewish guy who owned Palm Beach, was watching us along with John Maloney, another director of the place. I could tell by their reaction that we were sounding good together. The so-called audition had merely been a formality and it came as no surprise to me when I was told that I had landed the job.

We hadn't much time before our first gig together, which was the following Monday, Easter Monday, in the same venue. We only had one rehearsal that week to prepare for the show. Fortunately I already knew many of the songs in their set and other members of the Miami could sing as well so lead vocal duties were shared. This was pretty common in many of the showbands and it gave the main vocalist a well-earned break.

I remember feeling really anxious about the Palm Beach show. I knew the lads in the band were confident about what I could bring to the Miami's formula but this in itself put me under extra pressure to perform at my best. Then, of course, there were the fans to consider. Would they prefer the original singer? Would they think that I didn't fit in to the showband scene? This was all new territory to me but, nerves aside, I was looking forward to the Portmarnock show.

When we arrived that night we knew the place was packed. At this stage you could always tell how big a crowd was by the amount of buses parked outside, instead of just the bikes like back in the early days with The Melochords. The buses used to leave from the quays in town and bring the punters out to Palm Beach. If there were more than 15 buses we knew we had a full house. Then, of course, you'd have the local crowd, as well as the people who'd cycled from nearby areas such as Baldoyle or Malahide.

My blood was really pumping taking to the stage that night and I was shaking with nerves. After all, the rest of the lads had been in the Miami for around a year before I joined and had built up a following of their own. I knew I could sing well but I just hoped that we would gel as a group. I was also a bit concerned because I was something of an outsider in terms of my non-showband background.

I needn't have worried. The reaction from the crowd was amazing. We kicked off with 'Bernadine', the same Pat Boone hit that had landed me the job with The Melochords. The chemistry between myself and the other musicians was instantaneous. It seemed we could do no wrong with the audience, as song after song exploded from the stage. The crowd went wild and we kept them screaming for the best part of four hours. Nobody wanted to sit down and the dance floor was packed for the entire night – even during the slower, more romantic numbers. As the last notes from our final song echoed into the night, they were all sweating and crying out for more.

Our first performance had been a triumph and I could tell by the looks on the faces of the lads in the band that they were all thinking the same thing – this was going to work.

The Miami were a great band in their own right and I think it's fair to say that I brought an extra something to the mix. The band knew by the reaction I was getting from the crowd that first night that they had found their ideal frontman and the possibilities were now endless. We couldn't have known, however, that the combination of Dickie Rock and the Miami would prove to be one of the most successful musical partnerships of the '60s.

It was April 1962. I was still very young and had already witnessed the highs and lows of the music business. I'd gone from success with The Melochords to being a struggling singer with The Echoes to ending up beaten in a talent show by some Irish dancers. I was sure that joining The Miami Showband would put my music career back on the right footing.

FIVE

The Miami Showband

I became Dickie Rock after I joined the Miami. I'm not even sure exactly when or how it happened but that's what I became know as by my fans. The scene was already well established by the time I joined the Miami. By the early 1960s The Clipper Carlton had been usurped by The Royal Showband in the popularity stakes. Myself and the rest of the lads in the Miami immediately set our sights on becoming even bigger than they were, sparking a light-hearted feud between both bands.

The Royal had formed back in 1957 and they were one of the first Irish showbands to have an extensive fan base in Britain, paving the way for other acts like ourselves to follow. It's hard to believe that one time when the Royal played in Liverpool, they were supported by a relatively unknown local band called The Beatles! I remember hearing all about the Royal's singer, this guy from Waterford called Brendan Bowyer who was initially the trombonist but who was by then reputed to be Ireland's answer to Elvis. The Royal and The Clipper Carlton were the only showbands I went to see as a punter in the days before I joined the Miami. To be honest, the whole showband thing didn't really appeal to my tastes, musical or otherwise. When Tom Doherty asked me if I wanted to join the Miami, I still hadn't been convinced that the showband scene was for me so I'd decided to check out the Royal to get a sense of what was involved. They were performing at the Macushla Ballroom on the northside of Dublin and were at the peak of their powers at the time. The place was packed and the excitement from the audience was incredible as the Waterford boys took to the stage. There was no doubt that Brendan had a good voice, although I couldn't see the Elvis comparison myself. The Royal struck me as a hard-working band who knew how to pick a good song – I could certainly understand where their popularity came from. Most people my age will remember all the chart successes throughout the '60s – with various members of the group on lead vocals – but the Royal will probably be best remembered for their huge Brendan Bowyer led hit, 'The Hucklebuck'. I always thought that it was a great song and I liked The Royal Showband's version of it. It had been popular in America long before they recorded it. Frank Sinatra had sang it in 1949.

It was said at the time that there was intense rivalry between Brendan Bowyer and myself. This probably came about because I had made a joke about him in *Spotlight* magazine. I was quoted as saying that Brendan sweated so much on stage that he had to take his coat off. It was a tongue and cheek comment and Bowyer was quick enough to retort, in a later edition, that I didn't sweat on stage because I didn't bother moving at all, so there was no need for me to take off my coat. When people made comparisons between us, I used to quip: "Brendan Bowyer jumps around the stage whereas Dickie Rock *moves* around the stage." It was all a bit of a laugh, really, although there was a degree of truth behind the humour. I wasn't interested in leap-frogging over my fellow band members or performing all the on-stage acrobatics you'd see at the performances of many of the other showbands. I found that whole approach a bit irritating, to be honest.

The so-called competition between the Miami and the Royal was on my mind when I was performing on Brendan's home turf in Waterford. I'd had a few reservations about how we would be received when the Miami were booked to play his native city, particularly in the Olympia, which was virtually The Royal Showband's headquarters. I needn't have worried. We got an incredible reaction from the audience when we first performed there in 1963.

The Royal Showband had the edge on us because they were established long before the Miami. Before we came on the scene and challenged their supremacy, they were definitely the biggest band in the country. It was only natural for us to want to aim for their success and popularity. If there was an element of friendly rivalry between the leading acts, the Royal were certainly the ones to beat. In my naturally biased opinion, the Miami would eventually go on to steal their crown as Ireland's most popular showband.

I wouldn't say that we begrudged or were jealous of each other's success but there was a bit of envy involved. In my experience, jealousy can have a nasty side to it, whereas there's nothing malicious about envy. I would have been envious about the money that others in the business – like Brendan Bowyer – were reported to be making while I was on the same basic wage as the rest of my band. In the early days I might even have envied the number of hit records that The Royal Showband were having before my own recording career took off. That said, I think the success I went on to have with the Miami eventually eclipsed that of the other big showbands. In that sense, they probably would have been more envious of me in the end than I was of them!

* * * *

As the ballroom blitz continued apace, it seemed to me that new showbands were springing up in every town and village in Ireland. Some of them just enjoyed strong local loyalty and never made it big outside their home counties. Bands like The Royal Blues were treated like conquering heroes in their home turf of Mayo. They eventually went on to have moderate success on the national showband scene but not to the same extent as we did. They were huge stars in the west of Ireland, though. Others, like Brendan Bowyer and Tony Kenny, would go on to make a successful living in America. Van Morrisson, who started his music career in a showband called The Monarchs, was in another league altogether.

I think most people will agree with me when I say that the top showbands had some of Ireland's finest musicians among their ranks. I always thought that The Capitol Showband was one of the best. It had Butch Moore on lead vocals and Paddy Cole on saxophone. In Joe Dolan, The Drifters had one of the most unique sounding vocalists in the business. Joe always reminded me of Demis Rousso, with his high register style of singing and his appeal has certainly stood the test of time.

The Freshmen, who came from Ballymena in County Antrim, were also hugely popular. A lot of people considered them to be one of the best bands on the circuit but I would question that. Musically, they were extremely accomplished but I thought they modelled themselves too closely on The Beach Boys, right down to their signature harmonies. In my view it's one thing to cover the songs of another artist but I think it's quite another to try to clone them. I don't believe you can ever be taken seriously if mimicking another singer is your only claim to fame. By all means play a couple of Beach Boys' numbers but don't let it become your entire act. It's a shame, really, because as a band The Freshmen were excellent musicians.

The Dixies, from Cork, were also a big success and were considered to be the jokers in the showband pack. I first met them during the early days of the Miami when they were our relief band in Cork. It wasn't long before they became popular in their own right and their success was well deserved. They were a terrible bunch of messers and there was a very strong comedy element to their shows. There was more to their act, however, than just endless jokes and costume changes. I remember going to see them one time and being very impressed by their musicianship. Joe McCarthy, apart from being a very funny man, was an extremely accomplished drummer. Brendan O'Brien was a fantastic singer and a major draw for the ladies, who worshipped him. There were all sorts of stories about The Dixies, most of them involving their off stage antics. They had a reputation for playing tricks on the other showbands. Any time a rival band's wagon got pelted with eggs and flour, chances were that The Dixies weren't too far away. It was all just a bit of harmless fun. I got on great with them all and found them to be a brilliant bunch of lads.

I always thought it was great that there was a deep pool of music in America that the showbands were able to draw from. Many of the songs I performed with the Miami would have been lesser-known tracks taken off Elvis albums. As they weren't hits, they weren't very well known in Ireland and we were pretty much able to make them our own. People forget that Elvis didn't write his most famous songs, neither did Sinatra. They just became associated with them because of their great performances. For instance, if you ask people who wrote 'Blue Suede Shoes', most of them would answer Elvis but it wasn't his song – it was written by Carl Perkins; Elvis just made it his own. I feel it's more difficult to give a song an original interpretation if it's extremely well known. I think an example of this was Boyzone covering 'Father and Son' – one of Cat Stevens' best-known hits. I don't think they did justice to the original version. Westlife, on the other hand, had huge success with the Brendan Graham song, 'You Raise Me Up', because they made a really good job of it. The strength of the performance is the make or break of every song and I've always believed strongly in that.

Some critics dismissed the showbands because they performed so many covers. I didn't see anything wrong with the fact that all showbands lacked a certain amount of originality. We're a small country with just a limited number of good songwriters. I was never a fan of Country and Western or Irish music and that accounted for quite a large proportion of the original material that was being written here. On top of that, we were essentially dance bands and it would have been impossible to play over two hours of original music and hold the interest of the audience. As I've always maintained, it doesn't make it good just because it's an original.

As a singer with the Miami, I became synonymous with the big, romantic ballad and this is what set me apart from my showband contemporaries. My greatest influences were singers like Tony Bennett and Frank Sinatra and they produced an incredible body of work during their careers. I loved Sinatra's ballads 'Fly Me to the Moon' and 'Strangers in the Night', while my Tony Bennett favourites included 'I Left My Heart In San Francisco' and 'It Had to Be You', all songs that have stood the test of time. I have always been interested in and passionate about quality songs; the type you may not take to immediately but that really grow on you once you listen to the lyrics. America was always a fantastic source of popular music for the rest of the world. It's a country of 300 million people so it's bound to produce more than its fair share of talent. I really admire people like Irving Berlin who wrote 'White Christmas' or the likes of Neil Diamond and all those great songwriters from the Tin Pan Alley era. These guys were able to churn out incredible songs to order. Ireland may be renowned for 'Riverdance' and its folk ballads but there's no question in my mind that the best popular music originated in America.

No matter how much I liked a song I always knew that first and foremost, I was an entertainer. There was no point in performing obscure Frank Sinatra numbers just because I loved them. In my experience an audience needs instant gratification – you have to hit them with a bang as soon as you walk on stage – so a lot of the time we'd use a song that people knew and loved already.

All the successful showbands knew the importance of picking the right songs. I genuinely believe that the Miami elevated the showband to a new level, both in terms of the musicianship and the entertainment factor. Our band always believed in giving the audience – not to mention the owners of the ballrooms – value for money. I felt a sense of responsibility to my fans. If they were good enough to part with their money to come out and see the Miami, then as far as I was concerned we were duty bound to give them 110 per cent every time we performed.

I think the success of The Miami Showband had a lot to do with where we came from. I believe that everything is determined by your environment. Dublin kids from my generation would have been exposed to the Rock 'n' Roll scene and all the beat groups. But if you grow up in a place like Kerry or Mayo, you were more likely to be influenced by traditional or even Country and Western music. In other words, I think what you listen to and what you're interested in is dictated by your environment. I'm not suggesting for a second that one choice of music is better than the other. I just don't think it would have been possible for places like Mayo or Leitrim to produce a Dickie Rock or a Red Hurley. Likewise, Dublin wouldn't have been able to produce a Country and Western band of the calibre of The Mighty Avons. While I wouldn't class myself as a fan of that type of music, I have a huge amount of respect for Irish country singers such as Larry Cunningham and Ray Lynam.

We may have been doing what we loved on stage but there was a lot of hard work involved behind the scenes to make each and every performance happen. Life on the road with a successful showband was not always what it was cracked up to be. There were no such things as roadies for us – we were our own roadies. Before and after each show we would have to haul heavy amps and musical instruments in and out of our wagon, as our mini-bus was known. It was tough going but we didn't know any different. It had been the same back in the days of The Melochords and The Echoes. I remember a great guy by the name of Dermot Hurley who used to give us a dig-out when we worked the Carlton Hall in Marino. He made speakers that we called "crazy boxes" and would always oblige us if we were stuck and needed an extra amp at the last minute. Dermot eventually moved his business from his house in Marino to a place at Crossguns Bridge in Phibsboro. I've great memories of dealing with him from that time – he was a real gentleman.

Life on the road with the Miami could be a hard slog at the best of times but particularly if we were playing outside Dublin. If we had a show in a place like the Arcadia in Cork we'd have to leave Dublin at around two o'clock in the afternoon. We'd all meet in Parnell Square to travel down together on the wagon. The atmosphere on board was always great but the long journeys could often take their toll. We'd talk about music and new songs we needed to learn and things like that to pass the time. We all got on well together and there was never any tension. The only thing that got us going was the occasional minor disagreement over a choice of song or musical arrangement. We didn't socialise with each other outside the band but in some ways I think this was a good thing because it meant that friendships could never compromise our professionalism. We got on as well as any group of eight men could.

There were some fantastic people in the band. I was probably closest to Murty Quinn, the trombone player. Like me, Murty didn't drink so we'd usually share a hotel room when the band was staying overnight somewhere. Murty came from Sallynoggin on the southside of Dublin and I remember him as a very funny fella with a great sense of humour. I used to spend most of my time in his company when we were on the road. Our sax player Martin Phelan was the best looking member of the Miami and was something of a ladies' man. He was a nice guy to be around and I had great time for him. When I first joined the band, I thought that the trumpet player, Tommy O'Rourke, resented me a bit. Looking back, though, I don't think this was the case at all. Tommy was one of the oldest members of the Miami and was a conservative kind of character. The most intellectual member of the band was undoubtedly our guitarist, Clem Quinn, who was from the Navan Road area of Dublin. He certainly seemed to be more academic than the rest of us and was very knowledgeable about everything. He was a brilliant guitarist, too, and would later go on to record a big instrumental hit for the Miami called 'Buck's Polka'. Dennis Murray, the bass guitar player, was another nice bloke. I remember him as a small fella who was always very mannerly. Joe Tyrell was the bandleader and had the perfect personality for it as he was a real joker. He had two brothers in the priesthood and his sister was a nun. Tony Bogan, the drummer, was a very handsome man and was understandably popular with the female fans. As Tony and Joe knew me from growing up in Cabra, they were the only ones in the band who called me Richard. To the rest of them I was Dickie. Joe's brother, Brendan Tyrell, was our bus driver and he looked after us well.

I don't remember anyone drinking on the wagon. Most of the lads knew that they'd have to drive their cars when we were dropped back to the meeting point in Dublin after a country gig. None of them drank before a show, even when we'd stop off for a meal in a hotel to break a long journey. There would always be a quick stop en route as well, somewhere like Portlaoise, to buy some sweets or chocolate. We'd regularly be mobbed by hysterical, screaming fans looking for our autographs as we came out of the shop. It was great fun and we'd have a laugh about it when we got back to the safety of the wagon. In the early years of the Miami we'd all attract the same attention from our fans. It was only later, after we started to have all the hit records, that I became the main centre of attention.

We all had our own ways of passing the journeys. Some of the lads would use the time to catch up on some badly needed sleep. Sometimes Murty would be slumped against my shoulder and it would take me five minutes to wake him up. I could never fall asleep on the bus myself. I'd usually just read the paper. Unlike the Dixies, there wasn't really any high jinx or messing going on in the Miami's wagon. That probably gives the impression that we were a serious bunch of individuals but we weren't. It was just that the band was our full-time job – and like any job, it could be bloody hard work at times. That's not to say we didn't know how to enjoy ourselves. We used to have a great laugh discussing the latest gossip about other showbands. We used to give each other a bit of slagging over the girls. One night, after a show in the Ierne Ballroom in Dublin, I was getting a ribbing from the lads who had earlier seen me chatting up a beautiful, young woman.

"How did you get on with that bird tonight, Dickie?" one of lads shouted up from the back of the wagon. "I think she had the hots for you."

"You never know," I replied, half-seriously. "I might end up marrying her."

I used to love passing through all the towns and villages on our way to a country show. Our wagon had The Miami Showband name painted across the sides and everyone would go mad when they saw us coming. I remember waving out the window of the bus as people lined the streets to greet us.

We'd have to arrive hours before the performance to unload all the gear and set up for the night. Then we'd do a sound check. By the time the dance started at eight or nine, we'd be absolutely wrecked. Sometimes people would be queuing outside the venue while we were still lugging in our equipment. I never felt right about that. I thought it ruined the mystique of being a performer and it certainly wasn't the image you wanted to put across to your fans. It was a bit like Bono going to court to get his hat back off his former stylist. During the hearing, all these personal details emerged about the band. For me, that's ruining the magic that surrounds being in a band like U2. There are things in life that the fans just don't need to see.

When we played somewhere like the Majorca Ballroom in Crosshaven, County Cork, we'd only stay overnight in a hotel if we had a gig the following evening in Mallow or Killarney. If we didn't we'd return to Dublin immediately, after loading all our gear into the wagon first of course! It's another scene altogether these days, the main difference being that we have a guy who looks after all the sound and gear for us. Terry Finnegan goes down ahead of us and sets everything up and does the sound for us during the show. It's a tough job because afterwards he has to disassemble everything and he's always the last to leave. It would have been sheer luxury to have someone like Terry on board back in the Miami days.

The showbands didn't have it easy on stage, either. Dances could last anything from four to five hours and you might only get a break of 20 minutes to grab a cup of tea and a biscuit. Even then, half the band would have to stay on to keep the crowds entertained. This would give the others the chance to sing a couple of songs and then I'd be called back to the stage. I never really liked intervals because it meant you had to make two entrances. I always felt that this affected the continuity of a performance. I like to get out there and just do my thing all the way through.

I think the Royal was the first showband to introduce a relief group that would go on first to warm up the crowd. There was a lot of pressure on bands from ballroom owners to start the dance as early as possible – sometimes at eight o'clock – and there often wouldn't be a soul in the place as you took to the stage. Most of the lads would be down in the local pubs getting some Dutch courage into them before a dance. The girls would know this so they wouldn't bother turning up too early. You'd often be playing for around an hour before the place started to fill up. Relief bands solved this problem and the ballroom would be packed by the time the main act arrived on stage.

I remember seeing a relief band in Cork come on stage to play to a completely empty venue. They had no choice but to get on with the job and perform until the crowd gradually began to trickle in. We didn't start until much later when the place was packed. When English bands came over here, they couldn't believe that we were expected to play from two to four hours solid. To them, that was absolutely ridiculous. We were playing in Lisburn in Northern Ireland one night and there was an English band on the same bill as us. After the show, I remember their singer telling me that in the UK it was the norm for them to play no longer than an hour and 10 minutes. I joked that we would only be getting warmed up by then.

When I think back on it, we regularly had to play in dreadful conditions. Quite often you'd arrive down to a bleak, empty hall somewhere in the country – Cavan, Galway, Donegal, Limerick, Cork – and it would be freezing inside. The fact that we had to set up all the gear ourselves was the only thing keeping us warm.

The owners of many of these ballrooms – with a few notable exceptions – didn't exactly factor the comfort of the musicians into their scheme of things. Unlike modern venues today, there was no thought given over to things like changing rooms for the acts. Even then I thought this showed a real lack of foresight by the landlords because the more comfortable we were the better we played. The changing facilities would sometimes just consist of a breezeblock room with one toilet. You'd be shivering with the cold as you got changed. It must have been particularly difficult for the bands that had female members. The likes of Eileen Reid, who was the singer in the Cadets, had to get changed in the ladies' toilets – it was far from glamorous.

While the ballrooms could be miserable, some of the marquees we played in were even worse. Marquees became very popular during the 1960s and were often great places to play, particularly during the summer months. But if the weather was bad – which it usually was in

Ireland – they were a nightmare. I remember we were booked to play one marquee in Maam's Cross in County Galway. We arrived down and it had been raining all day. I asked the organiser where we could get changed and he pointed to behind the stage, where it was all wet and mucky. I was having none it. I told him: "You've another thing coming if you think we're getting changed there. You find us a proper place – a civilized place – to get dressed." He knew I was serious so he arranged for us to get ready in a nearby hotel.

On this and numerous other occasions I was forced to dig my heels in over poor conditions. Of course, that meant I developed a reputation among some promoters and venue owners for being a bit high maintenance. I was branded the type of performer who would cause hassle. But I didn't care – it was a point of principle. Nobody should be expected to go about their work in those circumstances. I didn't expect to be fawned over or pampered or anything like that – all I wanted was decent standards for the performers and I still expect that today. I believe that if you are treated with respect and dignity and have a comfortable environment, then you will go out on stage and perform better. It has to be said, though, that conditions improved dramatically for us when The Miami Showband became a big success. All of a sudden we were being supplied with food when we arrived at a ballroom and there would be tea or coffee available backstage.

If I had been shrewd enough to build a ballroom myself back then, I'd be a far richer man today. The success of the top showbands made millionaires out of many businessmen who recognised the need for more custom-built ballrooms. I remember arriving at one of these so-called entertainment venues and it looked like it had been thrown up overnight. There was little or no seating, save for some wooden benches along the walls. The idea was to squeeze in as many dancers as possible. All it essentially had was four bare walls and a stage. Others were classier affairs with a changing room for the bands, proper toilet facilities, a mineral bar, cloakroom and even balconies. We'd sometimes play the Seapoint Ballroom in Salthill which was a sophisticated venue with great facilities. Then the next night, just a few miles away in a rural Galway village, we'd end up playing a pokey dump of a place. Incredibly, however, these would often turn out to be the best shows. As we took to the stage, no matter where we were, I remember the air being thick with the pungent aroma of perfume, Brylcreem and sweat.

It's amazing when I look back on it that we were able to generate such a fantastic atmosphere in those halls, some of which were simply large sheds or barns. There was one ballroom in Drumkeen, County Limerick that fell firmly into this category. It certainly wouldn't have ranked with the more modern venues of the time but we loved playing there. It was a fairly big place and used to pack in thousands of punters. The audience was always fantastic and some nights I could hardly hear myself sing because of all the screaming.

The new ballrooms were built in every corner of Ireland and in some of the remotest parts of the country. The bigger showbands like ourselves were such a draw that our dedicated fans would follow us to the back of beyond. It wasn't unusual for people to travel anything up to 100 miles to see us.

A lot of the ballrooms we played in were independently owned but there were a few dominant players in the market. One of the largest chains that booked us regularly was run by Albert Reynolds and his brother, Jim. Their ballroom business started in the late '50s with Cloudland in their native Roosky, County Roscommon, and soon expanded to include Dreamland in Athy, Jetland in Limerick, Barrowland in New Ross, Roseland in Moate, Moyland in Ballina and Lakeland in Mullingar, to name but a few that come to mind.

Dreamland in Athy was one of my favourite ballrooms to play. Apart from the fact that it was only a short trip from Dublin, we seemed to attract fans from all over Kildare and beyond anytime we played there. It was a lovely, modern venue that was extremely well run and managed. Hours before we'd be due on stage, we'd often see an endless queue of fans waiting patiently outside. Sometimes they'd spot us arriving and deafening screams would suddenly shatter the tranquillity of Athy.

The Reynolds brothers' rival was another big player, Associated Ballrooms. The two companies used to compete to book the biggest, most popular acts. We were happy enough to play for either chain as long as the work was there for us. Albert and Jim Reynolds always looked after the musicians and their reputation for generosity was legendary within showband circles. They would make sure that you were given a hot meal in a nearby hotel before you performed. In certain other places that I won't mention, you would be lucky to get a glass of water but the

Reynolds brothers saw the wisdom in looking after the groups. I thought that their hospitality was often abused. It wouldn't be enough for some bands to be supplied with a meal; they'd have to be ordering the most expensive fillet steaks and putting wine and beer on the tab as well. That was just stupid behaviour and it used to annoy me because I felt they were taking advantage of Albert and Jim's generosity. I continue to have great respect for Albert Reynolds and I still run into him now and again. I bumped into him at the airport in Spain and it was great to reminisce about the good old showband days. Albert's a real gentleman who deserves all the success he's had – God knows he worked hard for it.

The ballroom boom created plenty of work for all the showbands as Ireland seemed to go dance crazy. My favourite ballrooms, such as the Arcadia in Bray, could pack in as many as 4,000 punters. While it was always in the back of my mind that the popularity of the Miami couldn't last forever, I was starting to relax a bit and enjoy the trappings of our success. It was finally dawning on me that I probably had the best job in Ireland.

Six

Spit on Me, Dickie!

By 1963 we were well on our way to achieving our ambition of being the biggest showband in the country. There was no time for holidays or socialising as we were booked up solidly by our management for the entire year. We were almost constantly on the road during that period. Even though the touring seemed relentless at times, we were all young men in our prime and well able to stand the pace. The more popular we became, the more we were starting to feel like stars. I would be lying if I said that I didn't enjoy the public recognition that came with being in a successful group like the Miami. It was a tremendous feeling and it gave my self-confidence a great boost.

Even those who don't know my music will have heard the expression, "Spit On Me, Dickie!" These words have followed me faithfully throughout my career, from the 1960s to the present day. Whether I'm playing Vicar Street in Dublin or the Gleneagle Hotel in Killarney, I hear it called out from the darkness of the audience in nearly every show I do.

It all started in Belfast during those first few years with the Miami. We used to play a place up there called the Boom Boom Rooms, which was always a great venue for us. It was run by two Jewish brothers, the Scotts, and was one of my favourite places to perform in Northern Ireland. It wasn't a huge venue like some of the larger commercial ballrooms and probably held about 1,000 people. As we were getting changed backstage before the show, the crowd outside – mostly young girls – were in ebullient form. I could hear them chanting: "We love you Dickie, oh yes we do; we love you Dickie, there's no one like you …."

I looked over at the other lads in the band and, like me, they were all grinning from ear to ear. They never minded me being the centre of the fans' attention because they knew that having a popular lead singer was good for the whole band. I used to get a bit of a slagging about it from time to time but it was always good-natured. "They're going to eat you alive tonight, Dickie," one of them joked, as the chants outside grew louder. We knew we were in for one hell of a show and we couldn't wait to get out there.

The atmosphere that night was simply electric. As we took to the stage a huge roar went up. I was taken aback by the incredible welcome and had to compose myself before launching into the first number. The crowd sang along with all the songs and the night just got better and better. We always received a great reception when we played Belfast but the sheer devotion and enthusiasm of the fans that night was unbelievable. On more than one occasion I was nearly pulled from the stage and into the crowd. I could hardly move with all the arms draped around my feet. Every time I reached down to shake an outstretched hand I knew I could end up being dragged into the audience. It was slightly nerve-wracking but also very satisfying. Nothing beats the adrenaline rush of playing to a crowd like the one in Belfast that night. I suppose the modern day equivalent would be like Justin Timberlake or someone appearing at the Point, but we didn't have all the fancy stage effects and smooth publicity machine that they have now. We were just judged on our live performances. It could be a bit tough because if we were playing a song that had already been a hit record, we were expected to reproduce it to just as high a standard when we did our version of it live.

We'd been on stage for a good hour or so when there was a bit of a quiet moment. Suddenly I heard a girl shout out, clear as day: "Spit On Me, Dickie!" The whole crowd, as well as all the other members of the Miami, erupted with laughter. It was such an unusual thing for someone to say. The expression took on cult status after that night and it has been with me ever since. Sometimes it pops up at the most inappropriate times. Years later, I remember performing this beautiful, slow number in the Olympia Theatre in Dublin. During the quietest part of the song, I heard someone shout out "Spit On Me, Dickie" from the back of the theatre.

Needless to say, that was the end of my nice, romantic song – the entire place was in stitches laughing after that. I never get sick of hearing it, though. It's been around for so long that I'd miss it if it disappeared.

* * * *

My first experience as a recording artist was in November 1963, the same month The Beatles came to Dublin. I can't remember exactly what I was doing the night they played the Adelphi cinema but I didn't get to see them. The hysteria that greeted their arrival was unprecedented. It gave us a bit of a hint of what lay ahead for the most popular Irish showbands. The Adelphi was just a cinema and it's incredible to think that it's where the biggest band in the history of pop music played their Dublin show. Before The Beatles came to Ireland, Cliff Richard's concert in the National Stadium had been the most talked about event of its day. There was no such thing as bands playing venues the size of Croke Park back then – not even for a group as massive as The Beatles. I remember that the four lads had to be smuggled out of the Adelphi and into the back of a newspaper truck to bring them to their hotel because of all the frenzy surrounding the concert. It was hard to believe that just a few years earlier The Beatles had been the support act for The Royal Showband! Now they were the biggest band on the planet. I was one of their legion of fans but I wasn't too disappointed at not getting to see them. I had never really been a regular concert goer. I used to perform some of their hit songs with the Miami, particularly the more up tempo ones like 'Twist And Shout' and 'I Saw Her Standing There'. As a band I always thought that they had a great look but, more importantly than that, they were brilliant songwriters. Not only did The Beatles pack out venues everywhere they went, they also had a phenomenally successful recording career. I was hoping that I'd achieve that myself some day.

It wasn't too long before the Fab Four came over that I had started to perform a lovely song called 'There's Always Me'. It was a relatively unknown track off an Elvis album I had at home. Tom Doherty loved my version and made plans for us to record it. He brought down John Woods, who was in charge of Pye Records, and arranged for him to hear us perform it at the Ierne Ballroom where we used to play on a Saturday night. John seemed impressed by what he heard and got one of his top guys, Jim Doherty, to work on it with us. Jim is a world-class jazz pianist and was one of the best in the business in Dublin at the time. It was released as a single about a month later and started to get a bit of radio play.

I will never forget the first time I heard it on the radio. We were on the way to a gig in Donegal and we dropped into a small hotel to get something to eat. Incredibly, the song was playing as we walked in. It was so exciting to hear ourselves on the radio and we looked at each other in disbelief. We had been told that the song was going to be played by Radio Éireann sometime that day but we didn't know exactly when. It was so coincidental that we happened to stop at the hotel at that particular time. I felt a huge surge of pride and immediately went looking for a payphone. I wanted to call my mother to find out if she'd heard it. I was delighted when she told me that she had. I still get that same thrill these days when I hear my music on the radio. When people like Ronan Collins play my songs, I always feel proud and thankful to be in the business I'm in.

Just after the song was released, Tom asked us to go around all the record shops to see how it was doing. I couldn't believe it – the single was flying off the shelves! It wasn't as if the release had been heavily promoted or anything. It was probably a combination of radio play and word of mouth that propelled the song to Number One in January 1964. We were there for six weeks in the end. All the other lads in the Miami were over the moon when they heard the news and a hit record brought even bigger crowds to our concerts.

For the rest of that year, it seemed that nothing could stop our domination of the Irish charts. That summer we reached Number One with 'I'm Yours', and again in October with one of my most best-loved songs, 'From the Candy Store on the Corner', which I still love performing today. It remains one of the most requested songs at my shows.

Our next big hit was another song called 'Just For Old Times' Sake'. By the mid-1960s the popularity of the Miami had reached fever pitch. It seemed that we could do no wrong. The band was getting bigger and we were witnessing record attendances at ballrooms all over the country. A highlight from that time was when we were invited to play in a televised show at the prestigious London Palladium in December 1964. The opportunity came about through an English showbiz agency we were attached to, run by a man called Paul Cave. I was on this revolving stage with the Miami and we played two songs, which went down great with the audience. I remember being struck by the very generous applause that greeted the end of our short set. Top of the bill that night was the legendary British singer, Petula Clarke. She had a huge hit that year on both sides of the Atlantic with 'Downtown', probably her most famous song. We got to meet her after the show and, despite all her stardom and fame, she was a really nice woman.

Through 1965 we had massive hits with 'Round and Round', 'Every Step of the Way', 'I Left My Heart in San Francisco' and 'Wishing It Was You'. I have a special place in my heart for 'Every Step of the Way'. It was the first Irish record ever to go straight to Number One. This beautiful ballad was a new departure for me in terms of its lush production. I recorded it in London backed by an orchestra. I was cut off from the rest of the musicians by dividers so the sound of the music wouldn't pour into my mike. I was singing like a swallow at the time and we recorded the song in just two takes, which would be unheard of today. The single was released as "Dickie Rock and The Miami Showband", even though none of the others had played on it!

Amazingly, I didn't make any money out of our records, despite all the chart success. In hindsight, I was probably naïve at the time, stupid even. I often think that if I had come from a business background, my father would have sat me down and said something like: "Now hold on for a second, Richard, this is your record. What percentage are you getting paid?" That said, I don't think that my naivety was taken advantage of – it's just the way things were at the time. The money went to the record company and the people who owned the publishing rights to the songs. Whatever was left after that was paid to Topline and they spent it on posters and other promotional material.

As the hit singles continued to mount up, I toured Ireland, the UK and even America with the Miami. We were making good money but not nearly as much as people thought. It's the same today – although bands are on great money, they don't make as much as people think. The only people making the serious money are the ones who are writing the songs or own the publishing rights. If you write them and sing them, then you're on the pig's back – that's how the likes of Elton John are so rich. I once read that Def Leppard had recorded a number of albums before they started to make any money. Record companies may sign a band up for, say, a €200,000 advance, which sounds like a lot of money. But people forget that this sum has to be spent on recording, publicity, hotels and all that goes with being in a band. Everything has to come out of that advance before the people in the band get a cent.

In the Miami we were all on a wage of around £50 a week, which would have been three or four times what my father was making. Dad would come home from work and tell me that people thought I was earning around £200 a week – and I could understand why they would think that. They'd go to a dance and see crowds of anything between 2,000 and 4,000 people paying at the door. Automatically they'd assume that the band would be sharing the takings but that wasn't always the case. Other expenses had to come off the gross earnings as well – the manager's fee, the venue, publicity – and we were usually paid a flat wage regardless of what was earned on the night.

While the hit singles may not have been benefiting me financially, they were certainly doing my profile no harm. Even those who weren't interested in me previously began to take notice. After The Melochords split up, some of the members had formed The Cadets Showband, fronted by the talented singer Eileen Reid. I expressed an interest in joining at the time but they wouldn't let me in. Some of the band apparently felt that I was changing groups too often after the demise of The Melochords. That may well have been the case before I formed The Echoes but it was only because I still hadn't found what I was looking for in terms of a new band. A few years later, when the Miami had three Number One hits behind them, I was rehearsing in the Top Hat in Dun Laoghaire one day when Paddy Murphy, the leader of the Cadets, rang me up and asked if I was interested in jumping ship and joining them. Out of pure curiosity – and possibly an element of mischief – I asked him what sort of money was on offer. On hearing his answer, I responded: "I pay that in income tax alone!" In truth, I wouldn't have left the Miami even if the money had been the same. As far as I was concerned, the Cadets had rejected me when I needed a break and were only interested in me now because of all the chart success I had enjoyed with the Miami. It would have been interesting if it had happened at the beginning. They had a great singer in Eileen Reid and I think we would have interacted well on stage together as a double act but it hadn't come at the right time and I was happy to stay with the Miami.

* * * *

Eurovision fever gripped Ireland in 1965. It was our first year to enter and I was really disappointed not to be offered a song by Telefís Éireann for the National Song Contest, especially given that I had a string of Number One hits under my belt at that stage. Butch Moore, the singer with the hugely successful Capitol Showband, was given one, along with a few other people I didn't know, including an Irish folk singer called Maisie McDaniel. The poor woman had an accident and wasn't able to make it on the night so I was asked to take her place and perform her entry. Entitled 'I Still Love You', it wasn't really my type of song – it's probably best forgotten, in fact – but I decided to do it because I knew that if I refused I possibly would not be offered a second chance the following year. I've always believed that you should never burn your bridges as you never know what the future holds. I performed the song to the best of my ability but it didn't win the National Song Contest and it fell to Butch Moore to represent Ireland in the Eurovision in Naples. He came sixth with the song 'Walking the Streets in the Rain', which was a great achievement for Ireland's first time in the contest. Butch – who was one of the founding members of my old band, The Melochords – had great support back home as he was very popular on the showband circuit. I remember him as a lovely man and a very good singer. Sadly, Butch passed away in America in 2001.

I was luckier the following year and I was offered a lovely song for the National Song Contest. This one was right up my street, a beautiful ballad called 'Come Back to Stay'. It was written by Dubliner Rowland Soper, who was a talented singer in his own right, in the vein of Nat King Cole. I sang it on the bus one day for the lads in the Miami when we were on our way to Galway and they all thought it was great, which gave me confidence. Butch Moore was again in the running but this time I beat him and won the contest. I was overjoyed because it was huge back then, not like the sham that passes for Eurovision selection these days. 'Come Back to Stay' became a massive hit. I'd sing it with the Miami all over the country, sometimes up to 10 times a night. The crowd would just stand there, listening intently – they couldn't get enough of it.

The 11th Eurovision Song Contest was held in the Grand Auditorium de RTL in Luxembourg on March 5, 1966. The hype surrounding my entry was hard to live up to. Even the Artane Boys' Band was at Dublin Airport to play us off. The Eurovision meant a lot to Irish people at the time. Back then we were a small country in every sense of the word and we certainly wouldn't have had the confidence as a nation that we have now. I was very nervous as I boarded the flight, knowing that the hopes and dreams of Irish people were resting on my shoulders.

During the rehearsal in Luxembourg there was an incident involving the Italian entrant, Domenico Modugno, who wanted to have girl backing-singers perform with him – even that wasn't allowed at the time. The Eurovision was a serious song contest back then, not the freak show it is today with its heavy metal bands, trapeze artists, half-naked women and all the gimmickry.

I went on stage that night in front of millions of TV viewers and sang my heart out. While I was feeling nervous inside, I was hoping that this didn't show too much. I went on to give the best performance possible. The most nerve-wracking part was when the votes started coming in: we were in the lead and then we were second, third, fifth and back to third again. Eventually we came fourth – and I was disgusted with the result. In fact, to say I was disappointed would be putting it mildly. The rest of the Irish contingent seemed delighted but I felt in my heart that it wasn't good enough. Even coming second would have been a disappointment. This should have been one of the biggest nights of my life but, true to form, I just wanted to get back to my hotel and relax after the whole thing was over while everyone else went partying. Jesus, I was an awful square when I think back on it. It was very untypical behaviour for a young man in his early 20s but that's just the way I was.

To further compound my disappointment, we were denied the opportunity to appear on Val Doonegan's television show after the Eurovision. Even though we had a contact on the show – a Limerick fella called Nealus O'Connell – we just couldn't get on. To add insult to injury, the Spanish entrant, a chap called Raphael, appeared as a guest with Val Doonegan – and he had only come tenth. I couldn't understand why Val, a Waterford native, couldn't have a fellow Irishman on his show. After all, this Raphael guy was even singing in bloody Spanish! I was very bitter and annoyed about it at the time. Somebody suggested that maybe Val

Doonegan didn't want another Irish singer on his show as it would have been competition for him, but that's just speculation. I still feel that he could have had me on instead of that Spanish bloke, though.

The homecoming I was given on my return from Luxembourg was phenomenal and helped to really lift my spirits. Even on the flight I remember telling Tom McGrath – a top Telefís Éireann producer and a great guy – that I didn't expect much of a crowd at the airport to welcome us back home. I certainly didn't think there'd be anything like the send-off we had received just days previously. How wrong I was.

After we landed I emerged from the plane to a scene reminiscent of The Beatles arriving in America. There were hundreds of people screaming and shouting up on the balconies. I couldn't see much because it was so dark but I could certainly hear them. There were more crowds inside the old airport building. It was amazing to realise that all these people had come out in support of me on a cold, wet Monday night. I was completely overwhelmed by the welcome.

Somebody had parked my car across the road from the airport at the Coachman's Inn. From there, I drove straight home to Cabra, thinking I was leaving all the chaos behind me but a crowd of fans and well-wishers were waiting for me at Dingle Road. It gave me an amazing lift, to be honest.

It finally started to dawn on me that I had done Ireland proud in the Eurovision. I may have only come fourth but people treated me as if I had won. To them, it was a huge victory and an improvement on the previous year's result achieved by Butch Moore. Of course, I realise today that coming fourth out of 18 countries was a great result for Ireland but I didn't see it like that at the time.

The fanfare surrounding my homecoming and Ireland coming fourth in the Eurovision may well have been the lead item in the following day's newspapers had it not been for another momentous occasion in Irish history. On March 8, 1966, the IRA blew up Nelson's Pillar on O'Connell Street, using timed explosive devices. Other than the damage to the pillar and the 13ft high statue of Nelson himself, there were no injuries or deaths. The Irish Army later had to blow up what remained of the pillar's stump. Needless to say, it was the main news story in all the Irish papers the next day. It's not every day that you get upstaged by a well-known Dublin landmark – Nelson stole my Eurovision glory!

SEVEN

Love and Death

To say that 1966 was an eventful year for me would be something of an understatement. It was a year of extreme highs, punctuated with some terrible lows.

For obvious reasons the Eurovision stands out as one of the highlights but even this auspicious event paled in comparison to my marriage to the love of my life that summer. Undoubtedly, marrying Judy Murray would turn out to be the best decision I ever made.

Despite what people may have believed, my experience with the opposite sex had been extremely limited up to that point, even with the female attention that came with being in a successful showband like the Miami. My first kiss during that game of spin-the-bottle in Cabra West was as steamy as it got for me – and I was 21 years old at the time! It was my first time to participate in a game of spin-the bottle – I was a bit of an oddball – but I remember being thrilled to finally get to kiss a girl. She was a young lady by the name of Maureen Stewart. That sort of innocence might be difficult to believe today, when you hear young people talking about "riding" at 15 or 16-years-of age. It wasn't that I was trying to cultivate an image for myself as this squeaky clean, holier-than-thou type or anything like that – it's simply the way I was.

I can fully accept, however, that there are certain preconceptions about singers and entertainers and not everyone bought into my boy-next-door reputation. Even Judy's mother was suspicious of me when she first brought me home to meet her parents. I could understand where she was coming from. It was a natural reaction for any mother to have after learning that their daughter was going out with a showbiz type. I'd probably feel the same way today if I heard that my daughter was seeing a famous star. While I never blamed Judy's mother for initially thinking that way about me, the reality was that I was a rather unconventional celebrity – a non-drinking, non-smoking, non-womanising one – and I hoped I would have the opportunity to eventually prove this to her.

Before I met Judy in 1965 I had been dating a few other girls but nothing too serious. I met a lovely girl called Collette Kavanagh at the Rose of Tralee festival. She was working there as a production assistant with Tom McGrath in Telefís Éireann. Since I wasn't much of a ladies' man, I never had the nerve to formally ask her out. Then I heard through somebody else that Collette would be willing to see me and we went out on a few dates after that. I really liked her a lot and we became pretty close in a short space of time, but not in a sexual way. I just got to see her once a week because I was working solidly and Monday was the only day I had off. In the summer I'd often be performing seven nights a week so it was difficult for us to meet up regularly and the relationship never became too serious. Shortly after dating Collette, I started seeing a teacher, Mary Kelly, who was from Galway – a truly lovely woman. The one thing I'll always remember about her was that all her friends were also schoolteachers. I never took any of these early relationships for granted. To me, every one of them had the potential to develop into something serious, perhaps even marriage. But from the moment I set eyes on Judy it was crystal clear to me that neither Collette nor Mary had ever been likely to become the future Mrs Dickie Rock.

It all happened in the Ierne Ballroom, off Parnell Square in Dublin, on September 11, 1965. From the stage I could see my father standing there with his cousin Vickie, who was his best pal. My Dad used to drop in to my shows occasionally on his way home from his union meetings. That night he brought me up a Club Orange, which was my favourite drink at the time. Later, during a break in the show, I went to meet him in the cloakrooms downstairs, where I found him talking to these two girls. One of them was Judy, whose pal's uncle, the Gunne family used to run the Ierne. They had been at the pictures earlier that evening and had popped into the dance afterwards. I went back up on stage and I positioned myself where I could see Judy standing to the side of the hall. I was trying to get her attention and eventually succeeded in passing a message to her, asking her to meet me down in the cloakroom. When it was somebody else's turn to sing a song, I grabbed the opportunity to go down and meet her. I was due back on stage within minutes so there was no time to lose. Judy came in and I got straight to the point.

"Do you drink?" I asked her.

"No."

"Do you smoke?"

"No."

"Do you want to go to the pictures on Monday night?"

"Yes, I'd love to," she replied.

That was one of the things I instantly loved about Judy – there was no messing around with her. What you see is exactly what you get. I'm extremely black and white by nature so it was important to me to find out if she drank or smoked because I didn't and it would have annoyed me if she did.

Like me, Judy also had unfinished business to attend to before we could go to the pictures together. We were both seeing other people at the time and we both had dates arranged for the Sunday night. With a heavy heart, I picked up Mary Kelly and we drove to the Glen of the Downs in Wicklow. Mary was a very good-looking girl and I think she was about a year older than me. I really liked her a lot but there was something missing in our relationship. After our drive I dropped her back to her flat on the South Circular Road. I knew, out of respect to the girl, that I had to be straight with her so I told Mary that I wouldn't be ringing her again. I didn't want to be going to the pictures with Judy behind her back so I had resolved to put things right first. That may sound stupid but it was just a personal value that I held dear. I've always tried to avoid hurting people throughout my life and it's something I've attempted to instil in my own sons over the years.

Much to my relief, Mary didn't seem too upset that I was breaking up with her and just said: "Oh, that's sudden." There were no tears or tantrums or anything of the sort. In hindsight, I don't think she really fancied me all that much. She certainly liked me but I don't think her feelings for me ran any deeper than that.

Judy, meanwhile, had finished up with the guy she had been seeing. It hadn't been serious between them, anyway.

The way had now been cleared for our first date. I brought Judy to the Cinerama on Talbot Street to see 'How the West Was Won'. It was a great place and had one of those new wide screens. After the movie ended, we went for a drive out to Sutton where they were building lovely new houses. I used to love taking a spin out there and looking at all the houses being built. Judy must have thought I was mad bringing her all the way out to north Dublin to look at a building site in the dark. Later, we went for a meal in Nico's on Dame Street. I remember looking at Judy and thinking she was so beautiful, absolutely striking. We had managed to cram a lot into our first date and I still succeeded in having her home – on her mother's orders – by midnight.

I've never been one to subscribe to the concept of love at first sight as I'm a firm believer that love is something that has to grow. My feelings for Judy, however, were as close as you could get to instant attraction on my part. I was besotted by this unassuming, gentle woman. She had jet black hair and I thought she bore a strong resemblance to the screen icon Ava Gardner. But not only that, she was a nice person as well. I love femininity in a woman in the same way that most women love masculinity in a man. Judy certainly possessed femininity in abundance. It's such a shame that so many women today don't seem to realise the importance of it.

Judy had lived a fairly sheltered life but probably not as much as I had. There was just herself and her brother growing up in their house in Rialto. The week I met her she had just started working as a secretary for National Cash Registers and I used to pick her up from there the odd time. I knew from the very first date that she was the woman for me – I was completely gone on her. But despite my strong feelings for Judy, she was starting to suspect that there was something not quite right about me – she must have even wondered if I fancied her at all. For starters, it took me three weeks to make a move on her and even then it was just a quick peck on the cheek outside her front door. The first time I kissed her *properly* was at the Ambassador Cinema at the top of O'Connell Street – and it wasn't what you'd even call a serious kiss.

I was still working six nights a week so I only got to go out with Judy on Mondays. For our third date I wanted to bring her up to a show we were doing in Northern Ireland, in a ballroom in Bangor called Caproni's. Her mother only agreed to let her go on condition that she brought along her cousin. Mary was about 8 years older than her and acted as chaperone. I had no problem with that and was simply delighted that Judy was able to go. I have a vivid memory that night of performing a beautiful song called 'More', while catching Judy's eye from the stage as I sang the words: "More than the greatest love the world has known …". After that night, the lyrics took on a special resonance for both of us. It became *our* song, the soundtrack to our love for one another. Every time I perform that song, it takes me back to the early days of our relationship and, in particular, to that memorable night in Caproni's.

It's funny, but I always got a sense that Judy's mother never really liked me. Maybe I got off on the wrong foot with her or perhaps it was just down to me being a performer, but even later, throughout our marriage, I got the impression that she didn't have much time for me. She was always up and down with me. I could always tell when she was in good humour because she'd refer to me as "Rich". In fairness, though, she was a very nice woman and I just had to accept that I couldn't do anything to change the way she felt about me. Perhaps she didn't realise that Judy meant everything to me and all I wanted to do was protect her and look after her. I used to get on well with Judy's father, though – he was a lovely man – and I think he liked me, too.

I'm not sure if Judy was as crazy about me as I was about her but she certainly had feelings for me. She told me once that she liked the way I treated people. In December 1965 – just three months after our first date – we got engaged. I had spoken to her father briefly about my intentions beforehand but Judy didn't know anything about it. I'd made sure that I'd got her a lovely engagement ring, not to mention getting a good deal on it too!

I showed it to my mother before I gave it to Judy and she didn't seem in the least bit surprised. "Sure I knew by you that this was it for you," she told me.

I was too shy to propose in the traditional manner and never officially said to Judy: "Will you marry me?" It was just kind of understood. We went bowling in Stillorgan one night and afterwards we were sitting outside in the dark. I complimented Judy on a ring she was wearing – it had been given to her by her mother – and asked her to take it off so I could take a closer look at it. I had the engagement ring in my other hand and I just slipped it onto her finger.

"Is this okay with you?" I asked Judy.

"Yes, of course," she replied.

And that was it – we were engaged.

It may sound like we approached the idea of marriage in a very casual manner but inside we were both thrilled about the prospect of spending our lives together. I'm not sure if Judy's parents saw it that way, though. The night we got engaged, Judy went straight home and showed her mother and father the ring. When they asked her when we were getting married, Judy told them June. But they assumed she meant June the following year and her poor mother nearly had a heart attack when Judy told them that the wedding would be held in just six months' time. I think they were definitely taken aback by the suddenness of it all and I'd say her mother and father were a little bit disappointed. They probably felt that, because we were only going out together for three months, things were moving too fast.

Now that I'm a father myself, I can fully understand and appreciate the concerns they may have had. But at the time it never once crossed my mind that we were rushing into things. I knew that we had six months or so before we got married. If it did not feel right at any stage before June, we still had time to break up, despite the hurt it would have caused. It would have killed me to have to do that to Judy but I would not have hesitated in calling the whole thing off if I had any doubts. In any event, the question of not going through with the wedding never entered my mind – or hers.

Once we got engaged I started to realise the enormity of the responsibility that would come with being a husband and, potentially, a father. I was marrying a woman whom I loved very much but I did begin to feel an enormous sense of duty weighing down on me. There was considerable expense attached to being a husband in those days. Unlike today, women were expected to give up their jobs once they got married. The thinking behind this was that the woman would be looked after by a husband so she had to make way to give someone else the chance of a job. It may sound stupid but one income per family was supposed to be sufficient. Even women working in the civil service had to give up their jobs once they got married. Judy didn't seem to mind, though. That's just the way things were at the time and there wasn't too much she could do about it.

It wasn't long before Judy was thrust into the public eye. In December

1965, a few days after we decided to get married, I was playing in a fabulous ballroom in Limerick called Jetland that was owned by Albert Reynolds and his brother. After the dance, at around 2 am, the papers arrived and there was a big photo of Judy emblazoned with the headline: 'DICKIE ROCK ENGAGED!' We never tried to hide the fact that we were getting married and everyone – fans, friends and family alike – were all very supportive of our decision. Once people got to know Judy they could see she was the right woman for me. There would be something seriously wrong with you if you didn't like Judy or get on with her. She is an amazing person and has the ability to touch everyone she meets with her kindness and gentle manner.

Just a few months before we got married, RTÉ – as Telefís Éireann was now known – screened a documentary about me called 'Portrait of an Artist – Dickie Rock'. Adrian Cronin, a great guy who used to be with 'The Late Late Show', was the producer of the programme and he followed me around the country with his TV crew. The whole thing was a fantastic experience and we had a really great time doing it. Judy featured in the documentary a number of times. They were filming at one of my shows in Galway and they got a shot of her looking at me on-stage as I was singing 'Strangers in the Night'. There's a funny scene where I'm doing my Eurovision hit, 'Back to Stay', while the camera pans in on Judy walking out the door in the middle of the song. That part was very cleverly edited to tie in with the words of the song and I thought it was hilarious. But there's one particular image from the documentary that stands out when I watch it today. In one scene you see me bringing Judy home to Cabra to have tea with my family. That was actually the first time I ever brought her home. It makes me sad to see my mother and father looking so young in it.

The reaction to the programme was just amazing. People genuinely loved it and it helped to expand the fan base I had built on the back of the Eurovision. To her absolute credit, Judy adjusted to being in the limelight remarkably well, particularly when she had come from a very private, conservative family. In a way, the documentary was a reality television programme of sorts, focusing as it did on real people and real lives. However, unlike reality TV these days, it never once felt intrusive or exploitative.

The rollercoaster ride that was 1966 continued to gather pace and

My first audition!

One of the few photos I have of my Ma and Da when they were young.

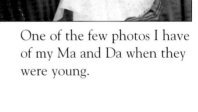

Outside Clery's in Dublin with my Uncle John.

1962 – 63 just after I joined the Miami.

Meet the boys

DICKIE ROCK

Dickie Rock (22) lead vocalist, is a keen admirer of Elvis. Has appeared with personalities such as Cliff Richard, Billy Fury and Adam Faith. Dickie had received several offers to go into show business in England, but became a Miami enthusiast from the start. His records have reached the number one spot in Ireland's top ten.

Promotional postcards were sent all over the country, given out at the dances and to the fan clubs to get our faces known. There also used to be a 'Miami News' article every week to tell everyone what we were doing.

(Reproduced courtesy of Francis Kennedy, www.irishshowbands.net)

The original Miami line-up – Murty Quinn, trombone; Tommy O'Rourke, trumpet; yours truly, vocals and tambourine; the leader Joe Tyrell; Martin Phelan, saxophone; drummer Tony Bogan; the late Clem Quinn on guitar and Dennis Murray on bass at the front.

The Three hit-makers – Murty Quinn, myself and Clem Quinn all had hits in the Top Ten when this picture was taken, 'One Kiss for Old Times' Sake', 'Come Back to Stay' and 'Buck's Polka' respectively.

The Guitarman – I remember playing for four hours in that polo-neck and it was no joke!

Some of my fans came to give me their best wishes at my parents' house in Cabra before I left for the church on my wedding day – June 20, 1966.

The seven Miami 'brothers' – looking for seven brides! The eighth 'brother' was missing in action.

My groomsman Martin Phelan is in the background with the Garda who was trying to clear a path through the crowd of well-wishers for myself and Judy.

PORTMARNOCK COUNTRY CLUB HOTEL

Telephones:
350611
Private Parties and Dances
Cash only

PORTMARNOCK

Co. DUBLIN

LICENSED
ACCOUNTS RENDERED WEEKLY
NO CHEQUES

Micks Rock W/Ree Nº 9390

June 20th 1966

Room No. Ballroom

	Week Ending _____ 19___				Total
Brought forward	120 Guests	@ 22/6	135 0 0		
En Pension	18 Teas & Sandwiches	@ 4/-	3 12 0		
Apartments	40 Teas	@ 1/-	2 0 0		
Early Tea	12 Red Wine	@ 14/-	8 8 0		
Breakfast	12 White wine	@ 13/6	8 2 0		
Luncheon	15 champagne	@ 40/-	30 0 0		
Afternoon Tea	10 Fruit cup	@ 4/-	2 0 0		
Dinner	6 doz club orange	@ 1/-	3 12 0		
Supper and Sandwiches	Bar Drinks		7 12 10		
Tea, Coffee, Milk			200 6 10		
Beers					
Wines, Spirits, Liqueurs					
Minerals	10% Service charge		20 0 6		
Cigars, Cigarettes	2½/. T.O Tax		5 0 0		
Telephone			225 7 4		
Papers			15 15 0		
Laundry			209 12 4		
Extra Attendance					
Amounts Paid Out					
Sundries					
Service					
Total	Total £ 225 - 7 - 4				
Deductions					
Carried forward					

The receipt from our wedding – I keep this framed in the house as a thank you to Judy's father who insisted on paying for everything that day.

At our wedding reception in the Portmarnock Country Club or Palm Beach as it was known then.

On honeymoon at the El Cid Hotel in Majorca – going down the slide the right way for once!

The Artane Boys' Band gave me a great send off!

Singing to some of our fans in the early days of the Miami.
(Reproduced courtesy of Francis Kennedy, www.irishshowbands.net)

One of the postcards used to advertise the new Miami line-up in 1967.

Jim'll Fix It! We were both at the Jimmy Saville Walk in aid of the Central Remedial Clinic (CRC) in Clontarf.

Just call me James Bond – the well-known '60s model Pam Conway is posing on the front of the Jag.

(Reproduced courtesy of Francis Kennedy, www.irishshowbands.net)

Singing 'Simon Says' at the Arcadia Ballroom in Bray with the new Miami. The fans seemed happy with the different line-up!

(Reproduced courtesy of Francis Kennedy, www.irishshowbands.net)

'Strangers in the Night' – the romantic ballads were always a showstopper.

before we knew it June 20, our wedding day, had arrived. We wanted to get married in the Church of Our Lady Queen of Heaven at Dublin Airport but Judy's local priest was being very awkward about it. I had nothing against the church in Rialto. I just felt we would have more privacy if we got married out at the airport, as it was a good bit out of the city. The priest in Rialto initially refused to allow it but I called out to see him and eventually persuaded him to change his mind.

When the day arrived I have to admit that I was a bit nervous. I got ready in my parents' house that morning and there's a great photo taken there with my mother fixing my bow tie. All the neighbours in Cabra gave me a fantastic send-off as I was driven to the church. Much to my relief, there didn't seem to be too many people outside the airport chapel. I thought that our desire for a private, low-key wedding was all going to plan. It was a different story, however, inside the church. It was packed to the rafters with hundreds of fans and well-wishers who decided to gatecrash our wedding. I didn't really mind, though. When you think about it, they had every right to be there. I don't think anybody should be banned from a church. These days, some celebrities even try to stop people from seeing them entering or leaving a church, by putting up tents or big screens. I find that sort of behaviour extremely vulgar. Just because they've sold the photography rights to some magazine doesn't give them the right to behave in such an appalling way. Who do these people think they are?

Amid all the chaos, Judy walked calmly down the aisle and she was absolutely stunning. I think I was looking well myself, all spruced up in my wedding suit, but I was nothing compared to her. Judy was flanked by her two bridesmaids – her cousin Mary Bowe and Leslie Lawlor, an old school friend. My best man was my brother, Brian, while Martin Phelan – the sax player from the Miami – was a groomsman. It wasn't a case that I was closer to Martin than any of the other lads in the band. The Miami was such a big part of my life it seemed appropriate that they should be represented on my wedding day. I could have chosen any one of them, really. A cousin of mine from America, Rev Tom Walton, officiated at the ceremony.

When it came to the part where we exchanged our vows and Judy was asked if she took this man to be her lawfully wedded husband, there was an audible sigh from my fans in the church and everyone laughed. It was all very dramatic, really. Back in those days there was no such thing as people clapping or talking during a ceremony and weddings were a far more sedate affair than they are now. My cousin deliberately ignored the incident and carried on with his priestly duties but myself and Judy caught each other's eye and found it difficult not to grin.

By the time we left the church, the few dozen or so curious onlookers that had greeted us on our arrival had swelled into a massive crowd. The guards had to clear a path so we could cut through the throng of frenzied fans. A film crew from Pathé News was there to capture the whole thing and the footage ended up being shown in cinemas. You can see us struggling to make our way through the crowds. We finally got to the wedding car and were taken on the short drive to Palm Beach in Portmarnock for the reception.

Despite our earlier hopes for a more private affair, I think that, in the end, all the attention from the media and fans added to the excitement of the day for us. I'll never forget the atmosphere outside the church. The feeling of goodwill towards us from the fans was very touching and meant a lot to me. I imagine it must have been great for Judy to get all that extra attention, too, especially as she was looking so beautiful – she really was like a movie star. True to form, she never seemed too phased by all the fuss and took the whole thing in her stride. Judy was under no illusions when she agreed to be my wife and knew what she was getting into by marrying somebody in showbusiness.

The wedding reception was extravagant for the time. According to the bill – of which I have a framed copy on my wall at home today – there were 120 guests, setting Judy's father back the not inconsiderable sum of £225. Even though I was a successful singer earning good money, Billy Murray was a very principled man. He insisted on paying, in keeping with the tradition of the day where the father of the bride was expected to foot the entire wedding bill. He was a very quiet, conservative man and extremely handsome. He managed a pharmaceutical factory that manufactured tablets and was loved and respected by his staff.

After the meal and the speeches, the wedding band took to the stage and our guests danced the night away. It was one of those rare nights when I didn't get to sing. In fact, Judy and I had to leave the reception early to catch our plane. Back in those days it was normal to go on your honeymoon directly from the wedding reception. Much as we had enjoyed the day, there was something nice and romantic about the bride and groom flying off into the sunset, leaving everybody else behind.

That night we flew out to Gatwick Airport in London, before catching a connecting flight to Majorca where we would spend the first two weeks of married life together. I remember that Judy was wearing this big hat as we got on the plane and I teased her about it, telling her to take it off because it made her stand out from the rest of the passengers.

In the short nine months since we had first met, the honeymoon was the longest period we had ever spent together. It would be virtually unheard of today, but we had never slept with each other before we were married. Even when we were filming the TV documentary and Judy came down to see me perform in the Seapoint in Salthill, Galway, we each had our own room in the hotel. People might think it was simply immaturity on my part but it genuinely never entered my mind that we should have been sharing a bed before we were married. It was a case of a quick kiss goodnight in the foyer before going our separate ways for the night.

Majorca was the first time we ever shared a bed. I had this idea – and Judy probably did, too – that refraining from sex until our wedding night would make it extra special. I'm still not sure whether it was a good idea or not. These days, couples tend to live together before they get married and there is certainly some merit in that. As the saying goes: "If you want to know me, come live with me." When you think about it, Judy wouldn't have known if I had any annoying habits, like say, for the sake of exaggeration, sweaty or smelly feet. And I didn't know if she had any personal traits that would irritate me. It was uncharted territory for both of us, really, as it was for most couples back then.

I suppose I was traditional in my outlook of sex before marriage. I also respected Judy too much to want to sleep with her before we were husband and wife. I've always tried to teach my sons to respect women. This might sound old-fashioned but, to me, every woman is a potential mother, a sacred kind of thing. When I see they way certain women are going around today, I fear for some of the mothers of the future. The point I'm trying to make is that it's easier for a man to choose to live with someone before marriage than it is for a woman. It's all very well if a woman falls in love with someone and moves in with him before they get married but what happens when it doesn't work out? This woman may end up living with numerous different guys until she finds the right fella. How many times is she going to go through this process in her life? The way the world is today, she is going to be branded a slapper, or something equally unkind, for living with different men. A bloke can live with as many women as he wants to and he won't be judged for it. In respectable society, a man doesn't want to end up with a girl who has been around the block 20 times – even though he may well have been himself. It's so unfair but the fact remains that there are still different levels of thinking today for men and women.

Back in the days when I got married, nine out of ten couples wouldn't have had sex until their wedding night. It was certainly my first sexual experience and I've no regrets about that – we're still together more than 40 years later and stronger than ever. But you can understand the other side of the argument, too. After all, being sexually together for the first time can be a traumatic experience, more so for the girl than the fella. In that respect, living and sleeping together before you get married can make sense. It's not enough to simply get on with your partner on a social or domestic basis; the sexual aspect to any relationship is very important, too.

You'd imagine that escaping to a sun-soaked haven like Majorca would afford a young honeymooning couple as much privacy as they desired. Not in our case, however. After our first wonderful night together I was relaxing by the swimming pool in the El Cid Hotel, waiting for Judy to come down and join me. She eventually arrived in all her finery and I was struck by the sudden realisation that this beautiful young woman was actually now my wife. Judy had never learned how to swim so I decided to teach her in the hotel pool. Suddenly, out of nowhere, up popped a newspaper photographer from the *Sunday Mirror*, and asked us if he could take our picture. He was nice enough about it so we were happy to oblige. This meant that everyone at home got to see us in the newspaper pictured together in the pool while we were still on honeymoon.

Later in the week, we bumped into a group of Irish women who worked for Aer Lingus and were in Majorca on their holidays. They were absolutely delighted to meet us and we posed for some pictures with them and had a great laugh. By coincidence, the girls revealed that just a few days earlier they had come over from the airport to see us leave the church after our wedding. I have very special memories of those two weeks in Majorca. It was a great start to married life together.

Fortunately for us we didn't have to worry about finding a place to live when we got back to Dublin. Not every married couple starting out together in the 1960s could enjoy the luxury of moving into a new home straight away. But my common sense approach to money – which probably stems from my working-class background – ensured that I had invested my earnings wisely.

I had got to know the well-known hotelier, PV Doyle, through performing in his hotels over the years and he became a good friend of mine. In 1964 – before I had even met Judy – I had approached him in the Montrose Hotel and asked his advice about how best to invest the few bob I was earning. I told him about all the hit records and the £50 or so I was making a week through playing with the Miami. It seems like a small amount now but it was big money at the time. You could buy a house for £2,000 or maybe even less then. I told Mr Doyle that, although I was single, I expected that I would meet a girl at some stage and want to get married in the future. My thinking at the time was that maybe I should buy a house now, while the money was coming in. That way, I reasoned, if I met someone special in two or three years' time and wanted to settle down, I would have bought a property at 1964 prices. This was typical of me at my most practical. The showband scene was booming but I often wondered how long it would last. The music business could be a precarious place – as I'd earlier discovered when The Melochords split up – and I thought that, at best, I'd get five or so good years out of the Miami.

PV Doyle told me that I should wait until I met the right woman first but I didn't want to wait. I was determined to invest my money regardless, so he advised me to buy something close to town and maybe rent out part of the property as flats to have an additional income coming in. After I met Judy, he helped me find a house in Leeson Park in Ranelagh and even organised a builder to convert part of it into flats. When we got married, Judy and I moved into the basement of the house, which was made up of two bedrooms, a big lounge, dining room and a small kitchen.

We were only back from our honeymoon a few weeks when Judy discovered she was pregnant. Naturally we were thrilled about it at the time but it probably wasn't the best thing to happen so soon after getting married. In hindsight, I always felt that we should have waited longer before starting a family. After all, we were still in the early stages of our relationship and only really starting to get to know each other properly. It didn't give us the time or space to ease into married life. I think it would have been better if we had waited three or four years before having children. I may have been practical and sensible when it came to financial matters but in other ways I was stupid and immature. We didn't see it like that at the time, however, and the news of Judy's pregnancy was met with great joy by both our families.

It was only a few weeks later when our newfound happiness came to an abrupt halt. Just four months after our wedding, my youngest brother, Joseph, was tragically killed in an accident. It was an event that would have a profound effect on all of us, particularly my poor parents.

It was October 1966 and I was over in England recording a new single. Judy picked me up at the airport on my return to Dublin and I couldn't help noticing on the drive home that she seemed a little bit subdued. When I asked her if something was wrong, she explained that Joseph, who was only 11-years-old at the time, had been in an accident. He'd been out playing with his pals on his bike and my mother had told him to come in and do his homework. He was quite a good student and attended St Vincent's school in Glasnevin. Just half an hour later, someone called to the door and told my mother that Joseph had been involved in an accident. She couldn't believe it because she thought he was upstairs doing his homework, like she had asked him to. But, typical of a boy his age, he had sneaked out of the house behind her back and gone off again on his bike. My poor mother, it wasn't as if he was out playing and she hadn't bothered to check up on him. She had simply assumed he was in the house. The accident itself was bizarre; there was no big crash or anything. Joseph was just sitting on his bike on the North Circular Road when he was nudged by a passing car. It wasn't the impact of the car hitting him that caused the damage; it was the way he fell. He crushed his brain stem at the back of his neck.

When I asked Judy how serious it was she told me that the outlook was not good.

I went to see my mother and father immediately and they told me that Joseph was in a coma in the Richmond Hospital. I was absolutely shattered. I was the eldest and Joseph was the youngest and we were extremely close.

I went up to the bathroom and remember sitting on the edge of the toilet seat and crying my eyes out. When I managed to compose myself, I came back downstairs and told my parents that I wanted to see Joseph.

My mother and father brought me down to the hospital and there he was, looking beautiful, with not a mark on him, lying on the bed. I rubbed his little face and forehead and whispered into his ear: "Hey Joseph, it's Richard." I could have sworn that I detected a little flicker from him when I said that. I spoke to the doctor but he said there was nothing he could do for Joseph due to the damage to his brain stem.

I refused to accept his prognosis and told him I was going to get another opinion. I organised for a neurosurgeon to fly over from England and examine Joseph. I explained to the doctor in the Richmond that I didn't mean any disrespect towards him personally but I simply had to exhaust every avenue of hope – for the sake of my brother, sisters and parents. However, the English surgeon gave us the same bleak diagnosis – nothing could be done to save Joseph.

My 11-year-old brother was gone within a week. I was rehearsing with the band down in Parnell Square – if anything, just to take my mind off things – when I got a phone call from my sister, Lillian. "Joseph has gone to heaven," she said.

I went straight down to my parents' house in Cabra. When you enter the front door you can see straight through to the kitchen. I'll never forget the heart-breaking sight of my mother with the ironing board out, the tears streaming down her face, as she got Joseph's altar boy suit ready for him to be buried in. I would later go on to experience the devastation of losing a child myself so I know exactly how my mother must have felt that day. There is such a sense of injustice to it all – you are not supposed to outlive your children.

I coped with Joseph's death by burying myself in my work. Even when he was in a coma I still continued to perform with the Miami. I was in bits, though. I just couldn't get him out of my mind. I remember being on stage in the Dreamland Ballroom in Athy, just before he died. As I was singing 'Come Back to Stay' I was expecting to see somebody arriving through the entrance to let me know that Joseph had passed away. I nearly cried every night on stage that week. It was tough keeping the show on the road after his death but a part of me didn't want to let people down – the band or the fans. The fact that I had developed this separate stage persona probably helped detach me from what was going on in my personal life, but every night on stage I thought about Joseph. He was this fabulous young boy who I was very close to. Judy was mad about him, too. Her brother, who was probably only around 16-years-old at the time, had also become great pals with Joseph. My brother was a lovely, lovely kid and very handsome. I have very precious memories of one particular day, not long before he died, when we brought him out to Howth for the day and took a motorboat trip around the harbour. He was so happy that afternoon and was full of life and energy. My brother was typical of any 11-year-old boy, although he would have been a lot more innocent than kids of that age are these days. If I had to describe Joseph in one word it would be "angelic".

One amazing thing about death is that it often brings out the true kindness and human decency in others. My parents were naturally devastated to lose a son but one man – who was a virtual stranger to them – kept them going through those difficult times. His name was Johnny Reid and he ran a motorbike shop on Berkeley Road. I had got to know him many years previously after buying my motorbike from him. Shortly after my brother was buried, Johnny just started calling up to the house to see my parents, even though they didn't know him. He was what you might call a real character. He used to have my mother and father in stitches with some of his antics. A favourite trick of his was pretending to have a seizure when other people called to the house. I remember my mother's brother was over from England and Johnny just winked at my father before throwing himself on the floor and clutching his chest in feigned agony. My uncle just went "Oh Jesus!" while my parents fell around the place laughing – and this was only a few weeks after Joseph's death. Nobody else could have made them laugh because they were so broken-hearted. Johnny became a very close friend of my parents and was always bringing them out for a drink or to different things. Sometimes it takes people from outside the family to help in times of tragedy. It made me realise that it's always worth taking a chance and running the risk of intruding on people's grief. Maybe there's something you can do to help, even if you don't know them very well. Just asking someone if they would like to go for a drink and a chat can often help. I was always grateful that Johnny Reid took that chance and thanked him many times before he died for everything he did. In my opinion, that man helped keep my mother and father alive.

Joseph's death left a big void in my parents' house. I had got married that year and moved out and so had my sister, Margery, who ended up with a super husband called Paddy Brown. With two of us now gone, only my brother, Brian, and other sister, Lillian, were left at home. The family had recently moved to a bigger house in Annamoe Park, which was in the older part of Cabra. There had been a draw the previous year for which Dublin Corporation tenants could put their names down for a site. Their neighbours in Cabra, the Morans, also had their name drawn. I was delighted to be in a position to loan my parents and the Morans the money to build the two houses. The way it worked was that the corporation would reimburse you the money once the houses were built. I remember giving around £2,500 to the builder at the time. I remember how happy my parents were when they moved in but with three out of the five children now gone, the new house must have felt pretty empty.

1966 had been a big year for me, both personally and professionally, but the highs were completely overshadowed by Joseph's death. A tragedy like that puts everything into perspective. I would have readily given everything up – the Eurovision, the hit singles, the success of the Miami – if it could have prevented him from having that accident or if it could have brought him back to us. The passing of time has helped ease the sense of loss but I still think about Joseph a lot and wonder what he would be like today if he had lived.

EIGHT

New Beginnings and Separate Ways

Judy gave birth to a beautiful baby boy on April 7, 1967.

I remember phoning my father from Mount Carmel Hospital and telling him: "We've been blessed with a son – we'd like to call him Joseph, if that's okay with you." Obviously they were delighted about that.

We brought the baby home with us after a few days and everything seemed fine. It would be nine months before we would learn the terrible truth about our infant child.

Being first time parents, I suppose we didn't really know what was 'normal' when it came to a baby's development. I remember Joseph was in his pram outside our home on Leeson Park and it was a lovely sunny day. I had a touch of flu at the time and a really wonderful doctor by the name of Mulvaney came to see me. After tending to me, she turned her attention to Joseph. She took him out of his pram and sat him up but he just slumped over. Slightly concerned, she asked us if he was crawling yet and we said no. She was a very good doctor and sensed that something wasn't quite right with Joseph. She just felt that he wasn't doing what a typical nine-month-old should be doing. On her advice we saw a specialist at Our Lady's Hospital for Sick Children in Crumlin who confirmed our worst fears – Joseph was severely brain damaged and would need special care for the rest of his life.

We were in a complete state of shock. It was the worst possible news any parent could hear. The frustrating thing for us was that, to look at Joseph, you'd never think there was anything wrong with him. He was beautiful, like his mother, with lovely eyes. Judy hadn't experienced any complications during her pregnancy. Perhaps a doctor who specialised in this area might possibly have detected a problem early on. Maybe Judy's mother, or even my mother, should have suggested we see somebody but these things weren't really discussed at the time. In those days people didn't like to interfere when it came to personal matters. It's impossible to know if it would have made a difference to how things turned out but you always ask yourself these types of questions in a time of crisis.

I've always felt – rightly or wrongly – that Joseph was damaged during his birth. That can happen sometimes, if the oxygen supply is cut off to the baby. His was a forceps birth and I think there is a possibility that maybe he was affected by it. The skull is very soft when a baby is born so I imagine it would be possible to cause damage to the brain stem with a forceps. I came up with this theory after discovering a flat spot at the back of Joseph's head, about the size of a large half crown or a two euro coin. I know I could be wrong and it's only a personal theory but that's what I've always believed happened to Joseph.

We were devastated to learn about our son's disability but Judy took it particularly badly – I think a woman always tends to blame herself when things like this occur. However, she later came to realise that it wasn't her fault. It was just one of those inexplicable things that happen in life. She didn't drink or smoke or do anything during her pregnancy that could possibly harm the baby. Joseph's arrival was a traumatic and challenging start on the road to parenthood and would present us with the biggest challenge of our marriage.

* * * *

People often talk about the principle of the matter when it comes to looking for more money. But for me it was never about the principle – it was always about the money. When people say principle they mean money.

I'd been with The Miami Showband since 1962. After a few years, it started to dawn on me that I was getting something of a raw deal. I was the one with all the hit records; I was the one signing all the autographs; I was the one being stopped by fans on the street. Huge crowds had greeted me at the airport and given me a hero's welcome on my return from the Eurovision; my wedding day had been besieged by fans and the media. While I had the greatest respect for the other musicians in the Miami, it didn't seem right to me that the lead singer – the public face of the band – was on the same money as the trumpet player. I think most people would accept that good and all as he was, there was something inherently wrong about this setup. In or around the time I got married, I sat down with our manager, Tom Doherty, and got straight to the point – I wanted more money. If I didn't get a raise, I was leaving the Miami.

Tom understood where I was coming from and agreed to an increase but it wasn't substantial by any means. It was somewhere in the region of £15 a week more than the others. I told Tom that there was no compunction on him to tell the lads in the band that I would be getting a few bob extra. As far as I was concerned, it was none of their business what I was being paid. If they were unhappy with what they were earning, they could approach him and ask for a pay rise themselves. I didn't even want to know what Tom was making out of his involvement with the Miami. All I was interested in was what I was earning.

While Tom agreed to give me an increase, he felt he had to first run it by two of my fellow band mates, Tony Brogan and Joe Tyrell. Apart from being in the group, they were also Directors of The Miami Showband. I suppose Tom didn't want to appear underhanded by giving me an increase behind their backs. I was never a Director of the band and had been one of the last to join but I felt that I had become their greatest asset. Personally, I don't see what the big issue was. It would be the same for a person in any job who feels they're working harder than others or realises that their value is worth more than somebody else's. In these circumstances it would be perfectly acceptable to go in and ask the boss for a pay rise and not expect him to let the other staff know about it. I think it was a mistake for Tom to tell anyone about my increase because it seemed to get on the wick of certain other band members. Some of them were apparently not too happy about my wage increase but it didn't seem to affect our working relationship. In fairness, Tony and Joe saw the sense in what I was saying and had no problem with me getting the extra money.

My discontent over money wasn't confined to the financial arrangement within the Miami. It rankled with me that the lads in the

Royal Showband, for example, were said to be earning considerably more than we were. While their success seemed to have peaked by the mid-60s, by contrast, as the decade progressed, Dickie Rock and The Miami Showband were growing in popularity. Even lesser-known bands – such as the Royal Blues, from Mayo – were reputed to be raking in the cash and that just didn't seem right to me. Don't get me wrong, I never begrudged anyone their success. Even today, I love to hear about the likes of Tony Kenny or Red Hurley or Joe Dolan doing well, because it means the audience is still out there for us. I'm happy to think that people are getting away from their televisions and going out to see a show. If the business is doing well, generally, it means that Dickie Rock is doing well, too. If I heard that business was bad for Joe Dolan I'd probably think to myself: "Jesus, this doesn't sound too good for any of us."

I can safely say that there was never any tension in the band in the five years we had been together. I may have been the frontman on stage every night but behind-the-scenes we operated as a democracy. We all had a say in the type of songs we wanted to play and relations in the band always seemed to be excellent. That's why I didn't expect it all to suddenly come to an end.

Much to my annoyance, the majority of the band announced they were quitting behind my back. I wasn't even in the country at the time because I was representing Ireland in the 1967 Sopot International Song Festival in Poland. I had been entered into the competition as a result of my success in the previous year's Eurovision. This festival was organised annually by Polish State television and the head of music at Radio Éireann, Kevin Roche, chose me to represent Ireland. The competition itself was held in a forest in a big outdoor venue that resembled a giant oyster shell, with a 60 piece orchestra in the background. All entrants had to sing a Polish song, translated into their own language – and not all of the songs lent themselves to English. I was given a song, entitled 'Our Love Will Stay', before we went over to Poland and it was translated for me. It was a great experience performing in such an unusual venue. On top of that, the musicians drafted in for the competition came from all over the world and were among the best I'd ever played with. Apart from my official entry, I also sang the Sinatra song, 'Fly Me to the Moon', which went down so well that even the orchestra applauded. Of course, one of their own won the competition – all these things were political because Poland was part of the communist bloc at the time. Sopot was a coastal resort by the Baltic Sea and I remember going down to the beach one day and it was freezing. The competition was an enjoyable experience that reunited me with many of the singers and musicians I had met in Luxembourg at the Eurovision Song Contest the previous year – people like Udo Jurgens, the Austrian who had won the Eurovision with the song 'Merci Chérie'.

On my return to Dublin I was met at the airport by a glum-looking Tom Doherty. He told me that most of the band – excluding Tony Bogan and Joe Tyrell– had handed in their notice. Unbeknownst to me, some of the lads had let their grievances over my pay rise fester to the point that they wanted to quit the band, but I genuinely hadn't seen it coming. My immediate response was: "Right, they've done it, let's get the ball rolling and bring in a new group of fellas."

The truth be known, I did get a bit of a jump of the heart when I heard the news. I was pretty disappointed by their actions, especially because they did it while I was out of the country. To this day, I'll always maintain that I never fell out with any of the original members of the Miami – they fell out with me. Their timing certainly wasn't great. After all, I was a married man now with a young son and those responsibilities weighed heavily on my mind. I would have completely respected their decision to leave the band if they had been upfront about it. I still get annoyed about the way it was handled when I think about it today – it was a mean thing to do. It seemed to me that I was the last one to find out they were quitting. At the very least they could have waited until I got back and discussed it with me before announcing their decision.

The last gig we played together was a few weeks later at the Arcadia in Bray. There was no obvious animosity between us, although the situation was a little awkward. The place, as usual, was packed to the rafters and I couldn't resist having a gentle dig at the lads during the show.

I sidled up to guitarist Clem Quinn, who had handed in his notice with the others, and said: "What to you think of this place? It's great isn't it?"

"It's fantastic," he agreed.

"Well, take a good look around and enjoy it, because you're not going to be seeing it again," I told him. "As for the huge crowd, well, enjoy that, too – you won't be seeing that again, either."

Clem saw the sense in what I was saying and reversed his decision to quit the band. Obviously, being a family man like myself, he knew he would be risking a good, solid livelihood by leaving the Miami. When word of the split got out, it was greeted with shock and dismay by our fans and made the headlines in all the newspapers. The timing of the split didn't make sense to anyone because we were at the height of our success and virtually ruled the ballrooms of Ireland. You could understand a band splitting up if they were experiencing declining popularity or weren't getting on with each other, but that wasn't the case with us at all.

Four members of the original Miami Showband – Martin Phelan, Murty Quinn, Tommy O'Rourke and Dennis Murray – immediately formed a new group called The Sands. They brought in teenage singer Tony Kenny, who had been a member of the beat group, The Vampires. Tony was a good-looking fella with a nice voice and it wasn't long before The Sands started to enjoy chart success. Their earlier singles with Tony included 'Help Me Rhonda', 'Yummy, Yummy Yummy' and 'Dance, Dance, Dance', which were all top 10 hits in 1968. Tony left The Sands in 1972 and went on to forge a hugely successful career as a solo artist, both in Ireland and in the United States. Like me, Tony is one of the few survivors of the showband era and managed to stay in the business long after the ballrooms closed their doors.

While the Miami split came as an unexpected blow, the nucleus of the group – Tony Bogan, Joe Tyrell, Clem Quinn and myself – remained committed to carrying on regardless. We immediately set about picking up the pieces. In this business, everyone's replaceable and there were plenty of other talented musicians out there who jumped at the chance to join a successful showband.

The Miami were back on the road in no time. We brought in some great guys including Brian McCoy on trumpet, Fran O'Toole, who sang and played keyboards, Paul Ashford on bass, Des McAlea on saxophone and Pat McCarthy on trombone. Pat's originally from Arklow, in County Wicklow, and is a great guy – we're still friends today. He was obviously a man with great taste, too, because he ended up marrying a girl from Cabra West. Band leader Joe Tyrell, who was a Director of the Miami, remained involved with the group but stood aside to let Fran O'Toole replace him on keyboards.

Fran O'Toole and Paul Ashford had previously been in a beat group

together called The Chosen Few so it was a completely new departure
for them to join a showband. It was similar to the transition I had made
five years earlier when I joined the Miami after playing in Rock 'n' Roll
groups The Melochords and The Echoes. Even though some of the beat
groups looked down on the showbands, joining the Miami presented
musicians with a great opportunity to earn some decent money. It was
more money than they ever could have dreamed of making in a Rock 'n'
Roll band. Some of the others would have been getting in the region of
£12 a week working in a factory so to jump up to £70 with the Miami
was a huge leap in salary. These were all young guys, going out with girls
and maybe intending to get married in the future, so joining a well-paid
band like the Miami made perfect business sense for them. Fran was
only around 21 at the time and I think Paul was just 18.

I was extremely happy with the new line-up of the Miami. Not only
had we brought in a nice bunch of guys, they were all talented musicians
and looked great too – it felt like a fresh start. We hit the ground running
and headed over to America for a short 10-day tour. I was able to bring
Judy with me, which gave her a little bit of a break from the new baby.
My mother minded Joseph for us; she really loved him so much. We
were in New York, playing a gig in a place called Sunnyside, which was
in Long Island and Judy was in the dressing room listening to the radio.
She heard this song called 'Simon Says' and thought it would be perfect
for us. She called me in to hear it and I was immediately taken by its
upbeat tempo and catchy, almost addictive, chorus. I took down the
name of the song and went back to the fellas in the band with the idea
of releasing it as a single back in Ireland. The song had originally been
recorded by a group called the 1910 Fruit Gum Co but wasn't really
known back in Ireland. When they heard it, the rest of the band was
just as enthusiastic about recording it.

We finished the US tour and headed straight into the studio as
soon as we got back to Dublin. We had a great time recording it. I was
something of a studio veteran by that stage but making a record was a
big deal for some of the new members of the band. I remember they
were all thrilled when it first went on sale in the record shops and started
getting lots of radio play.

To our delight, 'Simon Says' went straight to number one in the
charts in the summer of 1968, where it stayed for six weeks. It's always

been hugely popular and these days I still do it for fun, particularly if I'm playing at a wedding or something. It's great to see all the young kids waving, shouting and clapping their hands in the air, like the song tells them to. Having a Number One hit was just what we needed, after the original band breaking up. It gave us tremendous confidence and got the new line-up of the Miami off to a great start. Judy has to take full credit for the success of that song. If she hadn't heard it that day on the radio in New York, most likely we never would have recorded it.

Later that same year, we had a hit with a lovely song called 'Christmas Time and You'. It was written and arranged by Tommy Ellis, who has produced most of my major hit records over the years.

That same year I finally fulfilled my dream of living in Sutton. I bought a beautiful home in Offington Park. It was the same type of house I had brought Judy out to see on our first date. For some reason I'd always had an affinity with that part of the city. I loved living close to the sea and being near Howth, yet still on the same side of the city as my parents. I was a northsider at heart, I think. We kept our first place in Ranelagh and continued to rent it out as flats. It seemed like a good idea to give ourselves a nice additional income in case my music career ever went pear-shaped.

It wasn't long after we'd settled into the new house that Judy found out she was expecting again. Looking back, we were stupid. Joseph was still a baby when Judy became pregnant for the second time. Raising a child with special needs was hard enough without the extra pressure of another baby in the house. At the time Judy was naturally concerned on account of what had happened to Joseph, but her gynaecologist assured her that she had nothing to worry about. Joseph's condition was just one of those inexplicable things in life and there were no hereditary factors or anything like that responsible for it.

He was right, thank God. Jason Rock was born on July 24, 1969, perfect in every way, except for the fact that he cried solidly for about two years. He didn't stop. I'll never forget the day he was born. Judy wanted to visit a good friend of hers in Dundrum, Patricia Cahill, and had asked me to give her a lift. Earlier that day she had been feeling little twinges now and then and I told her I would prefer to bring her straight into the hospital. I didn't want her taking any chances. Judy refused to go, however, and insisted on being dropped off at her friend's house. I was supposed to pick her up later that afternoon but got badly delayed and was a few hours late. As I drove towards Dundrum on my way to collect her I saw Judy being driven at speed in her friend's car in the opposite direction. Much as I had feared earlier – she had gone into labour. I flagged down their car and brought Judy straight into the Rotunda Hospital. I can't even begin to describe the things Judy called me that day for being late. Under the circumstances I thought it best just to take it on the chin and not mention the fact that I'd wanted to bring her into the hospital in the first place. Jason was born shortly after we arrived at the Rotunda. I'll always remember that he arrived on this planet on the same day that Neil Armstrong and his crew returned to earth following their historic moon landing.

Having a healthy baby was a huge relief to us. We were so thankful when Jason arrived safe and well. Even though doctors had assured us that what had happened to Joseph had been a rare occurrence, it still didn't stop us worrying throughout the pregnancy. We were afraid that the second baby might also have a mental disability. This time, we could see the normal progress that a child should make. With Joseph we didn't know any better as we had no other children to compare him to. Having another baby in the house though was a major shock to both of us. All of a sudden we had two very young children in nappies, one with very special needs. It was a very hard time, particularly for Judy as I was working most of the time, either on tour or in the studio recording. That year, we enjoyed further chart success, first with 'The Wanderer' and later with another Tommy Ellis original, 'Emily'. The hits were great for the profile of the new Miami line-up and we were on the road constantly.

In hindsight, we were extremely foolish. I think we should have waited longer – perhaps four years – before trying for another baby because of the situation with Joseph. Today, I would always advise young couples to wait a while after they get married before having children. But nobody advised us to wait, including my own parents or Judy's. Conversations about personal issues were pretty much off-limits back then. Things like that simply weren't spoken about in the open way they are these days.

The real challenge now was to try to juggle my home life as a father with my job as a well-known entertainer. Even though Judy could have done with me being home more, having the responsibility of a second child made it all the more important to keep the show on the road.

Throughout the '60s it was virtually impossible for me to walk down the street without being approached by complete strangers. To be honest, I was always flattered and grateful that people would take the time to approach me and offer words of encouragement or support. To me, the fans are the lifeblood of our business. The way I see it is that, if the audience ever disappears, then so does my livelihood. I'm often asked if all the requests for autographs bother me and my answer is always the same – it will bother me when it stops. Most of the time, I get a great buzz from all the recognition. There are times, however, when being in the public eye can have its drawbacks.

Possibly one of the most frightening incidents of my life occurred in 1969 as I made my way home one night from a gig. When the Miami were playing down the country, we used to leave our cars at a meeting point in Dublin before travelling down together in our wagon. We'd often arrive back from a show in Cork in the small hours of the following morning. On these occasions, I'd pick up my car and stop on O'Connell Bridge on the way home to pick up the morning papers as soon as they'd hit the streets.

One night, at around 3.30 am, I stopped my car and rolled down my window to buy a paper off this little old fella who used to be a constant presence on the bridge. Suddenly, a car pulled up behind me and the driver started beeping his horn aggressively. I thought to myself: "What the hell is this all about?"

Trying to ignore his obnoxious behaviour, I paid for my newspaper and slowly drove off.

I took a right turn on O'Connell Street onto Abbey Street. As I did, I noticed this same car behind me, gathering speed. By now I was getting a bit concerned. The last thing I needed at this hour of the night was hassle. I just wanted to get home safely to my wife and two little boys in Sutton.

I reached Fairview and realised that the car had now pulled up alongside me. For the first time I noticed that there were two occupants, and both of them were shouting abuse at me and gesturing wildly. I wondered what the problem was with these guys? It's not as if we'd had an argument or anything.

As I continued on up the Howth Road, it appeared that I had lost my angry pursuers. Safe in that knowledge, I pulled into a late night petrol station in Raheny. I had just started filling up when the same car I had seen earlier screeched into the forecourt of the garage. These two thugs jumped out and ran towards me, effing and blinding at me for no apparent reason. They appeared to have lost all sense of reason so there was no time to ask them what their problem was. Two bloody head cases were coming at me like rabid animals. It was like being attacked by pit-bull terriers. I took one look at the sheer hatred in their eyes and said to myself: "I'm in big trouble here."

Unlike my father, who had been a keen amateur boxer, I was not used to having to defend myself physically. But self-preservation is an amazing thing and it forces you to make decisions you probably wouldn't even contemplate otherwise. I had the petrol pump in my hand and instinctively started to swing it all around me, while shouting at the garage attendant to call the guards. Still, the two thugs came at me until – smack! – one of them was lying unconscious at my feet. It was his own fault entirely. I hadn't intended to hurt anyone and had only used the petrol pump to stave off my aggressors. Typically, the other fella had scampered back to his car in a state of shock and locked himself inside it. These types of people are generally gutless chickens when not operating in packs.

I ran over to his car and started shouting at him: "Open that door, you little coward – go and help your friend."

He eventually got out as the guards arrived on the scene. The guy I had decked was still lying on the ground.

I explained to the guards what had happened and they let me go on my way. Still shaking, I drove home to my family.

The next morning I was lying in bed when Judy came in to tell me that the guards were downstairs looking to speak with me. I had to go with them to the Garda station in Raheny as I was wanted for questioning about an alleged assault. Apparently the guy I had clobbered with the pump was in hospital suffering from a fractured skull. Luckily for me, the fella working in the petrol station had confirmed my version of the story and I was never charged with any criminal offence.

Unfortunately, that was far from the end of the matter. The man who attacked me had the cheek to try to sue me for the injuries he had sustained. The whole thing came to court around a year later. Jesus, you wouldn't believe the ridiculous lies that were spun by his side during the court case. Their most outrageous claim was that I had stopped on O'Connell Bridge to pick up a prostitute, even though I was just buying a newspaper. I suppose they needed some justification for their behaviour that night in pursuing me as far as Raheny. But what did it matter to them why I had stopped my car on O'Connell Bridge? Even if I had been looking for a hooker – which I certainly wasn't – it didn't give them the right to come after me and attack me.

It was a really stressful time and to add to it we were in the middle of moving house. I don't know anyone who has moved as often as I have. We put our beautiful home in Offington Park on the market after living there for just two years. There was some method to my madness. I never knew how long my success in the music business was going to last, so I had this thing in my head about wanting to live in a property that was going to increase more in value. Sutton was always a good address in terms of selling property but the price was nothing compared with what it would have fetched on the southside of the city.

We found our next home by accident. I just happened to be driving through Churchtown when I spotted this lovely Tudor-style house for sale. From a work point of view, the south Dublin location suited me better as at this stage I used to meet the rest of the band on the Naas Road before travelling to a gig down the country. Churchtown was also more convenient for town, particularly if I was playing somewhere like the Olympia Theatre or the Television Club. I had bought the house in Offington Park for £6,000 in 1968 and sold it two years later for £10,800, which was a nice little profit. The people who bought it from me, the Sweeneys, still live there today. We would eventually stay in Churchtown for nine happy years and most of my children's childhood memories would be attached to that house. It was a lovely place to call home and it was also worth a lot of money in case my career ever suffered a setback – I was hoping the impending court case wouldn't damage me professionally or financially.

When the case finally came to court I found it all pretty stressful, despite the fact that the truth was on my side. One day during proceedings, I started to feel unwell and went to see a doctor but he just put it down to nerves as a result of the case. I took the stand to give my side of the story under sworn testimony, as did the man who worked in the garage. I was supposed to go back to court in the afternoon but was suddenly struck by severe stomach pains. I went home to Judy and she became extremely concerned about me. She called a doctor who came up to the house.

After examining me, he immediately phoned for an ambulance and I was rushed into hospital. So instead of going back to court that afternoon, I found myself carted to A&E with a burst appendix. I was operated on immediately as it was considered to be a life-threatening emergency.

When I regained consciousness, Judy came up to see me. She had some great news – the court case against me had been completely dismissed. The judge had even expressed annoyance that the case had been brought in the first place, declaring it a waste of the court's time and Mr Rock's time. I didn't really grasp the significance of what Judy was telling me. My stomach was killing me and I was only interested in moaning about that.

Later that day, my father came up to the hospital to thank the surgeon who had operated on me. His gratitude quickly turned to shock when the doctor told him: "I'm afraid your son's not out of the woods yet, Mr Rock." My poor father nearly died. After all, he had only buried his youngest son four years earlier. The last thing he wanted to do was go home and tell my mother that the life of their eldest boy was also at risk.

Thankfully, I made a full and complete recovery. There is always a risk with a burst appendix that it can poison your whole system. The doctors said only for the fact that I was fit and looked after myself, I could have died that day – it doesn't even bear thinking about. It's possible that the entire incident was brought on by the stress of the court case but I can't say that for certain. One thing is for sure, though: it was lucky I didn't go back to court that afternoon or I probably wouldn't be alive today to tell the tale.

That was the one and only time of my career when fame threatened my personal safety. I'm fairly certain that these guys recognised me on O'Connell Bridge that night and singled me out because of who I was. I'm also sure that the bloke who took the case against me for fracturing his skull probably thought I was loaded – which was far from the case. It was just sheer opportunism on his part and he eventually got his comeuppance.

I have no regrets about what happened that night in the petrol station. It was a scary situation and I had no choice but to respond the way I did. Once I saw the evil in his eyes and sensed that he was the type of person who didn't give a damn about other human beings, I had to defend myself. It was a case of two guys attacking one guy – ultimately, one of them got walloped. That's what happens when you go too close to someone swinging a petrol pump, I suppose.

I never found out any details about the men who attacked me that night. There is always the possibility that they copped on to themselves afterwards and went on to lead respectable lives. A good few years after the incident, however, I was in the foyer of the Adelphi cinema with Judy when I got a tap on the shoulder. I couldn't believe my eyes – it was the same individual I had clobbered in Raheny. "How's it going, Dick?" he said to me in a friendly manner, as if nothing had ever happened.

* * * *

As the 1970s dawned, it became clear to me that the Irish public's love affair with the showbands was past its peak. I don't think the cultural and social role of the ballrooms in Irish society can be underestimated. They were places where teenage dreams were realised and romances formed, with many resulting in marriage, children and all the rest. I'll always remember how happy people looked during a dance. Some of them may have been in jobs they didn't like and probably didn't have much money but the ballrooms were an escape from their everyday life. They were all about fun – and, of course, companionship. People never tire of telling me that they met their partners at a Miami Showband concert. They'll often say things like: "You were singing 'Every Step of the Way' at Seapoint in Galway when I met my husband for the first time." Be it Belfast or Castlebar, I'll hear the same thing again and again, although the songs tend to differ from couple to couple. The fact that many of my hits were sweeping, romantic ballads probably adds to their sentimental value.

The way I see it, the ballrooms were an integral part of changing Ireland's social structure. I know people were courting and getting married long before the ballrooms opened their doors in the '50s and

'60s but the dances meant that teenagers could meet up on a regular basis with people from different towns and villages. Before the ballrooms, I'm sure they met their partners at local parish hall dances or even through arranged marriages. In rural areas we used to play to crowds who'd come from miles away. All of a sudden, inter-county relationships began to thrive and it meant their lives weren't so claustrophobic. The showbands helped to open up a world with new and exciting possibilities.

I think that the showband era did more to change life in Ireland than it's sometimes given credit for. But, like everything else in life, it couldn't go on forever.

Nine

Taking Care of Business

There was good reason for me to fear the decline of the showbands. In some ways I had put all my eggs in the one basket when I agreed to join the Miami back in 1962. I wanted to make the most of the public's appetite for the showbands while it lasted and consciously decided to work mainly in Ireland. It didn't make sense at the time to be pursuing opportunities abroad when there was so much on offer back home. I'm extremely grateful for all the success I've had here, but because of the size of this country, the potential to make serious money is limited. Some people have compared my enduring appeal as similar to that of Cliff Richard, whose music career even pre-dates mine. The main difference between myself and Cliff, though, is that he still does the odd concert here and there and occasionally goes on tour, but he doesn't need to – he made his millions a long time ago. When you take the size of the UK market alone, he must have made around £60 million sterling. You just can't earn that sort of bread in Ireland. I still love performing and it's the main reason why I'm still doing what I'm doing, but I never felt that, financially, I could retire from the music business and put my feet up. If I had been born in England and could have emulated the success there that I've had in Ireland, I might have been in a position to retire years ago – not that I would have wanted to!

The problem was that we had no management representing our interests abroad, which severely limited our ability to spread our success beyond the Irish market. During the Miami years there were the occasional trips to America but nothing too regular. Tom Doherty was a good man but – like many other showband managers at the time – was only interested in Ireland. When we got the opportunity to play in cities such as London – like in 1964 when we performed with Petula Clarke at the Palladium – it would have been helpful to have a management representative over there with us in case somebody saw us perform and wanted to book us. We probably missed out on numerous opportunities because of this. It was the same in 1970 when we played the prestigious Drake Hotel in New York, just off Park Avenue in Manhattan.

There was a really nice club in the Drake Hotel that held around 300 people and the Miami were booked to play three shows a night there, for three weeks. There was a tea show, a dinner show and a supper show, with each performance lasting over an hour and a quarter.

One night I was getting ready for a late show at the Drake when I was approached by the maître d'. "The boys will be in tonight," he told me and pointed to the table where they'd be sitting.

I had no idea what he was talking about and just nodded.

During the performance I noticed four extremely well-dressed men, accompanied by three beautiful women, take their seats to the right of the stage. After the show, the maître d' came into my dressing room. "The boys would like to have a word with you," he said.

I went out and shook hands with them.

"Sit down, kid," one of them barked, as the maître d' got a chair for me. They complimented me on my performance and we chatted for a while. They mentioned that they had just come from the Copacabana nightclub where BJ Thomas had been playing. He'd just had a big Number One hit with 'Raindrops Keep Falling on my Head', the Burt Bacharach and Hal David song that featured in the movie 'Butch Cassidy and the Sundance Kid'. I asked 'the boys' how BJ Thomas was getting on.

"He's finished in this town," one of them snapped back, "thinks he's Sinatra."

The singer's crime had been to request that no drink be served during his performance. He had been fired on the spot, even though he was only half way through his run at the club.

I naively asked how they could get away with firing him like that. "Couldn't he sue?" I enquired.

"He won't be going to see any lawyer, that's for sure," came the response and they all erupted with laughter.

Suddenly it dawned on me that these were no ordinary 'boys'. They were 'made' guys, not to be messed with. I posed for a picture with them all later. Unlike Frank Sinatra, however, the photograph was never used by the authorities to prove whether Dickie Rock had mafia connections or not!

A different crowd came in for each sitting and the audience reaction we got was fantastic. The New York appearances led to us getting a great write up in *Variety* magazine. But again, we had no management over there to help us capitalise on the success of these shows which was a wasted opportunity in many ways.

It wouldn't be true to say I am bitter that international success eluded me. Sure, it would have been fantastic if my appearance in the Eurovision in 1966 had boosted my profile abroad more than it did. The fact of the matter is, however, that I had a number of chances to pursue opportunities abroad but I chose not to take them. In 1971, I turned down an opportunity that possibly could have launched my career in the UK. I was made an offer by the United Artists record company, who believed they could turn me into an international star. This would have given me the same advantages that people like Tom Jones were enjoying, although I would have been aiming more at the Frank Sinatra or Tony Bennett market. I'm not suggesting for a second that I was in their league or anything, but I was a good singer and had a lot of confidence in myself as a serious performer. The downside of the offer was that I would have to uproot myself and my family and relocate permanently to London. The record company also wanted me to get my ears pinned back as they said they stuck out too much.

I flew over for a meeting with them and remember one of the big shots from United Artists saying to me: "Dickie, you're a good singer – but there are lots of good singers out there. However, there are very few performers like you and the combination of both is what makes you a star."

I took time to consider the offer but eventually declined it. I felt that moving to England would be too high a price to pay for international success. I could have possibly lost the most important things in my life – my wife and family. If I had to base myself in London as a recording artist, Judy and the children would have remained in Dublin and that was unacceptable to me. All the travelling back and forth to the UK would have placed an unbearable extra burden on Judy, who was struggling as it was to raise two young children, one of whom was severely handicapped. Who knows what would have happened if I'd accepted the United Artists offer – but I've never had any regrets about turning it down. The main thing is that I've still got a beautiful wife and family to show for it after all these years.

It was some consolation that not long afterwards I found myself back on the international song competition circuit when I took part in the Golden Stag Festival in the Romanian town of Brasov. The formula for the competition was similar to the festival I had entered in Poland four years earlier, in that you had to sing a Romanian song translated into your own country's language. For the Miami, it was a case of the show having to go on without me. Due to booking commitments, there was no question of any gigs being cancelled while I travelled over to Romania for the festival. My brother, Brian – who is quite a decent singer himself – filled in for me for a couple of gigs. He actually had his own band for a while called The Hustlers and they were pretty good.

Brasov is located at the foot of the Carpathian Mountains, in the area of Romania famous for Count Dracula. I remember leaving my hotel to walk around the town and it was like stepping back in time. Even though Ireland back then wouldn't have been the modern, dynamic country it is today, Romania in 1971 seemed to me like it was decades behind us. While the town itself was in a picturesque location, I didn't have to go too far before I found appalling deprivation and poverty. I remember there was a foreign car parked on the street and there were literally hundreds of local people gathered round gazing in awe at it. For them, seeing a modern car would have been something of a novelty. I felt there was a real pre-war sense to the place, as if time had stood still for them since the 1930s.

At the time of my visit Romania was a communist country under the rule of Dictator Nicoalae Ceausescu. I can't remember if he was in the audience that night but if he was there I was unaware of it. I was told it was Ceausescu himself who initiated the Golden Stag Festival in 1968 in an attempt to show the western world that Romania was a free country. However, three years later he changed his mind and ended the annual festival, fearing it would give the Romanian people a taste of too much freedom. I performed in the final Golden Stag Festival before the plug was pulled on it. There wasn't another one until 1992 when, three years after the Ceausescu regime was toppled in the 1989 revolution, the event was revived by Romanian television. By that stage, however, I no longer had an interest in the competition and certainly didn't follow its progress any further.

In the first four years of the festival, the Golden Stag had played host to a number of well-known names including Cliff Richard, Kiki Dee, Connie Francis and our very own Joe Dolan, who performed there in 1970.

My participation in the Golden Stag Festival was eventful, to say the least. I performed over two nights, singing the Romanian song first, followed by Frank Sinatra's 'My Way'. Thinking nothing more of it, I flew back to Ireland to meet up with the guys in the Miami for a gig in Crosshaven in Cork. Half way through the show, word came through from Romania that I had won an award. I was needed back in Brasov immediately to accept it in the grand finale closing ceremony.

I really wanted to be there to collect the award so I made frantic last-minute plans to get back to Romania. First I called Judy and asked her to get my suit ready. There were no flights from Dublin or Cork that would get me to Bucharest on time so there was only one thing for it – I had to charter a private plane to get me to London. From there, I would be able to catch a scheduled flight to Romania. There was no question of RTÉ footing the bill, even though they had entered me into the competition. I had to fork out the £200 it cost at the time to hire the plane – an extravagant amount back then! In reality, it was stupid of me to leave Romania before the Golden Stag results were announced, just to play a gig with the Miami. But the simple fact was that I was committed to playing this particular show and the management wanted me there – it was one of the problems of being tied down to a band, I suppose.

The plane touched down in Bucharest in heavy snow conditions. I could hear the Golden Stag Festival being broadcast live on the radio of our minibus as we started our two and half hour journey to Brasov. The severe weather was hampering our progress and I began to wonder if I would make it in time.

When we finally pulled up outside the Dramatic Theatre I charged straight into the dressing rooms, where a touch of make-up was hastily applied. With just seconds to spare, I was announced to the audience and arrived on stage to a rapturous response from the audience. I could see all the other judges shaking hands with Kevin Roche from RTÉ, congratulating him on the fact that his entrant had managed, against considerable odds, to make it back. It was a fantastic honour to receive a Golden Stag Award, not that it made much of an impression back in Ireland – it wasn't even broadcast on RTÉ radio, unlike other European countries that had entered. There may have been a small bit of coverage about the award in the Irish papers but generally my Golden Stag victory went unnoticed back home. Perhaps there was wasn't any public interest because the event was held in Romania.

On a personal level, however, I felt a great sense of achievement. After all, I had come close to success in the Eurovision in 1966 and three years later had taken third place in the National Song Contest. And while I had previously represented Ireland in a song festival in Poland, this was my first time to win a competition. It was a great day in my life and certainly one of many career highlights. The Romanian award was a rewarding one personally although it didn't do anything for me financially. In fact, if anything it had cost me a fortune, having to hire a private plane and all of that. But singing and performing is not all about money – it's about enjoying the pleasure of being able to entertain people. That said, it's always nice in this business to get official recognition for your talent.

On the journey back to Dublin, I made sure to take extra care of my Golden Stag trophy, keeping it with me at all times for fear it would get damaged on the flight. I arrived home to Judy, still clutching the award in my hand, then stumbled through the front door and the bloody thing fell on the ground. I couldn't believe it – I had managed to bring this trophy all the way from Romania unscathed and then the first thing I did when I arrived home was break it. Luckily, I was able to fix it and the award took pride of place at home for many years afterwards – I'm not sure where it is these days, though.

* * * *

Despite the success of the new Miami, I was still constantly worried about how long it would all last for me. While in the late '60s you could sense the popularity of ballrooms beginning to wane, by the early '70s some had actually gone out of business and closed their doors for good. Slowly but steadily, pubs had started to encroach on the popularity of the dancehalls. Suddenly pubs were providing music and the whole scene started to change. This coincided with the folk and ballad boom, boosted by the success of acts like the Clancy Brothers. I wasn't really into the whole folk music thing, although I always felt that the Clancys were first-class and I had huge respect for what they were doing.

By the time the '70s arrived, however, it had become acceptable for women to go to pubs where they could have a drink and listen to music. I didn't have any objection to women being in a bar. To me, this was all part of the evolution of the pub scene. Alcohol wasn't served at ballroom venues, just minerals and sandwiches, so many pubs and lounges were refurbished or extended to take advantage of this new trend. Hotel owners were also starting to realise that they could provide entertainment in their function rooms while serving alcohol, sowing the seeds of the cabaret scene. Ultimately, ballrooms – and, by extension, the showbands – were damaged by this.

I believe that it was foolish to deny drinks licences to the ballroom owners. It would have kept the emphasis on the entertainment and social value of dancing events while staving off the emerging threat of the pubs. Many of the pubs just became places to drink and nothing more. Selling drink in the ballrooms would also have solved the problem of bands coming on stage to play to half-empty venues until the pubs emptied.

The funny thing is banning the sale of alcohol in the ballrooms didn't stop people drinking. Knowing that they couldn't get a drink inside the ballrooms, many men simply got boozed up for the night beforehand and this often led to trouble at the dances. Even a non-drinker like myself could see the stupidity of this situation. It would have been better to have people turn up earlier at the ballrooms and be able to drink at their own pace, rather than getting out of their minds earlier in the night. Once inside, the emphasis wouldn't have been on drinking but on the band, the dancing and, of course, the girls. I remember a drink-fuelled fight on one night in particular at the Olympic Ballroom in Dublin – there was blood all over the floor. When the fight broke out, I turned to the rest of the band and shouted at them to keep playing. Even though people were yelling and trying to get out of the way, it was a case of "the show must go on".

We saw some crazy fights over the years in the ballrooms – it was like the Wild West at times. Some of them were just minor scuffles, others were more violent but never to the extent that the music had to stop. While drink certainly played a part in the violence, it was nothing like as bad as you see nowadays with guns and knives involved – that sinister mentality wasn't there in the '60s and '70s. Then, of course, we didn't have all the drugs-related violence that you have these days either.

Even though there were no bars in the ballrooms, crates of Guinness were often left for the bands in the dressing-rooms of some of the more established ballrooms. This was a world away from when I started out with the Miami when you wouldn't get anything. By the mid-60s, however, there was greater competition between some of the ballroom owners to book the most popular bands and this led to improved conditions for all of us. Providing drink for the bands was a nice gesture by the owners, when you think about it. I suppose it was a way for them to express their appreciation to the bands and thank them for working so hard. Even though I didn't drink, I remember bringing bottles home from gigs to give to my father. I never saw anything wrong with people having a drink and certainly wasn't prudish about it or anything like that. That said, one of the things that originally attracted me to The Miami Showband was the fact that they were extremely disciplined and professional. I don't think I would have lasted with the Miami had they been a bunch of drinkers. I mean, some of them would have taken a drink on occasion but never to the extent that it would affect their performance. I was blessed to be in a band with such level-headed people as Tony Bogan and Joe Tyrell. We were able to treat the Miami as a serious business and always give our best to the audience. When people are paying money to come and see you, it's important that you're always on top of your game. How can you go out on stage and give it 100 percent – or even 90 percent – if you've been up drinking all hours the previous night? The fans have gone to the trouble of coming to see us and maybe the women have got their hair done for the occasion. In my experience, an audience doesn't want excuses – it wants to be entertained.

Alcohol played a big part in the lives of many musicians and some of the showbands had a reputation for being pretty wild and boisterous. The availability of drink after the shows probably didn't help the situation.

Being on the road with a band could be a lonely existence at the best of times and some musicians turned to alcohol for comfort. Many of them would have been on a high after coming off stage and having a few drinks probably helped them wind down. If they were staying away from home, they could continue drinking into the early hours back at the residents' bar of their hotel. You have to remember that for many musicians – particularly those with no wives or children – the showbands became their entire life, professionally and socially. In the summer they might be working seven nights a week so they had no outlet other than having the few drinks after a show. Their band wasn't just providing them with their livelihoods – it was their social life as well. The other lads in their band were not just fellow musicians, they were their friends, confidants and drinking buddies. I've seen drink take its toll on many performers over the years. Some – like Brendan Bowyer – have survived their battle with drink and lived to tell the tale. Brendan was very honest about his alcoholism but doesn't drink any more and is doing great, thank God.

Apart from the cultural shift away from ballrooms in favour of pubs, there were other factors involved in the decline of the showbands. I think the rise in popularity of Country and Western music was also partly responsible. The showband explosion largely came about as a result of the bands becoming the centre of attention at dances, pioneered by the Clipper Carlton and later the Royal and also ourselves. Country and Western music, however, took the emphasis away from the performers and became background music for dancing. Good as it could be, it didn't create the excitement that the showbands did. Some Country and Western acts were branding themselves as showbands but were in reality a different species altogether. I felt that the music played by these bands was very sedate and far removed from what the real showbands were doing on stage. Some of them were fine musicians and excelled at what they did, even though the songs they played weren't always to my taste but, in a way, Country & Western dragged the music scene back to where it had been before the showband era.

There was nothing unusual about the demise of the showbands – everything in life eventually gets replaced by something else. I remember reading about George M Cohan, the legendary producer, playwright, composer, actor and all-round entertainer who practically ruled Broadway. There's a statue of him in the middle of Times Square in New York and James Cagney played him in the 1942 film about his life, 'Yankee Doodle Dandy'. At one time he would have had six or seven shows running simultaneously on Broadway. Cohan was a phenomenal performer and a great dancer. But then movies with sound – the "talkies" – came in and damaged the popularity of theatre and live entertainment. Later on, movie theatres all over the world closed because of television. When I was growing up you had to book in advance to see a picture in town on a Sunday night. Some people would have pre-booked what were called "permanent seats" and they used to go to see a film every week. It was nearly impossible to get in to a picture in Dublin on Sunday nights. It was a big deal if somebody with permanent seats gave you a loan of their tickets if they weren't using them because they were like gold dust. Being brought to the cinema as a young child was always a fabulous treat. I have great memories of my mother taking me to the Capitol cinema, just off O'Connell Street. I got a terrible fright when the film started – I thought that these giant people on the screen were coming to get me. One of the films we saw together was 'The Jolson Story', which was based on the life of the singer Al Jolson. When I got older I used to go to the cinema with my friends at local picture houses such as the Cabra Grand or the Bohemian in Phibsboro. Cinema is directly responsible for introducing me to Rock 'n' Roll. After seeing 'Rock Around the Clock', starring Bill Haley and the Comets, in 1956, I was instantly hooked.

As we grew up without television, going to the pictures was our only real source of entertainment. Then RTÉ was established in the early '60s and it became easier to get into a cinema. Eventually, most of them had to close, places like the Carlton, the Adelphi and the Metropole. Television suffered when videos came out and now DVDs have replaced videos. The point is, nothing lasts forever and this was also the case with the showbands. I never felt any emotional attachment towards the ballrooms and didn't get all nostalgic or anything when they started to go out of business. I was simply worried about the impact it would have on my livelihood and I'm sure the rest of the lads in the band saw it that way as well. This was a time to be practical, not sentimental. All I cared about was keeping the business going for the sake of my family.

I like to think of myself as a survivor from the showband era, one of those singers that was able to adapt to the change. Joe Dolan was another and so was Tony Kenny. As the ballrooms started to close, I knew the time was right to leave The Miami Showband. There were other factors, too. By Christmas 1972, I had been with the Miami, in both its incarnations, for 10 years. I had negotiated a better deal for myself the second time round but I still longed for more control and wanted to be the Director of my own band. I had invested a lot of time in the Miami and felt that the time was right to move on. Under the new arrangement, Tom Doherty would still manage me but I needed to sever my ties with the rest of the lads. I wasn't too nervous about telling them and they seemed to fully accept my decision. They decided to carry on as the Miami without me.

The band's talented keyboard player, Fran O'Toole, took over as lead singer. I think there was an element within the band that welcomed my departure because it allowed them to shine in their own right. Apart from Fran, there were a number of other great singers in the band and I got a sense that some of them saw my leaving as an opportunity. Naturally, they probably felt a bit apprehensive at first about continuing on without me but they decided to give it a go anyway. It was a win-win situation for Tom Doherty as he was able to continue managing the remaining members of the Miami as well as keeping me on his books. In the Miami and Dickie Rock, he now separately represented two of the most bookable names in Irish entertainment.

Leaving The Miami Showband marked an important watershed in my career. It was the end of an era for me. The Miami had been good for me and I had been good for them. We had scaled the heights of previously unimaginable success in Ireland, packing ballrooms the length and breath of Ireland and notching up hit after hit in the charts.

I couldn't have known at the time, however, that my decision to leave the Miami would possibly save my life.

Ten

The Dickie Rock Band

It was extremely liberating to leave The Miami Showband and set up my own group. The musicians I recruited were already in an established band called The Arrows, who were also managed by Tom Doherty's Topline Promotions. I had seen them perform and knew what they were capable of musically so there was no need to hold auditions. The fact that they had been playing together helped make it a very smooth transition for me. They were also familiar with my style of performing so knew exactly what was expected of them. There were some very talented musicians in my new band, including Stephen Gilchrist on bass, Bobby Murphy on sax and Charlie Herbert on lead guitar. The drummer, PJ Coyne, was also a great singer. My decision to leave the Miami was met with the predictable "shock, horror" reaction in the newspapers and I'm sure some of the more diehard showband fans were disappointed to learn of the split. My friends and family, especially Judy, were hugely supportive of the move and felt the time was right for me to take more direct control of my career.

We played our first gig as The Dickie Rock Band in December 1972 – just weeks after I had left the Miami. The first show was in the Top Hat ballroom in Dun Laoghaire on St Stephen's Day. For me, there was little or no change in musical direction. I was still performing all my big hits and the popular songs of the time. The lads in my new band were superb musicians and we had immediate success, much to my relief. While we'd still play ballrooms from time-to-time – the ones that had survived – new entertainment venues were opening up all over the country. We were booked for places like the Drake Inn, in Finglas, one of the first big pub venues to hold up to 400 people for major gigs. We also played regularly at the Tudor Rooms, off Parnell Square, which, like the Drake, was owned by Paddy McKiernan, a lovely, lovely man.

Being a Director of my own band brought with it the financial control I had really wanted during my years with the Miami. Tom Doherty was on a percentage for managing us while the rest of the musicians were on a basic wage. The big difference this time, however, was that I was immediately getting considerably more than the rest of them and I had the say over how much I thought I should be paid. But I needed to work hard to earn it. The problem was that showbands were really dying by then. There was a noticeable drop in the numbers attending gigs. Throughout the '60s I would be playing to packed houses six nights a week – seven during the summer months. By the time I formed my own band, this had gone down to maybe four nights a week and even then we didn't always get the audience numbers, certainly nothing like we did in the '60s. Ballrooms that would have been packing in 1,200 paying punters, mid-week, during the showband era, were now either closed or lucky to get 500 people on any given night. I remember going down to Clonmel with my band to play the Collins Hall. Even though we were playing on a Saturday night, there were only around 700 people there. Just four months earlier I had performed in the same venue with my new band to a crowd of about 1,200 so that was a huge drop. This venue was part of Associated Ballrooms and I remember asking the manager about the low turnout and he said: "We had Joe Dolan and the Drifters last week and the numbers were terrible; the week before that we had the Miami and the place was empty – it's just the way the business is going, Dickie."

I can't say I wasn't worried. Here I was, a father of two young children with another one on the way, trying to make a living in an industry that seemed to be in steep decline. I was concerned that the standard of living my family and I were now accustomed to could not be sustained for much longer. I knew that staying relevant in the face of the death of the showband would be vital if myself and the band were going to survive. I realised that there wasn't much I could do, other than keep up the standard of professionalism and performance I had always prided myself on. I had to face the harsh reality that the entertainment business was going through a lull period. Even major international stars like Sinatra and Elvis experienced highs and lows during their careers. I decided to put my head down and just continue doing what I had always done – thankfully, it was a strategy that eventually paid off.

In some ways it was easier for me to survive than the more traditional showbands. Even during the Miami years, we were just a bunch of people on stage playing music and singing songs. Unlike some of the other bands, there was nothing theatrical or flamboyant about our performance. The Royal Showband would get dressed up before going on stage and some of their gigs were more like variety shows than concerts. The Dixies, from Cork, were the same, as were the Clipper Carlton. But the Miami had always been about performing rather than entertaining. To us, it was just about the music and connecting with the audience through our songs. My new band pretty much followed the winning formula that we had perfected with the Miami and that's probably why we stayed successful while others didn't.

I was in a better position than most to withstand a downturn in the music business. This was due to the fact that I was a shrewd and pragmatic investor when it came to property. I often hear people say that your biggest investment in life is your own personal property but in 90 per cent of cases, I don't think that's true. Property is really only an investment if you buy it intending to sell it on for a profit which is what I always tried to do with the different houses I bought. But most people will live in their so-called investment until they die and then leave the property to their kids. Some will have been paying a mortgage for 20 or 30 years by the time they're 65 years of age. Then they may have a house worth €2 million – and that price wouldn't be unusual by today's standards – but unless they sell it they are only sitting on a paper profit. If they sold they'd be able to buy an apartment outright for, say, €600,000 – giving them a new asset and all of a sudden they also have €1.4 million cash in their hand. Now *that's* what I consider to be an investment.

I have no problem admitting that I have always been careful with money – and still am, to a degree. My father was like that, too. That's probably why I got a reputation for being mean. It's something that has been said about me for decades and I've read loads of articles about Dickie Rock being "tight", "thrifty" or whatever. It's an undeserved reputation and it doesn't bother me a bit because the people who know me – the people that matter – would never think of me as mean.

To be honest, I think the meanness accusations came about because I didn't drink. When you're not part of a drinking culture, it wouldn't always cross your mind to buy a round of drinks. That said, I wasn't the type to walk into a pub and automatically start buying drinks for the whole place. There was one amusing incident back in the early '70s that probably helped propagate the meanness myth. At the time I was recording with an orchestra in Westland Studios on Lombard Street in Dublin. During a break in the session, the musicians went to a pub next door to have a drink. Not being a drinker, I didn't go with them so I stayed in the studio and had a cup of tea and a sandwich. After a while, the producer asked me to go in and drag the orchestra away from their drinks and back to the studio. When I entered the bar, I heard Benny McNeill – a real character who was probably the best trumpet player in Ireland at the time – shout in my direction: "Come here you mean fucking bollix, Rock, and buy a drink for the lads." He was joking I'm sure, but he was probably just feeding off my reputation for meanness. It honestly never would have crossed my mind that I should have bought all the musicians a drink. Even now, Judy will sometimes have to prompt me to buy a drink for someone if we're out with people. It just doesn't automatically register with me that this should be my round because I wouldn't be drinking myself.

I may have also, inadvertently, contributed to the meanness rumours over the years. I said in one interview that being Dickie Rock was great, because all my success meant I could get into the cinemas for nothing and I often joked that I didn't have to spend money anymore. The truth is, though, that I wasn't a wild spender. I saved every penny I could because I was insecure about how long my career would last. When I started out, I hoped for maybe two years, five if I was lucky – certainly not anything approaching 50 years! I wanted to make hay while the sun was shone, as the expression goes. If you are an astute saver, people will automatically assume you're mean. I may not have bought things for myself, but as regards my family – including my mother and father – I was never mean. They always had everything they needed and we regularly treated ourselves to great holidays abroad. There is a big difference between being cautious with money and being mean but I think people sometimes fail to make that distinction.

I've heard all the stories down through the years where I am portrayed as this penny-pinching miser. A couple of years ago, Murty Quinn – who was in the original Miami Showband with me – was even slagging me off in an RTÉ documentary. He described me as shrewd, which is true to some extent and I'd agree with him on that. But he also claimed that, after a show, when the rest of the lads in the band would buy sweets, I'd buy an apple instead – because you can't share an apple. He was saying it in a light-hearted way but it's the type of story that did the rounds about me.

I'm completely aware that people joke about me being mean. Even the comedian, Sil Fox, who I play golf with, makes up stories about going over to Dickie Rock's house for a game of snooker and finding a lock on the fridge. It's funny and I can laugh about it, simply because it isn't true. My wife and children know I'm not mean and so do my friends – that's all that matters to me. I'm still bloody careful with my money, though.

* * * *

Throughout 1973 I worked harder than ever to establish my new band. The birth of my third son, John, that year placed further onus on me as a father and provider to keep the money coming in. I relished the opportunity to play in new venues to a different type of audience. In the pubs and emerging cabaret lounges we were now playing to hundreds of people per night as opposed to thousands but there was more pressure to perform. During the showband days the audience were distracted by the dancing and the courting but all that changed with cabaret. Now the audience were mainly seated at tables and all eyes – and ears – were on the musicians. You felt that your performance was under closer scrutiny. I used to say that playing cabaret gigs in places like the Tudor Rooms separated the men from the boys because you couldn't put a foot wrong. The crowd profile was generally older, too, with cabarets mainly attended by married couples as opposed to the youngsters who had come to the ballrooms. Playing the smaller, more intimate venues came naturally to me and enhanced the experience of performing live. It became easier for me to connect with an audience and hold their attention and I believe the laid-back cabaret setting allowed people to properly appreciate the music. These places were generally very classy affairs. A lot of money was spent in the 1970s refurbishing pubs and entertainment venues and bands like mine no longer had to contend with dingy changing rooms.

. Even with many of the old ballrooms now closed, I still toured the country regularly with my new band in the hope of playing to as many of my existing fans as possible and maybe even converting some new ones. I have always believed – from the days when I first started out with The Melochords – that you should maintain a professional distance from your audience. Performers need to be one step apart from their fans. I don't mean ignore them. I love my audience and it's always a pleasure to meet my fans and have a chat with them after a show but, as the expression goes, familiarity can breed contempt.

I insisted, whenever I could, that girls should not be allowed to travel on the bus with the rest of the band. This was a condition I laid down when I first joined the Miami. It was nothing to do with wanting to keep temptation at arm's length or anything like that. I even felt that way when I was single, long before I met Judy and had kids. I just believed it wasn't a professional way for a band to behave. I was sure it took from the mystique of the performance. Even when girls were sometimes stuck for a lift home and the rest of the lads in the Miami let them on the bus, it would always have been against my wishes. Our fans from Dublin would often travel as far as Belfast to see us perform. On a few occasions girls would tell us that they had no other way of getting home and would plead for a lift back to Finglas or wherever. If it was raining, some of the lads in the band would feel sorry for them and let them on the wagon. I could sympathise with the situation and understood why the other members of the Miami found it hard to say no but I still wasn't happy about it. As far as I could see that sort of thing could often be misconstrued. Apart from anything else, I always felt it was risky in case we had an accident or something. I don't think I was being over-cautious about this, despite what my bandmates might have thought. I sometimes got a bit of slagging over it from the other lads but I didn't care because my motives were right.

The "no girls on the bus" policy was certainly at odds with the public perception of being in a band. People often said that we must have had a great time with all those beautiful young groupies throwing themselves at us but it wasn't like that for us at all. There was certainly a lot of promiscuity around and while I'm not going to name names, some of the showbands had wild reputations – they know who they are! – and embraced the Rock 'n' Roll lifestyle with reckless abandon. The opportunities to pick up women were certainly plentiful. There was a lot of glamour attached to being in a band and even the most average looking fella – myself included – could be transformed into a sex symbol as soon as he took to the stage. Women may have screamed at me when I sang but it was never a case that I was stalked by celebrity-obsessed groupies after a show. I don't think I appealed to that type of woman and most of my female fans would simply just look for an autograph or politely tell me how much they had enjoyed my performance. There were certainly all sorts of temptations and wild times to be had but that type of life wasn't for me. Even from when I first started out with The Melochords I had set ideas about what it meant to be an entertainer. I always believed anything that interfered with that was an unnecessary distraction. I never wanted the Rock 'n' Roll lifestyle. I simply wanted to be a professional.

These values, while sincerely held, sharply contrast with my deeply uncharacteristic behaviour one night in July 1974. While I have always been reluctant to comment on what is essentially a private matter – for the sake of everyone concerned but particularly Judy – I realise that I cannot give a truly honest account of my life story without referring to it.

That summer night, July 7, we had been playing in in Adamstown, County Wexford. The weather was beautiful that day and we were looking forward to the show as we made the two hour trip down from Dublin. Fans came from all over Wexford to see us and the place was packed by the time we went on. After the gig ended, I had gone back to the van to get changed while the rest of the band stayed for a drink and chatted to the fans. Being a non-drinker, I was never into hanging around after a show and was always eager to hit the road as soon as possible. I knew that by heading back to the wagon early, the lads in the band would be conscious that I was waiting for them to finish their drinks. I hoped it would place some subtle pressure on them to get going – otherwise they'd be there all night!

I was changing out of my stage clothes when a young Wexford lady, who had been at the show, arrived at the back of our wagon. She had lost a button on her trousers and had asked the lads in the band if they had a pin they could give her. They jokingly told her that we kept things like that in our van and directed her towards it. I heard the double doors of the wagon opening and looked up to see her standing in front of me. I have no adequate explanation for what happened next between us. All I can say is that it was an extraordinary lapse on my part and was completely my fault. How could it be otherwise? She was just in her late teens and I should have been the responsible one. There's little doubt that I showed incredible weakness and went against all my own moral and professional leanings that night. I was deeply ashamed of how I had behaved and was very upset with myself. I had let myself down, as a man, and had let my wife down, as her husband, but it was worse for the young girl. Unbeknownst to me, she became pregnant that night and later gave birth to a baby girl in 1975. I can't even begin to imagine how difficult it must have been to be a young, single mother living in rural Ireland in the 1970s.

I lived silently with the secret of my infidelity for many years, too ashamed to confide in even my closest friends or family. In some ways it changed the way I interacted with people. I withdrew from the innocent affections of my female fans. For a good while afterwards, I was always careful not to show any undue physical attention towards the people who came to meet me after a show. I was even conscious of putting my arm around someone if they asked me for an autograph or photograph in case it could be misconstrued. In my heart I knew I had let Judy down and I never wanted to do anything else that might hurt her in any way. It made me become more protective of her. I vowed that I would never let something like that ever happen again – I was 100 per cent certain of that. I prayed that I would be able to spare Judy the pain of learning about my stupid behaviour but I always feared deep down that it would come back to haunt me some day.

ELEVEN

The Miami Showband Massacre

I tried to put the Adamstown incident behind me and stayed as busy as possible with my band for the rest of 1974. Home life kept me busy, too, with three young boys to take care of. That winter, Judy announced that she was pregnant again so there were even more hectic times ahead.

With more and more ballrooms going out of business, bands like mine found it tough going but we had no idea how much worse things would get in the year ahead. In July 1975, one horrific incident marked the official end of the showband as we knew it. The murder of some of my former bandmates in the Miami shocked the nation and brought the already struggling music business to its knees.

The week they died I was playing with the band in the Seapoint ballroom in Salthill, Galway. The atmosphere in the city was fantastic that week, as it always is during the Galway Races Festival. I'd played the festival on many occasions during my Miami days and later with my own band. I never bothered going to the races myself. I'm probably what you'd consider to be a bookie's nightmare because I'm not interested in anything that involves the potential to lose money. Even though I had left the Miami three years earlier, our paths crossed frequently as we all travelled the country. That week, The Miami Showband were booked to play the Seapoint on Monday and Tuesday, with my band scheduled to perform there on the Wednesday and Thursday nights.

When we arrived in Galway that Wednesday afternoon, the Miami were already on the road. They were heading to Banbridge, County

Down, where they were booked to play the Castle Ballroom. I had always remained on good terms with my former band mates in the Miami. I used to see them regularly because, like myself, they continued to be managed by Tom Doherty and I'd bump into them in his office. In fact, I had just seen a few of the lads the previous week and we had chatted about how business was going for us. Sadly, this would be the last time I'd ever talk to some of them.

In the early hours of July 31, I was woken-up in my Galway hotel by a clearly distraught chambermaid. She told me that there had been some kind of accident or incident involving the Miami. The details were sketchy so I threw on some clothes and went downstairs to listen to the radio reports. I arrived down first and the rest of the band gradually followed, as news began to filter through. I remember we were really frustrated because the information available was very fragmented. This was back in the days before Sky News and 24-hour rolling bulletins. All we could establish was that there had been some sort of bomb and members of the band had been killed. The reality of what had actually happened didn't sink in with me initially.

Another four days would pass before we found out about the full horror of the ambush. We then learnt that the Miami's van had been flagged down by men dressed in military uniforms. The five band members were ordered out of the van, which they assumed was going to be routinely searched. This type of thing happened to all the showbands after the Troubles started. I remember being stopped one night in Belfast, after we played the Boom Boom Rooms. We all had to get out, as our van was searched and I heard one of the guys speaking on his radio saying: "Yeah, we're looking into it now", as if somebody had tipped them off about us. I'm sure none of the lads in the Miami realised the awful truth behind the checkpoint until it was too late. No showband would have believed that they had been targeted by UVF terrorists and had unwittingly fallen into the lethal trap set by them.

The more we heard the worse it got. They were lined-up at gunpoint while two of the terrorists tried to place a bomb in the Miami's van. There was panic and chaos when the bomb prematurely exploded, instantly killing two of the UVF men. Des McAlea was thrown clear by the force of the blast and was able to escape across fields, as the gunmen started a murderous rampage. The band's recently recruited bass guitar player,

Stephen Travers, was seriously wounded in the attack and was presumed dead by the terrorists. Mercifully, he survived, despite being critically injured. Fran O'Toole, Brian McCoy and Tony Geraghty were not so lucky. They were shot at close range and killed.

The sheer horror of the Miami massacre, as it became known, hit me hard, with a huge and sudden thump. I felt a sense of shock deep within myself. After all, I had brought some of these guys into the Miami in 1967 after the first line-up split; good, decent people like Fran O'Toole and Brian McCoy. I was particularly fond of Brian, who played the trumpet. Everyone loved him. When 'the Troubles' erupted in Northern Ireland in 1969, I remember we were all talking about it in the back of the van and Brian, who was originally from Tyrone, casually mentioned that he was a Protestant. We didn't know or care whether he was or not – and neither did he. None of us attached any significance to it. All Brian was interested in was being a musician. He was a beautiful person and a terrible loss to his wife and two young children. Fran, from Bray, County Wicklow, had joined the Miami the same time as Brian. He played the organ and sang, eventually taking over as lead singer when I left. He was also a married man with two children and was only 29-years-old when he died. Paul Ashford, who had joined the Miami with Fran, had left the band just a few months before the attack. He took it very badly as he was very close to Fran and the two of them went back a long way together.

The band's drummer, Ray Millar, was extremely fortunate to avoid the attack altogether. After the concert in Banbridge, he had decided to drive home to Antrim in his own car rather than travel with the band. He had been due to meet up with them again on Friday for their next gig.

I just couldn't understand why a group of innocent musicians, who came from both sides of the religious divide, could be so callously targeted. These guys, like the rest of us, were just trying to make an honest living and had no interest in the political situation in the North. I often wondered afterwards if I would have been killed had I chosen to remain with the Miami. Would I have died or would I have managed to escape? Maybe fate had simply intervened on my behalf when I made the decision to quit the band in 1972. In reality, however, it simply boiled down to the fact that any band playing the North could have been singled out that night by the terrorists. It could as easily have been The Dickie Rock

Band instead of the Miami. It was a small enough scene, on both sides of the border, and we all travelled in similar circles, playing the same venues, time and time again. The fact that the Miami had performed in the same Galway venue as me the previous night perfectly illustrated that point. The Miami Showband massacre changed all that. It had a terrible impact on the music scene in Northern Ireland. Many acts refused to play there for fear of being attacked.

I didn't play in Northern Ireland again for at least two years after the Miami murders. It was a shame because I loved playing the North and had a strong fan base there. Even after the hostilities flared up in Northern Ireland at the end of the '60s, it had never crossed my mind that it might be a dangerous place to perform. The only noticeable change from our point of view was the increase in the number of British Army and police checkpoints. We would have been stopped many times, in a similar way to how the Miami were flagged down that dreadful night. Only after the lads were killed did I think about how easily it could have been us.

Apart from the heightened security, there was nothing different about playing Northern Ireland in the early years of 'the Troubles'. There was one minor incident in 1969 when I was asked if I was a Fenian. Now this may sound like I was ignorant or uneducated, but I didn't have a clue what he was talking about. Things like religious or political identity simply didn't matter to us down in the South. People just didn't think like that. We didn't care if our trumpet player was Catholic, Protestant or Jewish – it meant nothing to us. The only criteria for joining a showband was that you could play your chosen instrument well. The ordinary people who came to see us play in Northern Ireland didn't care what religion the bands were either. We played to everyone, Catholics and Protestants alike. There was never the slightest indication of sectarian hatred at any of the dances we played in the North. I never formed an opinion on the political situation in Northern Ireland or followed it in the news with any great interest. We were just there to do a job – be it in Banbridge or Belfast – and that was simply to entertain people.

As an individual, I would have been happy to continue playing in the North after the Miami atrocity but I had to consider the other guys in the band who had families and may have had reservations about travelling up there. I never felt there was a real danger of it happening again. The attack on the Miami was a dreadful tragedy for the guys in the band and their families. To a lesser degree, perhaps, it was also a tragedy for the perpetrators of the atrocity and their relatives. We will probably never know what made them do what they did. That was all part of the conflict in Northern Ireland at the time. I can't understand it because I'm not that political – musicians generally aren't.

It's incredible to see how far the situation has come since those dark days. A lot of time, courage and energy have been put into building the peace process over the past 10 years and it is really starting to pay off. I mean, I never thought I'd live to see the day when Gerry Adams and Ian Paisley would be sitting down to do business together – it's unbelievable, really. Hopefully it represents the way forward for both sides of the community in Northern Ireland.

These days, I continue to perform in the North and love the people up there. I have a great memory of playing Romano's Ballroom in Belfast in 1967. It was managed at the time by a young Sam Smyth, who is now a well-known journalist and broadcaster. I was there on the same night that Sean Dunphy was representing Ireland in the Eurovision and I asked Sam to let me know the result as soon as it was announced. The place was packed that night and I remember looking down and seeing Sam trying to get my attention. He shouted up that Ireland had come second. While I was delighted for Sean Dunphy, I was raging that he had beaten my result the previous year with his song, 'If I Could Choose'.

Recently I had the pleasure of performing in a brand new theatre in the Shankill Road area and it was just fantastic. We all had a great time and were treated so well by everyone. I've always believed that people are people, no matter where they come from. Last year I sang at the Ulster Hall in Belfast – a really wonderful venue – as part of a Christmas Show, backed by a 35-piece orchestra. Standing on the stage, I started to experience strong feelings of nostalgia. I thought about my father, who would have boxed there in competitions as a young man. I also read recently that the late, great promoter, Jim Aiken, first put The Royal Showband on there back in 1959. Jim had apparently only expected a crowd of 1,000 that night but 2,500 turned up and they could barely close the doors. It had been a big gamble to book the Royal in such a prestigious venue but it paid off handsomely for him. When I last played the Ulster Hall, I just stood there in silence, looking around the venue, picturing the Royal up there on stage all those years ago. What memories that place must hold.

While writing this book, I learned with great sadness of the death of Jim Aiken, at the age of 74. Known as 'Gentleman Jim', he was a man of integrity and was universally liked and respected by everyone in the music business. It's hard to believe that he initially set out to become a priest and was still working as a teacher when he dipped his toes into the world of showbusiness. It's difficult to know where to begin when summing up Jim's contribution to the music industry in Ireland. From what I heard, he considered bringing Bruce Springsteen to Slane Castle in 1985 among his finest achievements. Significantly, however, Jim succeeded in keeping music alive in Northern Ireland during the Troubles when there would have been considerable reluctance by artists to play there. Jim brought all the great acts to this country, from Tom Jones and Roy Orbison to Johnny Cash and Pavarotti. His loss will be acutely felt, by his family and by anyone who had the pleasure of knowing him.

* * * *

As a postscript to the story of The Miami Showband tragedy, I'd like to jump ahead slightly – 30 years, to be exact. It never ceases to amaze me how newspapers can twist comments and present a completely warped version of the truth. Even a simple misunderstanding can be misconstrued and turned into a controversy. This was the case in the summer of 2005, when a distorted version of the truth was published about my non-appearance at a special concert at Vicar Street in Dublin to mark the 30th anniversary of The Miami Showband massacre. The newspapers tried to make out that I had snubbed the event but nothing could have been further from the truth.

Somebody had contacted my manager to say there would be a memorial concert for the Miami and asked if I would be available to take part. I already had a prior booking for a big date in Belfast and I hate letting people down by cancelling gigs.

Later, much to my annoyance, it came out in the papers that I simply had no interest in playing at the concert, which was not correct at all. Even on the day of the concert on August 1, I went down to the rehearsals at Vicar Street to wish everyone involved the best of luck. It would have been my greatest pleasure to perform in memory of my former Miami band mates in Vicar Street that night but it was too late to do anything about it – I simply couldn't get out of my Belfast commitment. I was deeply offended by the media's suggestion that I had ignored or snubbed the event – that simply just wasn't true. It was unfair of the media to depict me as being uncaring about the 30th anniversary of the Miami massacre when I had attended and even sang at the memorial service just days earlier.

I know the whole thing was a storm in a teacup but that's just how it goes with the media in my business – you have to take the good with the bad.

I think this type of negative publicity lost sight of the real story. This was simply the time to commemorate and honour the victims of the atrocity, all hard-working young men cut down in their prime. The 30th anniversary of the Miami murders made me reflect on a glorious period for Irish music, beginning with the first showbands in the 1950s and ending on a dark, lonely road in Northern Ireland in 1975. There were various different line-ups of the Miami in the months and years following the massacre but with most of the original members now gone, one thing was for certain – it could never be the same again.

Twelve

Surviving the Seventies

The Dickie Rock Band continued to thrive as the '70s progressed, although, as ever, I was well aware I could never afford to become complacent. We were doing well, relatively speaking, but the numbers attending gigs were still falling off and the performances were dropping too. It was becoming abundantly clear that I could no longer depend on a vast quantity of shows. I would need to focus more on the quality of the money involved in each performance.

In 1975, I parted company with my manager, Tom Doherty. It was an amicable split made because I felt I needed a new direction. Tom had managed me since inviting me to join The Miami Showband in 1962 and had always been fantastic to me. Our business relationship remained intact when some of the original Miami members split from the group in 1967. Even when I eventually left the second line-up of the Miami in 1972, I retained Tom's Topline Promotions company as my management. It was a case of being safe, I suppose, sticking to what I was used to.

I have a huge personal affection for Tom. He had a great rapport with everyone he did business with and was one of the most respected managers around at the time. There's no question that he was a very honest and honourable man. My one gripe with his style of doing business was that he didn't insist on getting a larger cut for the Miami when we were at our peak and the large crowds were there. I feel that this would have set us up better financially. Tom had agreed a 50 per

cent cut of the takings with venue owners during the peak Miami years
– out of which the band were paid a set wage – but I think he should
have insisted on 60 percent. In fairness, Tom wanted to look after the
promoters and the owners of the ballrooms in the belief that, in return,
they'd look after us. To some extent they did and we always got regular
bookings.

In some ways it was my own fault for saying nothing at the time. I
was foolish for not insisting on the band getting a bigger cut when we
were at the height of our popularity and I only have myself to blame for
that. It was never a case of being greedy, I just wanted to be paid what
I believed we were worth. The big money was there for the asking – we
just didn't ask for it. It's still a major source of regret for me, to be honest.
After the Eurovision in 1966 and the string of hit records I had with the
Miami, I should have been able to write my own paycheck.

When The Dickie Rock Band hit the road in 1972, we generally
played for an agreed fee as opposed to a percentage of the takings on
the night. That way, you could settle on a price you'd be happy with in
advance and be guaranteed of getting it, regardless of how large or small
the crowds were. When I set up The Dickie Rock Band, Tom was still
managing the business end of things for me. By that stage, however, the
crowds were deserting the dancehalls in their droves and the opportunity
to make serious money on the back of the ballroom boom had long
passed.

In the end, there was no falling out with Tom, or any confrontation
whatsoever. He was too much of a gentleman for that and I still had
huge respect for him. I rang him up one day and told him that I was
going with new management and it was as simple as that. I had first
met my new manager, a young Dubliner named Mick Quinn, when I
was doing small gigs around town with The Echoes before I joined The
Miami Showband. He was a red hot operator back then, a real whiz-kid.
Mick had a completely different philosophy to Tom when it came to
making money. He believed in getting as high a rate as possible for his
artists. In this respect, Mick was speaking the same language as me so I
decided to leave Tom to go with him.

The management styles of Tom Doherty and Mick Quinn were
worlds apart. For one thing, they were from different generations – Tom
was old enough to be Mick's father. Mick was more typical of the new,

younger breed of showbiz impresarios such as Oliver Barry and Jim and Mick Hand. During the Miami days, Tom used to take great pride in telling us that we were booked up solidly for the entire year. For him, keeping the band as busy as possible, while looking after the venue owners and promoters was the important thing. On one level a year's bookings may have sounded impressive but his system had one major flaw in that it didn't take into account the future success of the band, like the rise in our popularity after I entered the Eurovision in 1966. That year we were playing for the same fee that had been agreed when Tom made the original bookings. There was no provision in place to up the fees when we had hit singles. He didn't believe in going back to renegotiate a price once the Miami had been booked – it was a question of honour to him. But maybe there should have been a clause in the agreement that allowed for an increase in the fee if things changed and Dickie Rock and the Miami had a hit record out by the time the show came around. Again, I deeply regret that I didn't articulate these views more forcefully at the time.

Mick Quinn was different to Tom when it came to attitudes towards money: it was the financial reward from the shows, not their frequency that mattered most to him. As far as Mick was concerned, any band could get bookings 365 days a year if they were willing to work for little or nothing. He believed that the value of an artist should determine his or her worth when it came to negotiating a fee. After I told Tom that I was moving to a new manager, we arranged a meeting with Mick Quinn and the Irish Federation of Musicians to hammer out the details of the changeover. Top of Tom's agenda was the matter of honouring any dates that had already been booked. Mick was going through the list systematically, saying which ones we were and weren't interested in playing. We were all sitting around a table and Tom looked at me and said: "Ritchie Boy, I hope you intend to fulfil these commitments."

On hearing this, Mick threw down his pencil and told Tom that I would only be playing the shows where I could get the best money. He didn't care about keeping promoters and venue owners happy. To him, music was just a business and he believed in getting more money for artists that had hit records. It was a far more aggressive approach than I was used to but it was definitely the right one for me.

My memories of working with Tom are very positive and I deeply appreciate all that he did for me. After all, it was Tom who had offered me the job with the Miami. It turned out to be a good business decision for him but it opened many doors for me, too. Through the Miami I finally came into my own as a singer and was able to perfect the style of performing that would become my stock in trade. I may have been the one who could sing but Tom was astute enough to recognise my talent and help me capitalise on it. I just wish we'd capitalised that bit more. I went on to have a great business relationship with Mick Quinn that lasted over 10 years and he worked wonders for my career.

Apart from changing management, 1975 was another big year on the domestic front. In April, Judy gave birth to our fourth son. We couldn't believe it was yet another boy. We named him Richard after me. He was a fine healthy child, thank God, although he wasn't a great sleeper, like the rest of his brothers.

Before the year was out, Judy was expecting again. I was trying my best to help out at home but now I needed to work more than ever. Mick Quinn was doing a great job of keeping the band as busy as possible and most of the gigs he booked turned out to be nice little earners.

In March 1976, we finally introduced another woman to the family. Baby Sarah arrived safe and sound in Mount Carmel Hospital. I remember waiting outside the delivery ward when she arrived. I heard the midwife say: "Congratulations, you've finally got a daughter." Judy immediately asked if the baby was okay. She was always nervous giving birth on account of what had happened to Joseph.

Shortly after Sarah was born, I went on holiday to Greece. Judy had to stay home to look after the new baby so I brought my second eldest son Jason with me. I remember he was about to make his Holy Communion that year. It was a memorable holiday to say the least and left me with a lasting souvenir of Rhodes – an amputated finger!

I have two versions of what happened. The one I like to tell most – the made up one – involves a dramatic water-skiing accident. In this version, I am showing off my skills by letting go the ski line attached to the boat. I glide effortlessly towards the shore before attempting to grab hold of a jetty. But disaster strikes when the force of the motion rips off the top of my finger.

The *real* story is less dramatic and somewhat more embarrassing. The truth is that I was on a children's slide in the swimming pool when the accident happened.

Jason had gone down first and was waiting for me in the water below. For a laugh, I decided to go down backwards and head first. I grabbed the rails underneath the slide, not realising they were jagged. I started to move down the slide before I was properly ready and the next thing I remember is being under the water. I came up and there was blood everywhere. I was horrified to discover that the top of my finger was hanging off. I went immediately to the local medical centre and my finger was temporarily stapled and bandaged up.

As soon as I got home I went to see an orthopedic surgeon in Blanchardstown who tried to save my finger. It started to become gangrenous, however, and I noticed that there was a funny smell coming from it. I remember playing in the Seapoint Ballroom in Galway and feeling excruciating pain when I raised my hand in the air during the show.

Back in Dublin, I went to a plastic surgeon's clinic to see if there was anything else that could be done. Dr Prendiville, who was highly respected within his profession, examined my finger and said: "Cut your losses – take it off." I agreed immediately and he asked when I wanted to have the operation.

"Do it today," I responded.

The next morning I went into St Steeven's Hospital and the top part of my finger was amputated. The procedure went well and it has never given me any trouble since. The only disadvantage is that it affects my grip when I'm golfing. I always use it as an excuse when I'm not playing well.

It doesn't bother me at all when people ask me what happened to my finger, as it left me with a noticeable stump on my right hand. It also gives me a reason to tell the water-skiing version of the story.

* * * *

On August 16, 1977, the "King of Rock 'n' Roll", Elvis Presley, was found dead in one of the bathrooms in his Graceland mansion in Memphis – he was 42-years-old.

I remember distinctly where I was when I heard the terrible news. We were in the middle of a gig in Tramore, County Waterford, when word reached me that Elvis was dead. I immediately announced it to the audience. I can't remember any major reaction. If anything, the response from the crowd was rather subdued. Hearing that he'd died brought me back to when I first enjoyed his music as a teenager. I'll never forget how different and exciting he sounded. Back in the '50s Elvis was such a major influence on all the young bands. I remember learning some of his hits when I first joined The Melochords. The sad thing was that just before he died, you couldn't give one of his records away. Maybe that's why the news of his death was met with such indifference by the audience in Tramore that night.

I remember asking myself how such a phenomenally successful star could end his career on such a low. I came to the conclusion that it was simply the case of a once normal, beautiful looking man, who was a good singer with great rhythm, coming to the end of his career cycle. Once he reigned supreme as the king of popular music but then the '60s arrived and there were new kids on the block, such as The Beatles and The Rolling Stones.

Elvis may have been in the same game as me, professionally speaking – although he was an international star – but that's where the similarity between us ended. We were worlds apart in terms of the scale of our success and lifestyles. I was a happily married man with a great family; he was into prescription drugs and that whole other way of life. I was living a relatively normal existence, despite my success, while Elvis was a bloated version of his former self, living an isolated existence in his mansion, surrounded by his staff and various hangers-on. Our lives couldn't have been more different but I was deeply saddened to learn of his death.

I'm always amazed to realise that I have been performing for longer than Elvis was alive – and there's probably a good reason for this. There's little doubt that Elvis was a hugely influential pop star. He changed the face and sound of modern music when he exploded onto the scene in the '50s. But I don't think he had what it took to develop into a serious performer, like Frank Sinatra, Tony Bennett or the late Bobby Darin. His career started to nosedive in the late '60s and I don't think he ever fully recovered, despite the TV comeback specials and Vegas years. By the mid-70s, Elvis was practically a parody of himself. For any performers that tended to let the trappings of fame go to their heads, the passing of Elvis certainly provided a salutary lesson. The music business can be a fickle place indeed and his death showed that one of the greatest and most successful entertainers ever couldn't sustain the good times.

I've always been very conscious that just because you can sing it doesn't necessarily mean that every song will suit you. After the fall of the showbands, it was important for me to continue to pick the popular songs of the day that suited my voice. It was vital, however, to continue performing the hits that had got me to where I was in the first place. Songs like 'From the Candy Store' and 'Come Back to Stay' were as popular as ever but I was always mindful of the need to stay relevant and not to just trade on past glories. After leaving the Miami in 1972, I continued as a successful recording artist, although I didn't trouble the Irish charts as much as I had done in the '60s. I recorded a few original compositions I had come across in London in the early '70s but, even though they were great songs and well recorded, they weren't hits for me.

It wasn't until the summer of 1977 that I eventually returned to the top of the charts with a John Denver song I released called 'Back Home Again'. I have a fella by the name of Brian Carr to thank for introducing me to that particular song. Brian was the former bass player of a band called The Royal Blues, who formed in Mayo back in 1963. It used to kill me to hear that they were making three times as much as the Miami, even though we were getting the bigger crowds and having all the hit singles. After The Royal Blues split, Brian went on to run a small restaurant in Dublin's South Richmond Street called The Gigs Place. It wasn't a fancy restaurant by any stretch of the imagination – more like a café – but it opened really late and had a great atmosphere. I used to go there on my way home for a bite to eat after playing a show.

There was a great story Brian used to tell about the time he met this guy in Las Vegas who ran a beautiful, top-class restaurant there. They got talking and Brian mentioned to the American fella that he was also in the restaurant business and owned a place back in Dublin. He thought nothing more of it until one night a big limousine pulled up outside The Gigs Place and this same guy he'd met in Vegas arrives in with his wife and some obviously wealthy friends. Brian was mortified when they asked for him and he hid in the kitchen. Things went from bad to worse from there. The Americans requested a wine list only to be offered the grand choice of two bottles – red or white. When the bemused visitors' meals eventually arrived, some chancers suddenly burst in through the door, grabbed their food and ran off down the street with it. The Americans had their coats on and were away in their limo within seconds. Brian's was that type of place – anything could happen on any given night. It certainly didn't compare to a posh restaurant in Vegas.

One night I was having something to eat there when Brian gave me a John Denver tape featuring the track 'Back Home Again'. I told him that I wasn't into folk music but he insisted that I should listen to it. Driving home that night, I played the tape in my car stereo and realised he was right – the song would be perfect for my style of singing. I recorded it soon after and it was a huge success for me, going to Number One for many weeks. It's a song that my fans still regularly request and I always enjoy performing it.

While the atmosphere at my gigs was generally great, you'd occasionally get a bit of hassle. Back in the early days of the Miami, some lads would often act the eejit and make rude gestures at the band and especially poke fun at my ears. I could never understand how people could behave in such a hurtful way – maybe it was a jealousy or a begrudging thing. As we played around Ireland there were certain venues that just seemed to attract the same few troublemakers.

By the '70s I decided enough was enough and I started to bring some back-up any time I played in these places. I had got to know a well-known Ballyfermot character by the name of Dinny 'Boy' Desmond. I used to see him at The Gigs Place when I'd drop in for a curry after a show. Dinny, who has since passed away, was a real honest fella but tough as nails, one of those guys with no fear whatsoever. Knowing about his hard reputation, I started to bring Dinny to gigs where I'd encountered trouble in the past. It was for my own protection more than anything else.

One night The Dickie Rock Band was playing the Olympia Ballroom in Waterford. The crowd there were brilliant as usual but there were these four lads who seemed determined to ruin the show for everybody else. Their behaviour was really obnoxious and aggressive. They kept shouting up abuse at me and were generally making a nuisance of themselves. I looked over at Dinny, who was standing to the side of the stage, and nodded in the direction of the troublemakers. He made his way over to them through the crowd and had a quiet word.

I could see one of them telling Dinny where to go.

The Ballyfermot man calmly walked to the side of the hall and removed his jacket and bowtie. He went back over to the lads and it looked like he was whispering something to one of them. Suddenly, the guy started screaming in agony and held his hand up to the side of his head. Dinny had bitten his ear.

There was blood everywhere.

The young thug ran into the toilets, followed by his three mates. Dinny went in after them. The next thing I saw was the four lads staggering out of the place in a state of shock. They had been given the hiding of their lives.

I got a terrible fright when I realised what had happened. I had just wanted Dinny to give them a warning and hadn't expected anything like this. After the show ended I told Dinny 'Boy' that he had gone too far.

He responded: "That may be the case, Dickie, but I guarantee you that they won't be back again."

He was right there – I never saw their faces again. Although I realised that Dinny had probably meant well, I decided there and then that I would not be requiring his services in the future.

* * * *

When I wasn't recording or performing I made regular appearances on RTÉ television, which helped keep me in the public eye. In 1977, I made my fourth and final appearance in the National Song Contest and came in sixth place with the song 'I Can't Go On Without You'.

In the late '70s, the producer, John McColgan – who would go on to great things with *Riverdance* – filmed a one-off live show I did at the Stardust nightclub in Artane, which was later shown on television. The Stardust had only recently opened when I performed there. I remember it as a bleak kind of place and didn't really rate it as a live venue. Everything would change after it burned down with the consequent terrible loss of life. From then on, venues had to make announcements about fire exits and that sort of thing. Sometimes it takes a tragedy like that to make people more aware of issues such as fire safety.

In fairness to RTÉ and John McColgan, they did a good job with my Stardust show. People sometimes criticise RTÉ but I think that, generally, they do great work. After all, we're only a small country with a population of four million people. You can't compare it with the BBC or ITV in Britain which have 60 million people to target through licence fees or advertising. They have no shortage of money to put into big budget productions. But if you look at Ireland's impressive track record in hosting the Eurovision Song Contest down through the years, it's clear that RTÉ is well able to compete with the best of them.

Speaking of RTÉ, I'm proud to say that one of the station's most popular radio stars, Ronan Collins, was the drummer in The Dickie Rock Band in the late '70s. In my view, Ronan is a real all-round talent – great singer, brilliant drummer and a talented broadcaster. In fact, I'm hugely surprised that Ronan didn't get more television work over the years. I loved having him in my band because Ronan is my type of drummer – real solid and heavy on the snare. I've always been fussy about the quality of musicians I play with. I love a good, strong rhythm section, with drums and bass, accompanied by guitar and keyboards. I also adore the sensation of singing with the backing of an orchestra from time to time, which is a very different experience to performing with a band.

I generally demand and expect a high standard from my musicians, although there has rarely been any hassle with the lads in my bands over the years. I might have snapped at them occasionally if they got the timing wrong or something but not to any great extent – anyone can make a mistake. However, I am an absolute perfectionist when it comes to sound quality and have been very hard on sound engineers in the past! I believe that sound quality is vital and I always try to reproduce what my audiences are used to hearing on my records. There is nothing like poor sound quality to put me in a bad mood while I'm on stage, particularly if I'm singing well. I feel my good form is wasted on the crowd. I try not to let my frustrations show but I'm sure the audience occasionally picks up on it. I recently saw Jack Jones performing in the National Concert Hall and he didn't seem pleased with the sound quality and I could relate to that. Generally speaking, though, I'd like to think that musicians consider me to be an easy performer to work with.

Anytime I hear Ronan Collins on the radio these days it reminds me of the final years of the '70s when he was a member of my band. Business remained steady, thanks largely to the success of the John Denver hit and the Stardust TV special. As a result, I seemed to be on the road a lot with the band. I was glad of any work I could get as Judy was expecting again and soon we would have another mouth to feed.

In June 1979 we completed our family with the birth of our fifth son, Peter. He was a great little fella from the moment he was born. All the others had caused us endless sleepless nights as babies but Peter never gave us a wakeful moment – he was a model child. Even throughout his school years, he wasn't an ounce of trouble. But we didn't love him any more than the others for that. We always cherished all our children equally. As most parents will tell you, every child has different needs and demands as they progress through life.

I will always look back on the '70s as a time of uncertainty. It was a decade of great change for me, professionally and personally. I had taken big risks such as changing my band and moving to new management. As 1979 drew to a close, I realised I would have to work harder than ever to survive the '80s.

THIRTEEN

The Cabaret King

Mick Quinn played a significant role in helping to sustain my earnings as the entertainment business continued its sharp decline as the '80s arrived. Despite the passing of the showband era, I luckily didn't have to fall back on a career in welding. I was able to keep doing what I loved best – performing on stage. Having said that, I was doing fewer shows and being home a bit more made me realise that none of us – my own family included – fully appreciated how tough things were for Judy when the children were very young.

Having six kids must have been a culture shock for Judy, given that she grew up in a small family with just her brother. For me, however, a crowded house had been the norm as my parents had five children. To her credit, Judy excelled in every way as a mother and gave our children everything she had, emotionally and physically. I did what I could – when I was around, that is – but the lion's share of rearing them fell on Judy's shoulders. I definitely feel that I missed out on a lot of their early childhood by being on the road so often with the band. There was never a question of me quitting the music business to spend more time with my family, however, nor did Judy request or expect me to. She always understood that this was what I did for our livelihood, tough as it was on her. She knew from the beginning what she was getting into and fully respected that singing was not simply a lifestyle choice for me – it was my job, my career.

I remember one incident that typifies how hard things were for

Judy back then. I was lying in bed one morning having come home late from a gig the previous night. Judy had been dropping Jason and John to school in Dundrum and was rushing to meet Joseph's bus for St John of God, who were providing special care for him in Celbridge. Even when Joseph entered his teens, he still had the needs of a baby. She was obviously a bit flustered that morning, with all the rushing around. She was putting stuff into the back of our car – we had a Renault 4 at the time – when the boot came up suddenly and badly cut her forehead. I remember her coming home with blood running down her face. I immediately jumped out of bed and attended to the wound. The injury looked a lot worse than it was because of all the blood but it gave me a terrible fright to see her like that.

I absolutely loved being a father, difficult as it could be sometimes. A parent's love for their child is unconditional. You have to be there for them through good times and bad and we would certainly go on to have our share of both. Being a father gave me something to aim for and something to keep working so hard for. It gave me extra drive and ambition – but it also gave me endless hours of heartache and pain.

I will always think that we were foolish to rush into having children so soon after getting married. Couples need time to get to know each other first before they bring a child into the relationship. Naturally, with the benefit of hindsight, we would have done things differently but it goes without saying that we'd never give any of them back or be without them. I love my children more than I love myself and I know that Judy does too.

Being a famous singer and getting to perform in front of an audience on stage is a great buzz but it doesn't come close to the feeling you get from being a parent. Real success to me was being the father of such beautiful children. In fact, I used to pity those performers who had no families to go home to after a gig. They may have been worshipped and adored by their fans when they were up there on stage but many of them went home to empty houses. To me, that was a sad existence. While it was often difficult to strike a balance between parenthood and having a successful singing career, I never would have put performing before my love of my kids or wife. That said, I didn't beat myself up for not spending enough time with my kids when they were growing up. I remember going to cheer them on in football matches in Terenure College and bringing them to Funderland at Christmas, but I know there were certainly long periods of time when I wasn't around to do things like that. It was simply not possible to give them more of my time because of the type of business I was in. My successful career as a performer afforded my children certain comforts in life they may not have had otherwise. In that sense, I feel I was a good provider for my family.

I was lucky to have a great relationship with my children when they were growing up. Each of them would have expressed their affection for me in different ways but I know that they all loved me equally. It's hard to say which of my children I would have been closest to when they were young. Sarah was certainly her Daddy's girl, growing up as she did in a house full of brothers and because Joseph was handicapped, I would have brought my second eldest, Jason, to more places than him when he was small. John was a conservative character, while Richard was more demonstrative. Our youngest fella, Peter, was a complete and utter gentleman.

In some ways, having an older brother who was handicapped was a good learning experience for my other children. Maybe it toughened them up a little and – as unfortunate as the situation was – made them realise that the world could be a hard place sometimes. I used to say to them: "Life is never perfect." Certainly if there is one thing life has taught me it is that you can never take your health for granted.

Shortly after Peter was born in 1979, Judy started to feel twinges of pain in her fingers. Initially, her GP put it down to fluid retention on account of her recent pregnancy but the pain became progressively worse as the months went on and she eventually went to see a specialist. We were devastated when the consultant diagnosed a severe case of rheumatoid arthritis. It was even worse when he explained that it would eventually spread to other parts of her body – her shoulders, her feet, her wrists, her knees … .

It was incredibly sad to see a 32-year-old woman, in the prime of her life, struck down by such a debilitating condition. At one stage the arthritis got so bad that Judy had to have an operation on her feet and couldn't go up the stairs for a while afterwards. We had a beautiful home in Rathgar at the time called Highfield House but it was three storeys high and all those stairs posed major difficulties for Judy. Even though we mainly lived in the basement of the house, the problem was that all the bedrooms were upstairs. For this reason we eventually had to sell the place in Rathgar and move to Scholarstown Road in Knocklyon, which had a bedroom on the ground floor.

As the months went by, Judy's condition got progressively worse. Even the simple things we used to enjoy doing together – like going for walks around Howth or through the Phoenix Park – became more and more difficult for her. Judy recently had an operation to replace her knee, as this was the area giving her the most trouble. The procedure went well and has helped give her back some of her freedom. By nature, Judy is an extremely positive person but it can't have been easy for her dealing with severe pain on a daily basis for the best part of three decades and it certainly got her down at times. It upset me deeply to see her in so much agony and it was difficult going out on the road to do shows knowing that she was having to cope with five young children – one of whom was severely mentally handicapped – and a new baby. Raising a young family is hard enough when you're in full health so I can't even begin to imagine what Judy went through after she became ill. Some days, even getting out of bed was a challenge. After a while, ordinary, everyday tasks like driving a car became difficult for her. As her husband, I've done my best to be as supportive as possible and when I was home I tried to be as much of a hands-on dad as possible. It's important for any married couple to have the support of each other – it's the key to the success of any marriage. As the kids got older, they also became a great help.

We have been lucky to have a fantastic, caring rheumatologist, Doug Veale, who has helped improve Judy's quality of life considerably. Dr Veale is attached to St Vincent's Hospital in Dublin and is also associated with the Rheumatology Rehabilitation Unit at our Lady's Hospice in Harold's Cross. I realise that rheumatoid arthritis is his business and everything but in my opinion this doctor goes beyond the call of duty when it comes to dealing with his patients. He is incredibly sympathetic and caring, doing everything he can to help. The facility in Harold's Cross is unbelievable and Judy goes there a couple of times a year for physiotherapy and to use their pool. Every time she gets a particularly bad flare up, Dr Veale books her in and it makes a world of difference. The sad thing about rheumatoid arthritis is that there's no real cure for it. A lot of the time, it's just a question of managing the condition and trying to keep the inflammation at bay. But they're coming up with new treatments all the time and Judy – most of the time, at least – is able to function with the help of her medication, which we bring everywhere with us.

The start of the '80s was certainly a hectic time. Not only were we trying to deal with Judy's illness and looking after the kids but the business had irrevocably changed. By then, the showbands were just a distant memory, consigned to the scrapheap of history. Thankfully, I had managed to stay busy throughout the '70s, although I have to admit that I wasn't working as regularly as I would have liked. For many artists like me, the sweaty ballrooms of the '60s and cavernous pubs of the '70s were being replaced by cabaret venues and dinner dances and this was where I started to ply my trade.

In many ways the cabaret scene became the saving grace of showband survivors like myself. It was a case of constantly having to reinvent yourself in order to survive. In the '50s I had been a young Rock 'n' Roller with no interest in the showband scene. By the '60s, however, I had given in to the commercial reality that the real money was being made in the ballrooms. After the demise of the showbands in the '70s, I needed to find a new niche for myself so I set my sights on cabaret, concerts and corporate dos. The owners of live entertainment venues were constantly looking for new ways to make money and the emergence of the 'dinner dance' resulted in a lucrative new trade for many.

The inexplicable rise in popularity of Country & Western music continued and while I still wasn't a huge fan I did start to include certain country ballads in my set. In fact, in 1980 I had a hit single with 'Coward of the County', which was also a huge international success for Kenny Rogers that year. I've always been mindful of the need to be a commercial artist and perform songs that are instantly attractive to an audience. There's no such thing as a song 'growing' on you at a concert. It has to appeal to an audience instantly so the recognition factor of every number is vitally important. A typical Dickie Rock show – then and now – always combined my famous hits from the '60s, some Rock 'n' Roll standards and the odd decent country song thrown in for good measure. As far as I'm concerned, if people pay to come and see me, then you have to give them what they want. If a song is not popular commercially – even though it still may be a great song – I generally only get to sing it in the bathroom for my own personal pleasure. I'm a realist if nothing else.

From the early '80s on, I played all the main theatres and venues in Dublin, Limerick, Cork and Belfast. I also performed concerts in places like the Gleneagle Hotel in Killarney, Co Kerry, which is still a regular port of call for me these days. I even had the opportunity to play prestigious venues such as the Olympia Theatre and the Gaiety in Dublin. I have Mick Quinn to thank for putting those shows together, which were a huge success for me. When he became my manager he worked hard to build my profile. He was a brilliant organiser and had a keen eye for publicity. He booked me into the Olympia Theatre for a 12-night stint in 1980 and every night was a complete sell out. Also on the bill was Lonnie Donegan, who made his name from skiffle which was all the rage back in the '50s. I got some great reviews after those shows. One newspaper critic raved about my professional performance and described me as 'Dynamic Dickie'.

In May 1981, Mick put me on for two weeks in the Gaiety Theatre. Again, there wasn't an empty seat in the house as I took to the stage each night. It was a brilliant production, featuring the popular group The Bachelors, comedian Shaun Connors and X-Appeal, a beautiful bunch of dancers from Belfast. I remember *The Sunday Press* described the show as being the next best thing to Las Vegas. The Olympia and Gaiety shows helped me to reconnect with my old fans and it was great to see so many familiar faces in the audiences every night. Some of them even came to more than one show.

Aside from the success of the Gaiety shows, it was a hectic year for us. Judy's arthritis continued to give her great pain and in 1981 we decided to buy a place in Spain. It has been a home-from-home for us ever since. We always loved Spain and had holidayed there many times over the years when the kids were small. After Judy's condition was diagnosed, the doctor told us that living in a warmer climate would help alleviate her symptoms and this has certainly proven to be the case. Even if you don't have arthritis, warm weather can have a very positive effect on you. After all, we're warm-blooded creatures by nature and heat is good for us. It's no coincidence that if you wake up during the winter and you see the sun shining, it automatically makes you feel better. That's why older people tend to relocate to places like Spain during the winter months – it simply makes them feel healthier. Ideally, if you wanted heat all year round, you'd buy a place in Arizona or somewhere like that. But Spain is only two and a half hours away if you need to come home. Some Irish people I know who have properties in Spain leave Ireland in October and don't return until April or May. That wouldn't be for me at all. We tend to go over for two or three-week periods at any one time and always enjoy coming back to Dublin to see our friends and family.

We bought a lovely apartment in Southern Spain in a beautiful place called Mijas in Andalucia. We'd been there on holidays a few times and were naturally drawn to that region when we eventually decided to buy abroad. There's something about the atmosphere and pace of life in Spain that I love. Maybe because it's a big country, the facilities there – including their health services – are top class. I always reckoned we were better off buying a place on the Spanish mainland rather than somewhere like the Canary Islands, which, for starters, would mean a longer flight to and from Dublin. When you're on the mainland you have more options. You can hire a car and drive up to Seville, Granada or Cordova, whereas on an island you're stuck there and the scope to explore other places is limited.

When we first bought the place we contemplated moving to Spain on a permanent basis and in 1982 we decided to try living there for a year. We had the children in Spanish schools and everything. I was travelling back and forth to Ireland to play shows while the rest of the family stayed put in Spain. Looking back, I don't think the upheaval was good for the kids. In a way, it felt too much like a permanent holiday. As much as I like it there, I could never see myself living in Spain on a full-time basis. I like it for the warm weather, the nice restaurants, the golf courses and the Spanish people but it will never feel like home to me. The simple fact is I'm a born and bred Dubliner and when I'm away from Ireland too long I miss it. I love the simple pleasures here, like going for a game of golf with my friends, spending time with my kids, having dinner with friends – I don't have that type of connection with people in Spain. Then, of course, there's the language barrier. Even though we've been living there on and off for the past 26 years or so, we'd only have a working knowledge of Spanish. We're able to get by when it comes to ordering food in a restaurant or asking for something in a shop but nothing really more than that, although Judy is much better at Spanish than me.

These days, give or take, we probably spend 50 per cent of the year in Spain. There's little doubt that it has worked wonders for Judy's health – mentally as well as physically. As a mother she is very involved with her children and tends to worry about them more when she's in Dublin. Not that she doesn't worry about them when she's in Spain, it's just that she can't do anything about it when she's over there. In a way, this forces her to switch off and be more relaxed. All in all, buying that place in Spain was one of the best decisions we ever made and I'd strongly recommend it to anyone.

* * * *

In 1984 Gerry Houlihan, the owner of Clontarf Castle, approached me and asked if I would be interested in performing some cabaret shows there. It was one of the classiest places to play in Dublin and I immediately accepted the offer. Clontarf Castle became one of the most successful cabaret venues in Ireland and I have great memories of playing there throughout the '80s and '90s. I still do the occasional gig in Clontarf and recently played two sold out shows there for Mothers' Day, which were a great success.

Generally speaking, cabaret gigs were well paid. This was important in light of the fact that the regularity of the work began to diminish during the '80s. There was still money to be made but the live entertainment scene had been on the decline since the disco boom of the late '70s, as exemplified by the film 'Saturday Night Fever'. It was starting to dawn on hotel owners that, rather than have to go to the expense of paying a band, they could simply bring in one guy to play some records on a double deck. Add in some flashing lights and a bar extension and – hey presto! – you had yourself a nightclub. Once they were able to say they were serving a meal – usually chicken and chips – most venues were able to qualify for a late night dance exemption. Nightclubs started opening up all over the place, much in the same way ballrooms had back in the late '50s and early '60s. There's little doubt that the popularity of night clubs in the '80s seriously affected the livelihoods of performers like myself.

To compensate for the lull periods, it was vital to work as hard as you could during the holiday seasons. For instance, you might do 12 nights or so over the Christmas holidays but then there wouldn't be any work until St Patrick's weekend or even Easter. I always remember that January and

February could be extremely barren months work wise. To be honest, it did cause me a level of anxiety because I never felt comfortable enough to be able to retire. Money may well stay with those who respect it but you also need to keep working to sustain your lifestyle, particularly if you have a large family like mine.

I have great respect for singers like Tony Kenny, who carved out a niche for himself with Jurys Irish Cabaret and also got regular work in America. From a purely business point of view, this was a smart move on Tony's part. It allowed him to perform as much as possible in Ireland during the long running summer show at Jurys and then head over to the States where he had created work for himself. Tony is another survivor of the showband era and – like myself – was able to reinvent himself and somehow stay in the music business. I admire the fact that he's had success in America and does so well for himself over there – he's a hard worker and a good singer. Tony was still only in his teens when he joined the four members of the original Miami Showband in The Sands in 1967. He left them to go solo in 1972 – the same year I started The Dickie Rock Band – and has had a long and successful career ever since.

I'm sure Tony would agree that it's always great to get recognition for your work from people in the entertainment business. In May 1985, I was thrilled to receive an award from the Variety Artistes Trust Society (VATS). It was one of the most coveted awards in Irish entertainment and previous recipients had included Maureen Potter, Joseph Locke, Noel Purcell, Val Doonigan and Eamon Andrews. I was presented with the award at a special concert in the Gaiety Theatre. I remember people like Sonny Knowles, Cathy Nugent, Maureen Potter and Eileen Reid performed that night. When I went on stage to collect my trophy, the whole theatre erupted and I was given a standing ovation. I was honoured to accept the award, which was given for outstanding services to the Irish entertainment industry. I was never one for big acceptance speeches. I said a few brief thank-yous before launching into some of my hit songs – I was always happier to let my music do the talking.

My profile in 1985 was higher than it had been for some time. I was all over the papers after receiving the VATS award and the publicity did me no harm at all and led to more bookings. That year I was also approached by RTÉ who wanted to make a new documentary about me. It was made by Adrian Cronin, who had been the producer of 'Portrait of an Artist – Dickie Rock' back in 1966. This time, Adrian wanted to concentrate on my post-showband career and how life had evolved for me since my early days with The Miami Showband. The cameras followed me around the cabaret circuit all summer. A crew even travelled over to Spain to film me spending time with Judy and the children. The documentary, entitled 'Dickie Rock – Just for Old Times' Sake', was broadcast in November and I was very happy with how it turned out. Adrian did a really brilliant job mixing the new stuff with his old footage from the '60s. I felt that the programme perfectly captured my transition from showband star to a cabaret performer. After it was shown on TV, I was busier than ever. Your career always gets a big boost after something like that.

In 1986, Mick Quinn, the man I largely credited for my renewed popularity, decided to get out of the business and I was sorry to lose him as a manager. We remained on very good terms and I ran into him not so long ago in Spain, in a place called the Sunset Beach Club. I was singing a few songs in an informal capacity with a friend of mine called Pearce Webb, who works there. I was delighted to bump into Mick, as I hadn't seen him in years. He was in top form and looking great. Mick recently promoted Red Hurley, who had great success with his album, 'I Will Sing'. I jokingly told Mick that I wished he'd do that for one of my records. After Mick stopped managing me, a very nice fella called Willie Kane, who had worked in his office, took over and I stayed with him for around two years. By that stage I felt that I needed to be represented by a bigger company so I moved my management to Tommy Hayden, who Louis Walsh worked for as a booking agent. When Tommy eventually got out of that end of the business I was managed by one of the guys in his office, Tony Byrne.

As any manager in this game would agree, sometimes you get offered the gig of a lifetime, the type of show that's just that extra bit special. In 1989, I was flattered to be invited to perform at a gala dinner in the world-renowned Hotel de Paris in Monte Carlo, which was being hosted by Ireland's Honorary Consul to Monaco, Dr Michael Smurfit. I've known Michael for many years and have done a number of corporate events for him. I even played at his son Tony's wedding, backed by a big band – it was a fabulous occasion. I've always got on very well with Michael and consider him to be a complete gentleman. I didn't have to think twice when he asked if I would play at the dinner in Monte Carlo, which was to be attended by Prince Rainier himself. I was among a selection of entertainers, including The Dubliners and some Irish dancers, flown over to Monaco by private jet for the ultimate corporate gig.

There are many things I'll always remember about that night – the opulent surroundings of the Hotel de Paris, performing in front of Prince Rainier and his family but, above anything else, the pure decency of Michael Smurfit will remain with me the most.

It was a simple gesture on his part. After we performed our last song, Michael came up to the stage and shook hands with me and every member of my band, thanking us for coming. Quite often, the musicians are overlooked in favour of the lead singer but Dr Smurfit made a point of acknowledging each one of them personally. I know for a fact that it meant a lot to them. I remember thinking to myself: "This guy has class, pure class."

Later, he invited me down to his table to meet everyone and have a chat. He may be a multimillionaire and a hugely successful businessman but he is an extremely nice man, with no airs and graces about him.

There are certain well-known people who could learn a lot from Michael Smurfit. A few years later we were invited over to London to play at a special testimonial dinner for an Irish football hero who was leaving his club after an impressive 20 year career. Some of the lads in my band were big fans and were looking forward to meeting him after the show. One of them had even written a special song, to the tune of an old melody, paying tribute to him. The guys in the band were just ordinary Dubliners who would have loved your man to come over afterwards and say something like: "How are ye, lads? Thanks for coming over and playing; I really enjoyed that song you wrote about me." It would have been great for them to be able to go home and tell their kids or their friends that they had met someone who was such a big name in football at the time. However, he simply got up and walked out before the performance was finished. Frankly, I was very disappointed by his behaviour. None of the musicians received any recognition from him. I know we were just there to do a job and were being paid for it but it wouldn't have killed him to come up and say hello.

That's just life, I suppose – not everyone has the class of Michael Smurfit.

Pictured in Judy's mother's house when we were expecting our first child Joseph.

I never get tired of meeting the fans after the shows. When they stop wanting to talk to me I'll know I'm in trouble!

At an All-Stars friendly with Sean Thomas, the then Manager of Bohemians FC and Bobby Charlton.

GRAND OPENING OF THE NEW

STARLIGHT ★ BALLROOM

eland's No. 1 Showband   WESTPORT 1969   FRIDAY NIGHT, FEBRUARY

DICKIE ROCK and the MIAMI

(on stage from 11.15 p.m. to 2 a.m.)

also THE SAN-ANTONES also the TONY CHAMBERS ORCHESTRA

(THE GREAT MAESTRO HIMSELF)

HEAR THEIR GREAT NEW RELEASE—"LIFE WITHOUT LOVE"
—C/W. "HEY LITTLE GIRL"   DANCING 9-2   ADM 10/-

We played on the opening night of the Starlight Ballroom in Westport and our Mayo fans gave us a great reception.

In New York in 1970 when I met Engelbert Humperdinck in the Americano Hotel. (Reproduced courtesy of Francis Kennedy, www.irishshowbands.net)

I wouldn't try wearing those white trousers now but at the time they were all the rage! (© Tony O'Malley)

At home with Jason and Joseph.

Judy with Joseph.

Joseph used to love the swings in
Palmerstown Park.

Sarah in the front with Richard,
Jason, John and a friend in
Churchtown.

DICKIE'S BAND

Topline Office

55 Parnell Square W., Dublin 1.

1972: Steven, Fran, PJ, myself and Johnny at the back with the late Bobby Murphy and Charlie at the front.

My mother and Judy's father with Joseph on his Communion Day.

Judy's mother and father.

Mary, 'our chaperone', and later Judy's bridesmaid, Judy's grandmother and her aunt.

My mother in her later years.

The famous velvet suit from the '70s – it weighed a tonne.

The Cabaret King – Clontarf Castle. By the '80s dinner dances accounted for nearly all the gigs I was doing.

With Maureen Potter when she came to see me play in Clontarf Castle.

The atmosphere at the dinner dances, with everybody sitting down and staring right at you, was very different to the old ballrooms. It had to be a very concentrated performance.

The Pianoman – my mother would have been proud!

When the fans realised I was with Paddy Cole they couldn't wait to get their picture taken!

The Dickie Rock Golf Classic in Donabate Golf Club with Leslie Brooks, Judy, Kathleen Brooks and myself.

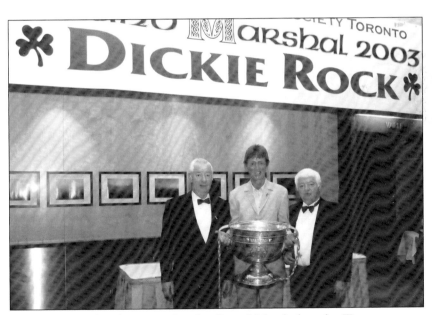

I was honoured to be invited to be Grand Marshal at the Toronto St Patrick's Day parade in 2003. Jim Ellis and Paddy Ellis are pictured with me as I'm holding the Sam Maguire which had been brought over for the occasion. They were brothers of Tommy Ellis who produced most of my records and composed a lot of my songs.

A chip off the old Rock! I'm proud that my son Richard has followed me into showbusiness.

Judy and I have been through everything together over the last 40 years and I hope we have many more happy times to come.

For most of my career I've enjoyed being recognised and it's great to have the chance to meet people of the calibre of Dr Smurfit. Occasionally, however, you pay a price for that fame, as I found out later that same year. I had what turned out to be a highly embarrassing brush with the law, which almost landed me in jail. It was a situation partly of my own making, I have to admit, but it all got blown out of proportion by the media.

I got stopped by a guard one day because I didn't have tax or insurance for the car I was driving. From the way the case ended up being portrayed in the papers, however, you'd think I was involved in a high speed car chase through the suburbs of south Dublin.

Sometimes in life you take what you believe to be small, calculated risks. More often than not, they turn out to be the wrong decision. That was the case when I took a chance and drove my 1964 Silver Cloud Rolls Royce without tax or insurance. It was a beautiful car but it needed some work and had been off the road for a good while. The mechanics had originally intended to send somebody up to my house to collect it. When nobody arrived, I rang the garage, only to be told that they couldn't make it up to me that day. Out of sheer frustration, I decided I would drive it down myself and be done with it. There's no denying that it was a foolish thing to do – it hadn't been taxed since 1981 and I wasn't insured to drive it. Foolishly, I had convinced myself that I could get away with it. After all, it was only a short drive to the garage in Churchtown from where I was living and I was taking my time. I was very conscious of the fact that I had no insurance and was behind the wheel of a big car. I shouldn't have done it but I did – simple as that.

I couldn't believe my bad luck when I was pulled in by a guard at Rathfarnham Bridge. I mean, of all the times to get stopped! I handed over all my details and didn't really give the matter much more thought, even when a court summons was eventually delivered to my house.

When the case was finally heard, I was nowhere to be seen in the court, much to the annoyance of Judge Sean Delapp, who threw the book at me. In my absence he fined me £3,000 and sentenced me to three months in prison.

I was completely oblivious to my fate as events were unfolding in Rathfarnham District Court. I had been invited to a wedding around the same time and had got the dates mixed up. The first I heard of it was the following day, when I got a call from a newspaper reporter asking me how I felt about going to jail.

I was gobsmacked and simply couldn't believe what he was telling me. I had certainly never intended to cause any offence to the judge by not turning up – it was a genuine error on my part. My solicitor was furious with me and said that if anything like this happened in the future, I was to give him a copy of the summons immediately so he could deal with it. I never blamed Judge Delapp for passing that sentence and knew he was simply doing his job. He's actually a very nice man and I later went on to become very friendly with him. I do think, though, that a court should give you the benefit of the doubt if you don't turn up for your case. Surely they must assume that something unusual has happened and that there is a reason for you not making it. For all they knew I could have broken my leg or been involved in an accident on my way to court – anything could have happened. If I had ignored the court a second time, then fair enough. I think it was unfair to slap a big fine and a jail term on me without any attempt to find out why I wasn't there.

I nearly died of shock when I read reports of the case the next day. The newspapers painted a very different version of what had happened at Rathfarnham Bridge that day. The court reporters weren't at fault. They were just going on the account of the guard who had stopped me. Giving evidence, the guard claimed he had to reach speeds of up to 80 miles an hour on Ballyboden Road to catch me. Maybe he was – but I was not. Maybe he saw me in the distance and sped after me but that did not mean I was tearing down the road. This was simply ridiculous. My car was a big, old Rolls Royce, for God's sake, not a high-speed BMW. I doubt it was even capable of going at that speed given the condition it was in at the time. I was also consciously driving slowly for fear of being uninsured and having an accident. I knew I had been taking a risk that day by bringing the car out on the road in the first place; I certainly had no intention of doing anything to increase that risk. I was barely moving in that car; you couldn't even say I was cruising, let alone speeding. As far as I was concerned, the court had been told complete and utter lies. Anyone reading a newspaper that day could have been forgiven for thinking that Dickie Rock had been engaged in a dangerous car chase, with the Gardaí in hot pursuit of a vintage car.

I firmly believe that everyone should a pay a price if they do something wrong. That said, the punishment needs to be proportionate to the crime. In my case, I think a misleading impression had been given to the court and I hadn't even been there to dispute what was being said. Needless to say, I immediately instructed my solicitor to appeal the sentence.

Shortly before the appeal case came to court, the guard who had given evidence against me visited my home. I couldn't believe it when he asked me if there was any way I could keep the story out of the papers. I've no idea why this was so important to him.

I said: "It's only in the papers because of what was said in court."

Maybe he was embarrassed by all the publicity the case had attracted. He certainly knew how annoyed and upset I was over what had been printed. Quite simply, the reports didn't make any sense. He had stopped me for not having tax or insurance but how could it be said I was driving at 80 miles an hour.

I avoided jail – no thanks to that guard – but the hefty fine of £3,000 still stood. I was also given a two-year driving ban. Generally, in such a case, you can appeal the driving ban after one year and this is exactly what I intended to do. It was extremely difficult for Judy having to drive me around everywhere, particularly with the crippling arthritis that was making her life a misery. When the appeal was heard, my solicitor explained to the court that my wife was in poor health and the driving ban had been an added burden on his client.

"So it should be," the judge snapped back, without a flicker of emotion on his face. Throwing out my appeal, he told me I would not get my licence back until the two-year ban had expired. I was really taken aback by his complete lack of compassion.

I had the opportunity to confront him in Terenure a few years later after he had retired. I went up to him on the street and said: "Do you remember me? I just want to tell you that you're the most insensitive, disgusting individual I've ever come across in my life. You have no compassion for people – you're a bloody disgrace!"

It was great to be able to get that off my chest, I can tell you. I was upset for Judy, really, and the impact my driving ban had had on her. One of the things I hate most in people is unfairness and I genuinely believe that judge treated me unfairly by not taking my wife's health situation into account. It wasn't as if I was looking to appeal the fine or anything like that. I was simply trying to make life as easy as possible for my wife but that judge clearly couldn't find the humanity in himself to see it that way. In most cases, unless there were exceptional circumstances, it was usually possible to get your licence back half way through a ban if you appealed it. While the judge clearly had the legal option of restoring my licence open to him, for some reason he didn't see fit to show me any latitude.

I'm the first to admit the situation was partly – if not mostly – of my own making. I made the stupid decision to drive the car that day and I deserved to be punished for it. However, I didn't deserve to read untruths in the newspapers that caused me and my family considerable upset and embarrassment. I'll never know why that guard said what he did that day in court. Maybe he thought he'd be considered a big shot among his colleagues for putting manners on Dickie Rock, but I doubt it.

Whatever his motivation, it caused me no end of hassle. As I entered the 1990s I decided to put the incident behind me and move on. If I thought my troubles were behind me, however, I couldn't have been more wrong.

FOURTEEN

Growing Up In Public

In September 1990, I faced the biggest personal crisis of my life. I took a call from Tony Byrne, my manager at the time, that stopped me in my tracks.

"Hiya son," he said – he always called me that even though he was younger than me. "Are you sitting down?"

When I told him I wasn't, Tony advised me to get a chair. He had the worst possible news. It was a prospect I'd dreaded for many years: the *Sunday World* was about to run a story about what happened in Adamstown.

I had hoped the story was dead and buried. I'd only met the girl a few times over the years. The first time was when she approached me and told me I was the father of her child. Initially I didn't believe it but when I heard all the facts I eventually realised it was true. When I accepted this, I suppose I panicked. I was terrified, realising the hurt it would cause Judy if she found out. I knew it would be like a knife slicing through her heart. The sheer thought of having to put my wife and family through something like that killed me. I was heart broken at the idea of causing them so much pain. I'd managed to deal with the situation privately at first and didn't tell anyone but once I accepted paternity there were legal and financial matters that had to be sorted out behind-the-scenes. My friend and musical director, Eugene McCarthy, was fantastic throughout that whole period. It was an extremely stressful time and I hated not being able to tell Judy the truth. Not that I had ever considered telling her was an option. I genuinely felt it was in her best interests not to find out about what had happened, particularly because there was a child involved. For 15 years I had managed to keep my indiscretion a secret from her. After Tony's call, I was hit by the sudden realisation that I had no other option – I would have to tell Judy everything.

With the *Sunday World* about to break the story, I had to act immediately. I put down the phone and tried to figure out my next move. I knew Gerry McGuinness, one of the founders of the *Sunday World*, so I called him to see if he could use his influence to get the story pulled. Gerry said he was sorry but there was nothing he could do. He didn't want to interfere with the editorial independence of the newspaper. He also told me that if the *Sunday World* didn't publish it, other tabloid newspapers would be only too happy to go ahead. Gerry also believed that his newspaper would treat the story more sensitively than some of the other British-owned papers.

That was the end of that idea so and I headed into the kitchen to find Judy. I suggested that we go for a drive through the Dublin Mountains. After a while, I pulled the car over and switched off the ignition. Taking her hand, I looked her straight in the eye and told her everything.

Telling Judy what had happened was the hardest thing I've ever had to do. She couldn't believe what she was hearing. I can only begin to imagine how deeply upsetting it must have been for her to find out that I had fathered a child with another woman. She knew that I wasn't the type of guy who went out socialising and living the high life. If I had been the partying type, maybe it would have been less of a shock to her but as it was I rarely went anywhere without Judy. I was the one that went straight home after a gig, even if I was playing down the country. She knew I wasn't a promiscuous type of fella, who was going down to the pub and drinking every night, trying to pick up women.

Judy didn't get angry but she was extremely upset – we were both crying. I kept telling her that I loved her more than anything else in the world. I said that there was nobody else for me except her. I pleaded with her saying that we had six beautiful children together and we couldn't throw it all away because of one very serious lapse on my part.

We sat in the car for what seemed like hours. I just couldn't apologise enough to her. There were other matters to consider as well, such as how we should break the news to the kids before the story was published.

When we got back home I rang them all to warn them that there would be an upsetting article appearing in the papers in five days' time. I didn't really go into too much detail and just gave them the basic facts.

In the terrible days that followed I was so thankful to realise that if a relationship or a marriage is strong – likes ours is – then you can overcome anything. It certainly caused a kink in our marriage, there's no doubt about it, but I worked hard to rebuild the trust I had lost. I hardly left Judy's side those days as I wanted to prove that I was more committed than ever to our relationship. There was never any question of our marriage breaking up and Judy didn't ask me to leave the house or anything. Despite what we went through together that dreadful week, we are stronger than ever today, thank God.

It sounds hypocritical now, but down through the years I had always been the one who discouraged people I knew in showbusiness from having flings behind their wives' backs. Quite clearly, I had then turned around and broken one of my own golden rules that night in Adamstown. The only reason I can give to explain why it happened is that I'm just a man, with normal heterosexual urges. That's not an excuse as I know full well that it was gross stupidity and sheer weakness on my part – but it was a one-off weakness. I wasn't like some of the other men I've known in the entertainment business over the years who effectively led double lives. Behind the façade of being happily married with young families, they were off having affairs and some even brought their mistresses on holidays with them. While I certainly can't claim to be pure as the driven snow or anything, I've always hated that type of behaviour. These guys seem to think they can have it both ways and, as I discovered, the fact is that you can't. If you go down a road of deception, you run the risk of harming the people you love, like I hurt Judy. I never for a second set out to be unfaithful but the consequences of my actions were still devastating for my family.

I'll never forget the day the story came out. It broke on the front page of the *Sunday World* on September 23, 1990. When I read it, I was relieved that I had decided to tell Judy the *whole* truth about what had happened. I didn't want there to be any nasty surprises in store for her when she read the article. All the details in the story were pretty much exactly the same. I hoped that it would show Judy that I had been completely honest and had left nothing out. When the article came out,

Judy didn't really say anything.

Even though the story was all over the papers, I still had to go on that night and perform before a live audience. I was doing a big show in the Olympia Theatre to honour the legendary singer, Austin Gaffney. I was dreading it, to be honest. I didn't really want to leave Judy and the family alone at such an upsetting time and I was terrified about what sort of reaction I would get from the crowd. Much to my relief, I got a fantastic reception from the audience that night and it gave me a badly needed boost. I think most people there recognised that it was a tough time for me and my family and I really felt their support that night. Backstage, people who knew me offered words of encouragement and concern. Others found the subject too awkward to broach and I could understand that.

After the exposé, my private life was open season for debate. I remember I heard one fella say: "Sure what's the big deal about Dickie? All he did was have a ride." That was a stupid thing for him to say. I knew it was far more serious than that. As a married man, I had willingly accepted certain responsibilities: I had vowed that I would be faithful to my wife. And it wasn't just about sex – the young woman had become pregnant so there was a child involved, too. The problem is that society seems to accept as a fact of life that men are weak and prone to temptation. It's a far more damning thing for a woman – particularly if she's a mother – to be unfaithful to her husband than the other way around. It's very unfair for women, really.

I had no one to blame but myself for the hurt I had caused to my family but their pain was compounded by the media interest in the story. While they didn't say it to me at the time, I'm sure my children were angry about what I had done, mainly because of the hurt I had caused their mother, whom they all adored. Being the only girl in the family – her Daddy's girl – I think the whole thing was devastating for Sarah. At one stage she was even approached in Rathmines by a girl who said she was her sister. That must have had an awful effect on someone of that age. You can imagine what it would have been like for her in school with all that stuff in the papers about her father – some teenage girls can be very cruel. A few of the parents probably even told their kids to keep away from her. In my experience, most people are decent but some can be very unfair or unkind.

Obviously I would have preferred it if the *Sunday World* had never published details of what was essentially a private matter for me and my family but I know that journalists have a job to do. Writing stories about celebrities is part of their work – it's what they're paid to do – and from a tabloid newspaper's point of view, it was a good story. In saying that, I think it was unfair for certain reporters to be ringing the house and hassling my family, looking for quotes and interviews off them. I can't remember the names of these particular journalists but I feel that they went too far by contacting Judy and the kids at such a sensitive time.

Sometimes a crisis can make a relationship stronger and I definitely think this was the case in my marriage. I rarely go anywhere without Judy these days, apart from my game of golf or when I'm performing, and we are closer than ever. It probably hasn't always been easy being married to me but, throughout all the hard times, Judy has been an incredible wife and devoted mother to our beautiful children. I feel that I have been forgiven by my family for all the hurt I caused them.

Today, when I look back and think about the consequences of my behaviour in Adamstown in 1974, I feel very sad for everyone concerned – my family, the girl from Wexford and her daughter. As far as I'm concerned, they're all innocent victims in this. I've met the girl on a number of occasions in the past but I don't have any father-daughter relationship with her. I sincerely believe that for her sake and for the sake of my family, this is probably for the best. I've nobody to blame but myself for what happened that night and there's nothing I can say now to undo all the hurt I've caused. For what it's worth, though, let me clearly state this: I was the one completely at fault and I slipped up – badly.

* * * *

To say that life wasn't perfect for my family over the years is probably something of an understatement. We certainly had our share of tragedies and crises, but no more so than any other similarly sized family. There are parents out there who have probably been through twice as much as we have. The only difference between us is that it didn't make the newspapers when their children got into difficulties – things that are all too often part and parcel of growing up and becoming a young adult.

In an ideal world, I sometimes think you should be able to lock your children in the house when they enter adolescence and keep them under your constant supervision until they're old enough to know better. In reality all you can do is offer them guidance throughout those difficult teenage years and hope for the best. I've always used my father as my yardstick in terms of being a good parent. As role models go, I couldn't have raised the bar any higher than that. Like my Dad, I always tried to take my responsibilities as a father seriously. I think in some respects I was a strict father, particularly when it came to pushing my children towards getting a good education. I may not have been academic as a child, but I still wanted my children to have the educational opportunities that I didn't have growing up. This approach, of course, is pointless if your kids are not academically inclined. Pushing them in that direction can just drive them round the bend. It doesn't matter what type of career you have yourself. You could be a senior counsel or a consultant in the medical profession, but if your children are not academic then you're better off putting them into a trade – like my parents did with me. If you insist on your kids going to college and they aren't up to it, they may hate it and end up with nothing to show for it career wise.

I'm not professing to be an expert on parenting or anything like that, but I have one piece of advice for couples starting out in life today: when your children enter into their early teens, believe nothing they tell you – absolutely nothing! Teenagers will love you but they will also lie to you. They will lie to you and try to kid you to get their own way – it's simply in their nature. Adopting a healthy scepticism of every utterance that comes out of their mouths will help protect you – and *them* – from the pitfalls of adolescence. Of course, they will resent you for it at the time and think you're just giving them hassle but they'll be better off in the long run.

Whatever about the worrying times my children have caused me, over the years they have suffered because of my fame. Most families can deal with their troubles behind closed doors, in the privacy of their own homes, but in their case it was often a different story, especially for my son Richard who ended up doing a lot of his growing up in public.

The day I found out that Richard was a heroin addict was one of the lowest points in my life.

It's no secret that my third born son fell victim to drugs when he was just 18 years old. I'd like to tell you that we saw it coming but, in truth, we hadn't a clue what was going on. For the sake of Richard's privacy – and God knows he deserves it after what he's been through – I'm not going to rehash the sordid details that were all over the tabloids, but just want to talk about it from the perspective of a father. I think it's important for me to tell his story from the point of view of a parent who has been to hell and back but who, most importantly, has come out the other side. Perhaps it will send a message of hope to other mothers and fathers out there who are currently at their lowest ebb trying to confront the scourge of drug addiction in their house. It's not as if heroin discriminates when choosing its victims. Richard wasn't more likely to become a heroin addict just because I was working in showbusiness or anything like that. The perception some people have of the modern drug addict as a down and out vagabond, begging on the streets, is often wide of the mark as well. As we discovered, the shocking reality is that you could be anyone, from a doctor or a lawyer to someone on the dole, staring across the kitchen table at your heroin addicted son or daughter.

Like all of my children, Richard had always shown a great interest in music – they were all a chip off the old 'Rock' in that respect. He's a great-looking kid, extremely handsome and a real cool dude – probably too cool for his own good, sometimes. When Louis Walsh was putting his boy band together in 1993, Richard went down and auditioned for the job. I remember Louis rang me up and said: "Richard was absolutely terrific today, he's in." He was just going on 18 at the time and about to do his Leaving Certificate.

Richard was absolutely thrilled when he heard he'd been selected. I remember the excitement in the house when, with the financial help of John Reynolds from the POD nightclub, Boyzone was officially born. He was really nervous the following night when he appeared as part of Boyzone's original line-up on that infamous episode of 'The Late Late Show'. The lads were treated as a bit of a joke, really. It was a little bit surreal seeing Richard on the Late Late. I thought he came across as being too shy in comparison to the others. Gay Byrne slagged them off for not being able to sing or play any instruments, much to the amusement of the studio audience. I laughed when he said that because there was an element of truth to it. Richard was given a big clap when he was introduced as Dickie Rock's son which made me feel proud. I cringed, though, when the boys started into their routine. I thought their performance that night was a disaster – they were very badly rehearsed and hadn't a clue what they were doing – but it got them the national exposure they needed to launch their career. It was a gamble that ultimately paid off – but that was typical of Louis Walsh – there was no such thing as bad publicity in his book.

I've always admired Louis's business acumen and professional judgement. He was able to see what Take That had done in Britain and he had enough self-belief and vision to replicate the successful boy band formula in Ireland. I think those lads – as well as Westlife – should get down on their knees and kiss Louis Walsh's boots for what he has done for them. These were all just young guys who probably would have ended up in ordinary jobs. Instead, they went on to tour the world, playing to millions of adoring fans.

I never imagined Boyzone would become as big as they did. No one did, really. Richard completed his Leaving Cert that year and decided that he was going to dedicate himself full time to the band. This concerned me a little because he was a bright kid and could have done well in college but I reluctantly supported his decision. I had just a few words of advice for him: "Be professional and do it properly."

Just as Boyzone were on the cusp of stardom, however, Richard was kicked out of the band. He has always recognised that it was entirely his own fault. He just messed up and got involved with the wrong type of people. The sad thing is – and I'm not just saying this because I'm his father – he was genuinely one of the most talented in the band. The truth is, all the other members of Boyzone were working-class fellas from the northside of Dublin – they wanted success and were hungry for it – but Richard wasn't.

The official line was that Richard was dropped because he didn't fit in with the image that Louis Walsh was trying to cultivate for Boyzone. The reality was that he was hanging around with a bad crowd and started missing rehearsals and important meetings. Louis could obviously sense the direction that Richard was going in so he sacked him after a couple of months. He wanted the cleanest-cut bunch of lads possible in his boy band and Richard was acting too cool for his liking. He had far too much of a bad boy attitude and gave the impression that he was answerable to no one. Louis needed someone who was 100 per cent committed and dedicated but Richard was giving off a 'couldn't care less' attitude.

It never dawned on him that he would be booted out of the band and he was shocked when Louis fired him. I was so disappointed when I heard what had happened and told Richard that it was his own fault. In the hope that he had learned his lesson, I decided to see if there was anything I could do to rescue the situation so I went down to Louis's office in Ranelagh.

I somehow convinced him to let Richard back in the band again. I was always grateful that Louis gave him a second chance. I think everyone deserves that, at least, particularly young lads who are prone to making mistakes. But it wasn't long before Richard messed up again and this time he was out for good. I've always accepted Louis's reasons for throwing Richard out of the band and, despite what people might have believed, I never thought he was a bollix for doing it. There were no hard feelings either between Richard and Louis and they've spoken many times since those dark days.

Richard took his ejection from the band extremely badly. Just a few days after he was sacked for the last time, Boyzone went on to sign a recording contract with Polydor that would catapult them into the big time. I can only imagine what it must have been like for him, a young lad of not yet 18, having to see his former band mates on the television all the time and listening to them constantly on the radio – you couldn't go anywhere without hearing their hit single, 'Working My Way Back to You'. While Richard probably felt sorry for himself, he certainly didn't feel hard done by. He knew he had only himself to blame but it must have been devastating for him all the same.

In the summer of 1994, Richard smoked heroin for the first time in Spain. There's little doubt in my mind that the whole Boyzone experience contributed to Richard's problem with drugs. He had already been associating with the wrong types so it was inevitable that he'd end up in some sort of trouble. His sense of frustration over blowing his shot at stardom made him even more vulnerable to dangerous temptations. We only found out later, from other parents in the same predicament, that the warning signs were there: the secretive behaviour; the locked bedroom door; the staying out all night. At the time we didn't know what was going on, especially as none of my children – including Richard – were drinkers. Eventually we started to suspect that there was something more seriously wrong.

One night I came home to find Judy in tears in the kitchen. She had found drug paraphernalia belonging to Richard in his room. On another occasion, Judy was up the walls with worry when he didn't arrive home and I ended up trawling the nightclubs of Dublin looking for him. I met Keith Duffy in one club who told me that Richard had been in earlier but was now gone. When I arrived home, at about 3am, Richard was sitting on a chair in the kitchen, with Judy beside him, crying. I asked him directly what he was on and he told me it was heroin. I lifted him up and just put my arms around him and said: "Listen, now we know what we're dealing with, let's see what we can do about it. Let's solve this problem and get on with it – whatever it takes, we'll do it."

Dealing with something as harrowing as heroin addiction was uncharted territory for us as parents. We had no idea how difficult the road to recovery was going to be. It is a completely debilitating addiction. All of a sudden it was like having another handicapped child on our hands. The severity of heroin addiction hits families hard. You can read about it in the papers and everything but only when you experience it in your own family can you fully understand the complexity of the problem. It was an extremely worrying time for us but, like everything, the mother always seems to suffer more. Judy took it extremely badly but never stopped loving Richard for one second – neither of us did. It was so tough on Judy having to see her son go through all that.

Richard's recovery from addiction was a slow journey. It was a road filled with trips to hospitals, treatment centres and court appearances. Inevitably, perhaps, Richard's addiction got him into trouble with the law. On June 2, 1998, he was arrested and charged for possession of £40 (€51) worth of heroin and for allowing his car to be used to carry drugs. This was because the guy who was in the car with him was found to be carrying substantially more drugs than Richard.

I fully supported Richard in court when the case was heard nearly two years later, which was a stressful experience for both of us. It's a well-known fact that I broke down in the witness box. I wanted the judge to know that I felt my son had suffered more than others in his position because of my fame. I told the court that Richard had already effectively received a sentence on account of all the media interest in the case.

I can understand there being some degree of publicity because Richard is my son, but certainly nothing like the amount of coverage the case got. It was just too much. There are thousands of young lads and women who find themselves in Richard's predicament but it's rarely in the papers. One detective working on the case told me that there were sons and daughters from very respectable backgrounds who were in similar trouble to Richard – it just didn't get publicised. I was also amazed to learn of a number of very prominent families who had children caught up in drug addiction.

As hard as it was for me to go to court and publicly stand by Richard, I was glad to do it for him. I wanted the judge to know that my son was a good person at heart who had paid the price for having a famous singer as a father. We were incredibly relieved when Richard was handed down a two year suspended sentence, as there was always the possibility that he could have been sent to prison. I'm happy to say it was an opportunity that Richard didn't waste.

One thing you quickly learn about heroin addiction is that full recovery is a long process filled with disappointment after disappointment. Richard had been in and out of different rehab clinics with no real success. We had no choice but to keep on trying – there's nothing else you can do. It was the intervention of the well-known entrepreneur and author, Bill Cullen, that eventually put Richard on the right road. Bill is a director of a residential rehabilitation centre in County Wicklow called Forest and he organised for Richard to go there. With the help of his excellent counsellor, an English lady named Lynne Kirby, he was able to beat his addiction. I will always be extremely grateful to Bill and everyone at Forest for saving my son's life and giving him back his health.

I admire Richard for having the determination to go down to that place in Wicklow of his own volition and kick his drug habit – it took courage. I've heard stories about parents having to throw their kids out of the house because of heroin addiction. When they get completely out of control, you have no choice but to practically disown them. But even though it was very bleak at times, things never got that bad with Richard. Throughout his addiction, he remained a loving son. He went through hell but was able to come out the other side. Richard has acknowledged the pain he caused to Judy and myself, as well as to his brothers and sister. We had to stick together as a family and unconditionally support him – that's what families do. There's little doubt that Richard feels a lot of guilt for what he put us all through but the main thing is that we have him back.

My other kids were fantastic to Richard, always talking to him and minding him, but I'm sure, at times, they felt a bit neglected by me. During that whole period I would have given Richard an awful lot of my time. Later, I explained to them: "Look, Richard needed me more at the time than any of you did. It doesn't mean that I loved you any less. I will be there for all of you equally if and when you ever need me." To me, Richard was like the prodigal son. It's shocking to think that we could have lost him to heroin. It was a six-year-long nightmare for all of us, an experience I wouldn't wish on any parent.

I've always tried to be there in times of trouble for my other children, too. I fully supported Sarah when she found herself in the headlines after an incident in a Dublin nightclub in 1995. She was just 19 when she was charged with being in possession of ecstasy after a Garda raid on the club she was in that night. I firmly believe that she was simply in the wrong place at the wrong time but she needed my help and I was glad to give it. Sarah told the court that the whole thing had been a big mistake and the judge just ordered her to pay £250 (€320) to the poor box.

These days, Richard's back in the newspapers – but for all the right reasons. He's had a starring role in the hit show 'Dancehall Qs and Hucklebuck Shoes', which pays musical homage to the showband era. The show features Claudine Day, who is playing her mother, Eileen Reid and Brian Dunphy takes the role of his father, Sean. Richard stars as his old man, Dickie Rock. He certainly does me justice in the role and has developed into quite a good singer and performer. The whole thing has been a fantastic experience for Richard, who has been to the forefront of the show's publicity campaign. He's been interviewed by numerous newspapers and magazines and was even a recent guest on 'The Late Late Show'. Not surprisingly, many of the interviews have focused on Richard's past problems with drugs but he seems unfazed by it all and has been talking frankly and openly about it – more than we would like, sometimes.

Richard's passion is now music instead of drugs. Everything he does in life has some sort of connection to music. He works for a company called Micro Media, who design and distribute all the posters and flyers for the POD, the Olympia Theatre and the Electric Picnic. He's also returned to DJing and has some gigs coming up this year. His main musical focus now is on his electro-dance band, Lectrosoul, which he's incredibly enthusiastic about. It's to Richard's immense credit that he was able to come through the abyss of heroin addiction and start reclaiming those lost years. He may have missed out on fame and fortune with Boyzone but he may well get his big break yet – he certainly has the talent and the looks for it.

We're not just proud of Richard's success – we're simply relieved and overjoyed to have our son back.

FIFTEEN

An Unbearable Loss

On March 10, 1992, we tragically lost our firstborn son. He was 24-years-old.

Joseph, our baby – our six foot three baby – was tragically taken from us and our lives were changed forever. Even though he had been born severely mentally retarded, it was not his condition that killed him in the end but a simple accident.

Raising a mentally handicapped child was difficult for Judy, particularly because my work kept me away from home so often and she had to cope on her own a lot of the time. It was a delicate balancing act for her, having to rear six children, one of whom took up considerably more time than the rest because of his intellectual disability. Joseph was a big, strong lad, even when he was a young child, and could be difficult to handle because of his size. When he was around eight or nine he went into residential care and it made the world of difference to Judy's life and Joseph's. We were fortunate to have the help of the staff of St John of God at St Raphael's, in Celbridge, County Kildare, who cared for Joseph for most of his life. We could only take him home on the weekends when I wasn't working because of Judy's rheumatoid arthritis and I used to go up and collect him on a Saturday and bring him home with me.

I will never forget the kindness shown by Brother Aloysius, who looked after Joseph at St Raphael's. Words cannot express my admiration for the nurses and staff there who deal with people with disabilities and everything that entails – their bodily needs, their education and their general well being. These carers give so much love but they are also thorough professionals in the way they go about their work. They often have a tough job to do, in very difficult circumstances. I believe that any child with a mental disability is better off in full-time professional care. I've heard some parents who were in our position say: "Oh, I could never send my child anywhere, they're better off at home." That's the wrong attitude, if you ask me. All my other children were living at home, but they were going to school every day, getting an education for themselves. Joseph, despite being handicapped, was as entitled to a full-time education as they were. We could only do so much for him at home, particularly due to the competing needs and demands of our other children, so I believe we were right to send him to St John of God, where the professionals could bring out the best in him.

It broke my heart to look at Joseph sometimes. He was such a handsome fella and it saddened me to think that he would not be able to fulfil himself as a young man. I'd look at his brothers and sister and see how healthy they all were by comparison. When he reached his early 20s, it used to kill me to think that this beautiful-looking young man could never experience the normal things in life, like having a girlfriend or starting college or a job or becoming a husband and father – he was missing out on so much. He was never able to call me "Dad" or Judy "Mum", like our other children. I remember when he was just a boy some woman told me that Joseph was a "blessing from heaven". I know she meant well but to me that was absolute rubbish. I consider all my other children to be blessings, whereas poor Joseph, through no fault of his own, was a cross to carry. It didn't mean we loved him any less than the others but describing a mentally handicapped child as a blessing seemed like a cruel joke to me.

One of my most enduring memories of Joseph as a young boy is of him coming into our bedroom in the middle of the night. I'd wake up and see him standing there at the end of the bed, just looking at us. Quite often it would have been because he had wet himself and he was probably feeling uncomfortable. I'd bring him back to his room and change him, then let him get into the bed beside us. As I'd drift off to sleep, I'd see Joseph's beautiful big eyes staring at me from the pillow. God, he was a lovely, lovely child, with those incredible eyes and shock of black hair, like his mother's.

Joseph may have been brain-damaged but physically he looked like any other young man of his age. He did have difficulty swallowing sometimes because of his condition, but otherwise he was perfectly healthy – that's why his sudden death came as such a shock to us. I remember the events of that painful time vividly. I had been over in the Lebanon performing for the Irish troops and the day I flew back to Dublin I got a phone call to say that Joseph wasn't well. He had pulled something hot off the cooker down on top of himself in the St John of God centre. It was a pure accident and was *nobody's* fault but Joseph was in a bad way and needed to be rushed to hospital by ambulance.

Judy and myself went straight down to James Connolly Hospital in Blanchardstown where we found Joseph slumped in a chair in the casualty department. The staff said they weren't able to get him into the bed so I put my arms around him and lifted him up. As my head touched against his, I remember that Joseph was holding me. There was always a lovely smell from him, almost like what you'd get from a baby. I started talking to myself, saying: "God, please take this poor young man from us." Even though I said it I didn't really mean it. I just felt such pity for my son – this helpless, beautiful man who was suffering so much. I wanted all this pain to be taken away from him.

The doctors examined Joseph and decided to keep him in overnight for observation. St John of God were good enough to send down a nurse to look after him. He was brought down to another unit of the hospital and I lifted him into his bed. I asked him to give me a hug and he put his big arms around me. Then I gave him a kiss and left, not realising it would be the last time we would see our son alive. Judy was quite upset as we said goodbye to Joseph. Even though I was deeply concerned about his condition, I tried to stay strong for her sake and assured her that everything would be fine.

We left the hospital and went to pick up our youngest son, Peter, from school in Ballyboden. Then I rang my mother in Cabra to update her on Joseph's condition and we went home.

Later that evening, Judy took a call from the hospital. We were asked to go back in because Joseph's condition had deteriorated. My heart jumped – I knew this didn't sound too good but I hid my fears from Judy. I drove slowly towards Blanchardstown, taking my time to collect my thoughts, hoping that everything was all right. We arrived at the hospital and Joseph's room was just to the right of the front door. I held the door of his room open for Judy who walked in before me. Suddenly, she screamed and doubled over. I looked over at the bed and saw that Joseph's entire body was covered with a sheet – he had died half an hour earlier.

We learnt afterwards that the shock from being scalded had given him a heart attack. It was an appalling way to find out that our son had died. The hospital had phoned us as soon as it happened and understandably they didn't want to break the news to us over the phone but I think a nurse or some other member of staff should have been stationed there to meet us before we went into Joseph's room. They should have prepared us for what we were about to see behind those unlocked doors. Somebody should have been told: "Stand at those doors until Mr and Mrs Rock get here and then bring them to me." It was a highly insensitive way to treat two parents who had just lost their son. I wasn't angry about it – I don't get angry – but I was certainly upset, especially for Judy.

We were brought down the corridor to an office, where there was a phone call waiting for me – it was my mother. When I told her that Joseph had died, I'll never forget the sound of her screaming at the other end of the line. She took the news extremely badly; in some ways it probably brought back the pain of losing her own son – my youngest brother, Joseph – all those years earlier.

I had no interest in an autopsy being carried on him and told the doctor: "I don't want his body touched. Our son is dead now, he's gone, and that's it." I didn't need to be provided with specific answers as to how Joseph had died. I didn't want anything appearing in the papers about the cause of death or anything. He was no longer with us and nothing – including an autopsy – would bring him back to us.

Joseph's death was undoubtedly one of the saddest times in my life and I went to bits after it. It was worse on Judy, though. It always is for the mother – she's the one who carried him inside her and brought him into the world. Before we had the funeral Mass in Celbridge, Joseph was lying in the coffin in a separate room to the main church. I remained behind with him on my own to say goodbye to him one last time before the service. I bent down over his beautiful face and said: "I'm sorry, son." I don't know why, but I was kind of blaming myself for what happened to him, even though it wasn't anybody's fault. We had great support that day from my colleagues in showbusiness with people like Joe Dolan, Red Hurley and many others, coming to the funeral

For the sake of our five other children, Judy and myself had to try to pick up the pieces and get on with our lives. The kids all loved Joseph and took his death very badly. I remember going out to Bray, where Richard was in school at the time, to break the tragic news to him – it was awful. All the kids were deeply upset over losing their big brother but I think Sarah took it the worst. I will always say, though, that the experience of having a handicapped brother had a positive effect on my children and taught them not to take life for granted.

There is nothing sadder for a parent than losing a child. It goes against the natural order of things when we outlive our children.

The saying "time is a great healer" may sound like a cliché but it really is true. As the years went by, although it was very difficult, we managed to get over losing Joseph. We still get occasional bouts of sadness, however, when we look at his photograph and can't help wondering what he'd be doing if he was still with us.

On another level, I felt a great sense of relief for Joseph when he died – and for Judy, too. We certainly never wished for him to die, or anything like that, but it brought us some comfort to know that his years of suffering were finally at an end. Like any other parent in our situation, we used to worry about what would happen to Joseph when we died or got too old to care for him. With Joseph's passing, that worry was taken away from us. His life may have appeared tragic but we have many precious memories of our 24 years with him. Despite the pain, we'd rather have had it than to have been without him.

While it would be inaccurate to say that some good came of Joseph's death, I have been privileged to have been in a position to give something back to the people who cared for him so well over the years. After Joseph died, we became friendly with another couple whose son attended St Raphael's in Celbridge. Leslie Brooks and his wife Kathleen are keen golfers and long-standing members of Donabate Golf Club in north County Dublin. In fact, the Brooks family lost their son, Robert, just six months before we buried Joseph. We got to know them very well and built up a good friendship with them. In a way, I think we helped each other by talking about our sons and the similar experiences we had in common. Leslie had decided that he wanted to do something to raise funds for St Raphael's St John of God, by way of thanking them for all the care they had given his son. His first fund-raising event was held 16 years ago and started off as a low-key affair. I turned up to lend my support and ended up singing a few songs, accompanied by a keyboard player. At the end of the night, I said to Leslie: "Listen, let's do this properly next year and I'll perform with a full band."

The Dickie Rock Golf Classic has taken place every year since and I am honoured to attach my name to it. Since its inception, it has raised over €160,000 for St Raphael's and it is always well supported. The golf starts early in the morning and runs until about 5 pm. It's followed by a buffet and fantastic night of entertainment in the clubhouse. The event has been generously supported over the years by other showbiz luminaries such as Sil Fox, Joe Dolan, Red Hurley, Paddy Cole, Dale King, Tony Kenny, Rowland Soper and Finbar Furey, with the formidable George Hunter acting as compere. I am also grateful for the support of the members and staff of Donabate Golf Club.

Apart from the fact that it's a good cause, the Dickie Rock Golf Classic is a day when I get to officially recognise all the love and support that the staff of St Raphael's gave to Joseph.

SIXTEEN

Loving Too Much

On January 4, 1999, my father passed away.

I will remember that period as being one of the most traumatic times in my life for a number of reasons. Not only did I lose my father that week but I came close to losing my wife, daughter and grandson, too.

My father was in his 85th year when he died. When somebody reaches that age you can prepare yourself for their death, up to a point. He spent his final hours in a nursing home in Westmanstown, near Lucan, in Dublin, where he was looked after by a wonderful lady called Maureen and her staff. A few years earlier my father had been over with us in Spain and I noticed that he was becoming confused a lot and his memory didn't seem great. As time went by he got worse and my mother, because of her age, was unable to handle him. He appeared to be going downhill rapidly so I discussed it with my brother and sisters. We all felt it would be best – for his sake and my mother's – to get him into full-time care.

Even though he hadn't been feeling great for a while, it still came as a complete shock to me when I heard he had died. I had just visited him the day before. My sister Margery rang me the next morning and advised me to get over to the nursing home immediately. By the time I got there he had passed away. My sisters Margery and Lillian were with him in his room. We were all in bits. I remember putting my fingers over my father's face and gently closing his eyes. I was the eldest child and I suppose it was only natural that my father's death would have a profound effect on me. All my earliest memories of him suddenly came flooding back: picking chestnuts together in the Phoenix Park; going to football matches with him in Tolka Park; the love and devotion he showed towards my mother and how he had been an amazing father to all of us.

As preparations for my father's funeral got underway, I received a phone call that I will never forget – I still shudder when I think about it. Judy and my daughter, Sarah, along with her new baby, Benjamin, had been involved in a car accident in Ballsbridge. My first grandchild had been born on July 8 the previous year and was only six-months-old at the time. He was a lovely little fella and we all adored him. They were making a right turn onto Waterloo Road from Morehampton Road when a car jumped a red light and hit them side-on, at speed. Judy took most of the impact and badly injured her ankle – as if things weren't bad enough for her already with the rheumatoid arthritis. Sarah suffered mild concussion but was badly shocked because the baby was in the car with them. Miraculously, little Benjamin was uninjured. When I saw the state of our car, which was a total write-off, I could not believe that the consequences had not been more serious. Their car had literally been lifted off the ground by the force of the impact. I can't even begin to think about what could have happened but thank God their injuries weren't too serious.

When Judy rang me from St Vincent's Hospital to say they had been in an accident, I was in the middle of organising my father's funeral arrangements. I remember thinking: "Jesus, this can't be happening." It's hard to find the words to express the emotions I was feeling – it was absolutely devastating. The next day we buried my poor father.

It must have been difficult for my mother to stare into his coffin and remember him as a 23-year-old man when their love was young. That's the thing about loving too much – you know that some day it will have to come to an end. It was heartbreaking to watch her say her goodbyes to him. Just before they closed the lid on his coffin, my mother leaned over his body and said: "Goodbye, my love. Please give my love to the other two Josephs up there in heaven."

I remember Judy was on crutches with her leg in plaster at his funeral which was very uncomfortable for her. Sarah was there, too, as were my other children. They were all close to their grandfather and he adored them. They were very upset when he died, even though they accepted that he was old and in poor health. I had brought them to see him in the nursing home in his final years. After the funeral Mass so many people told me what a wonderful man my father was. I knew that myself, but it was nice hearing it said by others.

When my father died, I sometimes agonised over whether or not I had been a good son to him. I was afraid that because of what I was going through with my own family – particularly all the trouble with Richard – I had probably neglected him a bit in his final years. It wasn't a case that I felt really guilty about it or anything like that. It was just one of those situations where there were simply other things going on in my life that required my immediate attention. But it made me realise that children should never take their parents for granted. It's so important that you appreciate and love them while they're alive because you won't have them forever. If you're a fella, take your dad out somewhere occasionally. If you're a girl, spend as much quality time with your mum as possible.

We all made an extra effort to look after my mother after Dad died. She took his death badly and grieved heavily for him. My sister Margery and her husband Paddy did more for my mother than the rest of us. I'll never forget their kindness and how attentive they were to her. The days and weeks after my father's funeral were tough but after a while I found it easier to deal with his death. I stayed focused on looking after Judy, who was still recovering from the car accident. She was a bit of a nervous driver for a while afterwards, which was understandable. Who wouldn't be?

* * * *

Another tragedy befell my family in May 2001 when my foster brother, Vincent, died suddenly at the age of 43. Even before my youngest brother was killed off his bike in 1966, my parents had decided to give a foster child a good home, so not long after Joseph's death, Vincent became part of the family. He was nine when he moved to Cabra to live with my parents. I remember him as a lovely kid, a real happy child, although he had a completely different personality to Joseph.

I was never sure of the reason behind my parents decision to foster a child but it says a lot about the type of people they were. I suppose they just wanted to give some other youngster the chance of a secure family life. Whatever their motivation, I fully supported their decision and even remember driving them down to the orphanage in Rathdrum, County Wicklow, to discuss the fostering process with the nuns who ran it. In a way, I think having Vincent in the house helped my mother and father with the grieving process and filled part of the void created by Joseph's death. They really loved Vincent and he made them happy, which was good enough for me.

While Vincent became an important part of our family, I never considered him a brother, although I was extremely fond of him. As far as I was concerned, I only had two brothers, Brian and Joseph. I think part of the reason was that by that stage I had moved out of my parents' house, so I really only saw Vincent when I was visiting there. I got to know him a bit better when he was in his late teens and he used to come to my shows any time I played Dublin. It was always great to see him.

I never really knew about the full circumstances leading up to his death, but the inquest found that it was caused by a heroin overdose. It was extremely sad because Vincent had battled with a drugs problem on and off for many years. With Richard's problems, I had first hand experience of the devastation caused by heroin. I was well aware that chronic addiction couldn't be solved overnight. As far as I knew at the time, though, Vincent was off heroin. He had just successfully completed a drugs rehabilitation programme so it came as a huge shock to us all to learn of his death.

I don't understand why Vincent's life turned out the way it did. I didn't have much contact with him in the years before he died. I hadn't drifted from him or anything. It was just that I had my own family to take care of and they were naturally my main priority. My son Jason was quite close to him and would have known him much better than I did. Part of the reason might have been that my foster brother moved out of my parents' place at quite a young age and probably got caught up in everything that was going on in the city at the time. He became a troubled young man. I think a lot of people who spent time in orphanages when they were children also became deeply affected by that whole experience but in many ways his life seemed to be going well. He was an extremely talented hairdresser. I helped get him his first job by introducing him to a hairdresser by the name of Harris who I'd met in Spain. He served his time with him before going on to train with David Marshall – a good businessman and a very decent person – who was a great help to him. Vincent had a really promising career ahead of him because of his fantastic skills and his partner was a beautiful South African girl who absolutely loved and adored him. It was so shocking to see such a good life wasted. In a perfect world, Vincent would have been happily married with children but it just didn't happen that way for him.

We were away in Spain when we heard about Vincent's death. We all flew home the next day but weren't in time for the funeral Mass so we just went straight to the reception afterwards. My kids were all pretty cut up about it, particularly Jason. It was terrible to see my poor mother so upset. She really loved Vincent and was shocked when he died so suddenly. Vincent's natural birth mother and her sons – his half-brothers – came over from England for the funeral. My parents had always encouraged him to keep in touch with his natural family. It was the first time I got to meet them and they were really lovely people.

Vincent's death was a very sad time for all of us. I worried about the effect it would have on my ma and made an extra effort to spend as much time as possible with her afterwards.

I was glad that I had done this because just a few years later my mother died on February 9, 2003. She would have been 89 that year. I really feel that she had a great, full life, largely due to how well my Dad treated her throughout their marriage. He was mad about her right up to the end of his life. When Judy and I would visit him in the nursing home, he'd always say to us: "Where's your mother? Is your mother coming up today?"

I'm happy to say that I have very precious memories of my mother's final years. We had sold our house in Rathmines and were waiting to move into the apartment we have now in Terenure. While it was being done up, Judy and I lived in my mother's house on Annamoe Park in Cabra for around two months. It was wonderful to be able to spend so much time with her again, back in the area where I had grown up. I had never lived in that house before because my parents only moved to Annamoe Park from Dingle Road after I got married in 1966.

It was funny, though, to be living under the same roof as my mother again after all those years. She used to get picked up by mini-bus and brought to the church or the old folks' club and, when she'd arrive home, Judy would have her dinner ready for her. Sometimes, we'd sit down together and watch 'Judge Judy' on television, which we all loved. Even though I was now an adult with a grown up family of my own, I still got the mammy treatment dished out to me from time to time. Occasionally I'd return to the house in the middle of the night, after travelling up from somewhere like Cork, and I'd be trying to slip into the house quietly when suddenly I'd hear my mother calling out from the dark: "Richard, is that you?" She was living downstairs in an extension they had built after converting the garage into a bedroom and bathroom. I'd go into her room and there she'd be, with the curlers in her hair, sitting up in the bed. As I'd bend down to give her a kiss, she'd say to me: "Did you get something to eat? There's a nice bit of apple tart out there if you'd like it."

It was like being transported back in time to the days when I was starting out with The Melochords and later with The Miami Showband. My father used to tell me to try to get home as quickly as possible because my mother wouldn't be able to go to sleep until she heard me come in. After all those years, nothing, it seemed, had changed in Cabra.

I consider myself blessed to have been able to spend those months with my mother as she neared the end of her days. When she eventually died in hospital in Blanchardstown, I felt a terrible sense of loss. Losing both parents is a terrible thing but, for me, the death of my mother was particularly poignant. All of a sudden it really felt like the end of something. This person, from whom I came and who had been there for me for as far back as I could remember, was now gone. My mother had done everything for me throughout my childhood and she was still very much a part of my life after I got married and had children and responsibilities of my own. A mother loves her children above everything else and absolutely unconditionally. After she was gone, there was a noticeable void in my life. It was the simple things I had taken for granted that I missed the most. I couldn't ring her up any more after I had been on 'The Late Late Show' and ask her how she thought I had done. Quite often, she'd say: "God, Richard, you were looking very tired on the telly tonight. Are you working too hard?" She wouldn't mean it in a critical way, or anything, but simply out of genuine motherly concern.

My mother and father were fantastic to all of my children, particularly Joseph. Your relationship with your parents continues to evolve at various stages of your life and when they become grandparents another stage begins. My parents were what I'd call no-hassle grandparents and were simply there to provide love and hugs, not criticism or discipline. As far as they were concerned, it was down to the parents to give out to the kids. They never criticised myself or Judy's parenting skills, although I was always happy to accept their advice when it was offered.

For most of us, it's inevitable that our parents will die before us. In perhaps 90 per cent of cases, that's a simple fact. It doesn't make it any easier to accept when it happens though, particularly if – like me – you were very close to your mother and father. To me, the father is the heart of the family but the mother is the soul. It's incredibly sad when a love as strong as theirs has to come to an end.

My problem is that I always think too deeply about these things. I don't always wear my heart on my sleeve – even with my own kids – and probably have a tendency to internalise my feelings. I fully realise that it's better if you let these things out but I can't help the way I am. After my mother died, I grieved heavily inside over a prolonged period. I wouldn't say that I was depressed or anything but I certainly felt a very deep sadness within myself. It was the same feeling as when my son died. Sometimes, though, I think it's a good thing for a human being to take time out and think about the important things in their lives, even the sad things, because it helps you to get over them.

There's an old saying that goes: "It's better to have loved and lost than never to have loved at all." I wonder sometimes if that's true. One thought that makes me sad is the mere fact that we're all getting older and it's all going to come to an end some day. In the same way that my parents' love for each other had to end in this life, it will be the same for me and Judy, this woman who I love more than anything else in the world. She is part of me and I'm a part of her but it's going to come to an end some day. It's the same with my children. I know I'm going to have to leave them at some stage in the future and I can only hope against hope that they're going to be all right. I don't want to be on my deathbed worrying about all these people who I love more than myself. Have they all established themselves? Are they getting on well in their lives? Will they be able to cope without their Dad? In some ways the point I'm trying to make is that if you've never experienced love in the first place – the love of a woman or the love of your children – then maybe you've less to lose. I know from the experience of losing a son and a brother how painful love can be when it's suddenly taken away.

Some people find comfort in their faith but I'm not really one for religion, to be honest. I wouldn't go so far to say that I'm agnostic – that's a bit of a copout if you ask me. However, I sometimes find it difficult to believe that there is a God, a benign presence up there looking after us, when you consider all the evil things that happen in the world. I'm not even talking about the tragedies that have occurred in my life, just things that happen in the world in general.

I was in Spain recently on a golf trip with a group of people I know very well. On one of the nights I found myself in the hotel on my own and a terrible wave of sadness came over me as I sat down to dinner. All these powerful feelings of nostalgia were flooding through me. I started thinking about my father and my mother; my poor son Joseph and my youngest brother and when he was killed all those years ago. My thoughts then turned to my own children: was I paying them enough attention and doing enough for them? I honestly don't know what brought it on but I put my head in my hands and cried. It didn't help that Judy wasn't with me that time, even though we rarely go anywhere without each other. To make matters worse, I had to perform two nights that week in Spain as part of the golf event I was taking part in. I was really cut up for some unknown reason and it took me a few days to get over it.

I eventually came to the conclusion that perhaps having these sort of thoughts is all just part and parcel of getting older. My mood improved when I thought about all the fantastic people in my life – my family, my friends and my fans. I realised that as long as I had my health and my children and Judy around me, there would be plenty of good times ahead.

SEVENTEEN

The Fame Game

After my mother's death I continued to divide my time between Ireland and Spain. I never missed an opportunity to come back and play at home. Corporate events and weddings accounted for the bulk of my work, along with the occasional concert in venues such as Vicar Street. When I wasn't performing I continued to maintain a low public profile. I avoided social events and parties like the plague. That whole scene had never been for me. I was always happier spending time at home with my family.

The very notion of celebrity is a major bone of contention for me. I may be well known, or even famous, but I simply consider myself to be a professional performer and entertainer. I think the term "celebrity" has been debased by the gossip magazines and social diary pages of the newspapers. It seems to me that anybody can be a celebrity these days. I don't mind if there's a degree of substance to their celebrity status, like prominent sports people who have brought pride to this country, such as Eamon Coughlan, John Giles, Sonia O'Sullivan, Barry McGuigan and that great gentleman, Ronnie Delaney. The fact is that their achievements still stand up after all these years and they deserve great respect, even when these athletes have retired from sport.

I was flattered to recently learn from Eamon Dunphy, when I was a guest on his radio show, that Johnny Giles is one of my biggest fans. It's always lovely to hear things like that. Eamon is a person I have great admiration for, even though his mouth sometimes gets him into trouble and he has a tendency to annoy people or drive them mad. He came from a humble working-class background on the northside of Dublin, like I did, and went over to England at a very young age to make something of himself. While his career as a footballer may have been modest, I think it's great that he reinvented himself to become Ireland's most successful journalist and broadcaster. Eamon certainly speaks his mind and he sometimes goes too far but I respect his honesty and decency. I've met him a good few times over the years and have always found him to be a lovely fella.

Outside the world of sport and music, there are certain Irish people out there, who seem to be famous for the sake of being famous. They come from good homes and backgrounds but go around the place behaving badly, letting themselves down. I think they need to get out there and get a bloody job or settle down or something. I'm sick of reading in the papers about some of these women and who they are supposed to be sleeping with or seeing pictures of them flashing their flesh. I can't understand how these people are considered to be celebrities. Maybe it's a Lillies's culture or a Reynard's culture, or whatever, feeding the egos of these false celebrities. They're a bit like Paris Hilton. I mean, what does she do? She comes over to Dublin and she's all over the papers, just because she's going to inherit a fortune.

At the other end of the scale you have people who have good reason for getting the publicity. I'm pictured in the newspapers from time to time myself but only because it's part of the business I'm in and I need to promote my gigs or records – in other words, I've something to sell. I certainly think I've worked hard enough and long enough to be thought of as famous, unlike some of these nobodies, trading solely on their looks, who feature regularly in the gossip pages.

I've huge admiration for people like former Miss Ireland, Andrea Roche, who's married to PJ Mansfield, the son of developer Jim Mansfield of City West. She may have initially become famous for being beautiful but she's now a very respected businesswoman and handles herself well. When you see Andrea in the papers, usually it's because she's doing something useful. She may still be a good-looking woman, but she's a true professional as well and I admire that about her.

There are women out there now who seem to be pictured in the papers partying every other night. I'd love to grab them by the shoulders and say to them, in a father-like way: "Listen, you're in your 20s now but where are you going to be at 36, 40, 45 and beyond? Will you still be floating around the clubs and parties doing what you're doing now? What will you have to show for it?" I think these women are really heading for trouble by embracing a culture of falseness. There's nothing worse than being over-exposed – literally, in some of these young ladies' cases – particularly if you've no talent to show for it. I used to warn my own daughter about the dangers of going down this particular road. As Sarah's my only girl, I suppose I worried about her more in that respect than I did about my other children. I'm very proud that she turned out to be such a wonderful mother whose main focus is her young son.

Appearing in the gossip pages of the newspapers is like a drug to some people – it's pathetic nonsense. As far as I can see they get withdrawal symptoms if they're not seen at a particular party or some trendy bar or club or at all the 'important' social occasions. It's different if you're Bono, Joe Dolan, Linda Martin or Van Morrison – they've earned the right to be considered a celebrity because they're talented performers. I met Van Morrison once. I know his partner, Michelle Rocca, and they came to see me when I was playing in Clontarf Castle. Van was able to hear me perform my version of his ballad, 'Have I Told You Lately', which is a gorgeous song. Don't ask me what he thought of it – we didn't say a word to each other. It's very hard to know what to make of Van Morrison as he's an intensely private individual from what I've heard.

Van isn't the only one who came to see me at Clontarf Castle. I remember I was living in Rathmines when my old 'minder', Dinny 'Boy' Desmond, called up to the house one day. He had a favour to ask. He wanted two tickets to my cabaret in Clontarf Castle for a friend of his – Martin Cahill, the notorious criminal known as The General. Needless to say it was a request I couldn't refuse. I told Dinny I'd look after that for him and didn't give it any more thought.

A few weeks later I was getting ready for the show when Ann Darcy, who booked the acts for Clontarf Castle, arrived in my dressing room with a concerned look on her face. "You're not going to believe who's sitting out there," she told me. "The General's here with his wife."

I'd forgotten all about it, to be honest. Ann was taken aback when I told her: "Yes, I know – I invited him." I explained what had happened and she seemed relieved that there was a simple explanation for his presence there that night. When she first saw him I think she was worried that he was casing the joint or something.

I went out and performed the show but couldn't see my special guest because of the darkness of the cabaret lounge. Afterwards, when I was getting changed, I was told that Martin Cahill was outside and wanted a word. I could see a few worried faces when I said that would be okay.

The General quietly entered my dressing room with his wife and was extremely polite, as he thanked me for the tickets. He shook my hand and said: "It's such an honour to finally meet you, Dickie. That was a great show. It took me back through the years, hearing all those songs again."

We didn't have much of a chance to get into any kind of conversation because of all the various people sticking their heads in the door wanting to say goodnight to me. I knew well that they just wanted to be able to tell their friends that they'd seen The General. I don't know if he realised this but he soon asked me if there was backdoor he could leave through, to avoid any fuss. We said our goodbyes and I showed him out.

It wasn't long afterwards that Martin Cahill was assassinated by a professional hit man near his house in Rathmines in Dublin. I was shocked when I heard about his death on the news, particularly as I'd only recently seen him.

* * * *

I think that men and women alike are attracted to famous people. When I was in the Miami we were mobbed by women everywhere we went. I never felt that this was because they thought we were wealthy stars and were after our cash. It was simply that they were drawn to all the glitz and the glamour that comes with being in a successful band. I don't believe that the modern phenomenon of women marrying for money is anything new – it's always been part of the game. Since time began, certain beautiful women – the shallow kind – have used their looks to get where they want to in life. The cute cave woman, for instance, would have gone for the man with the biggest cave. It's part of nature, really, because man has always been considered the hunter and provider. It's all down to whether or not a man has something better to offer in his particular cave – that's what some women have gone for down through the ages.

I think marrying for money instead of love can often result in an unhappy family life, but not always. This was sometimes the case in Ireland back in my parents' generation. Love can grow and develop as opposed to being just a flash of infatuation at the beginning. I was certainly attracted to Judy on the night we first met but it wouldn't be true to say that I fell instantly in love with her or vice versa. Once we got to know each other it didn't take us long to feel this way but the point is that our love for each other had to grow first.

I'm no great expert on what makes a marriage work but I do have certain theories on the subject. This may be an old-fashioned view, but I believe that for a marriage to be successful, people should marry within their own societies or classes. Say, for example, a college educated guy marries a girl from a different background to him, just because she's beautiful. In later life, this decision could come back to haunt them as they may find that they have very little in common when you take away the physical attraction that brought them together in the first place. Likewise, you often have girls from middle-class homes marrying lesser fellas – they might be violent men or big drinkers or something. How can you explain a decision like that? Are these women just stupid? I call it the "lame duck syndrome". Some girls tend to have pity on lads like that and they're attracted to the rebel or the troublemaker. I can never understand it because these girls would have lived in lovely homes, gone to the best schools and had everything they wanted in life – then they choose these fellas who are from completely opposite backgrounds. Maybe they do it to antagonise their parents.

It's getting harder to define class these days. I have to laugh when I see stars such as Colin Farrell driving around town in an old banger, wearing torn jeans. If an ordinary guy did that he'd be called a bloody skanger but Colin Farrell can get away with it because people know he has a few bob. If a young working-class fella wears torn jeans it's because he can't afford a new pair. The rich guy, on the other hand, wears torn jeans because he's choosing to highlight his status. It's as if he's saying: "Of course I could buy new jeans but I simply couldn't be bothered."

I get a bit fed up reading about everything stars like Bono are involved in all the time. I think he's a bit of an egotist, to be honest. I suppose we're all egotists in a way – myself included – being in the business we're in. However, I know Bono's a great father and a real family man and I admire him for that. You could never take away from the phenomenal success he's had along with the rest of the lads in U2 and they still seem to have their feet on the ground. There's little doubt they've worked hard to get to where they are. It's incredible, when you think about it: a bunch of lads from a little country like Ireland, from the northside of Dublin, being *the* biggest group in the world. I'm not a great listener of their music, but from what I've heard of U2, I'd consider them more of a rock/pop group than a pure rock band. I think it's easy for people to criticise them for moving their operation to Holland for tax reasons. At the end of the day, however, you have to remember that music is a business and it can often make sense to base yourself in a country that has a kinder tax regime. They still spend a lot of time here and have contributed to Ireland's good reputation abroad for many years. Having said that I don't think they did themselves any favours when they went to court that time to get their stuff back from their former stylist. I mean, for the sake of a Stetson hat and some other trivial items you had all these personal details about the band coming out in court and being printed in the papers. I think that whole episode damaged the image of U2 – it just wasn't worth it.

Nothing like that ever happened to me back in the Miami days. Sometimes I'd throw one of my ties into the audience after a show but that's the only memento the fans would have got from me. I'd be flattered to think that people would keep them. I certainly wouldn't be going to court looking for them back!

Maybe because of my working-class background I've never really felt comfortable hobnobbing with the high society crowd. It annoys me when certain people approach me and pretend that they're Dickie Rock fans. I said to one woman recently: "You can stand here and chat to me now, but I know you've never bothered to come and see me when I've played Vicar Street; you'll go to Elton John's concert in the RDS, though." The fact of the matter is that I still rely on 90 per cent of my own people – working-class people – to come to my concerts and support me.

I've said it before and I'll say it again: from the time I first started out and throughout my career, the people of Cabra West, Ballyfermot and all the working-class areas of Dublin and Ireland have made me who I am today and I'll never forget them for it. In fact, they're the only VIPs that matter to me.

* * * *

In 2005, RTÉ screened a documentary about my life and career, somewhat predictably called 'Spit On Me, Dickie'. It was made by Mint Productions which is run by 'Prime Time' presenter Miriam O'Callaghan and her husband, Steve Carson. Miriam was the one who approached me and I was interested immediately because she's someone I've always admired. I met her in Coman's pub in Rathgar to discuss the project and we hit it off straight away. I asked why she was interested in me, as opposed to someone like Joe Dolan and she said she felt that my story – and that of my family – would make for more interesting television. I discussed the matter with my family and my manager, Connie Lynch, a great guy who I'd been with since the early '90s until recently. They all thought it was a great idea. Once I agreed to do it, Miriam approached RTÉ and they jumped at it.

I loved working with Miriam. She is a complete professional, yet one of the most unpretentious, down-to-earth people you could ever meet. I admire all the success she's had on television and it's hard to believe that she's had to juggle her career with being a mother to eight children. Miriam conducted all the interviews for the documentary in my apartment and we had a great laugh together doing them. I remember while we were there one day, my phone rang and Miriam answered it, saying: "Hello, Dickie Rock's personal assistant speaking." She's a striking looking woman, too, very tall.

I remember Miriam sent a crew over to meet me in Spain. I was playing golf one afternoon with two good friends of mine, Tony Robinson and his wife Margaret, and they filmed us for two hours. Every swing and every putt was captured on camera with painstaking attention to detail. When the documentary was eventually screened, however, none of the Spanish segment was used, much to Tony's frustration! I suppose Miriam had to get everything into a one hour programme and it was inevitable that some scenes wouldn't make the cut.

I really enjoyed making the programme. It bought me back to the time I had featured in my first documentary in the '60s when RTÉ screened 'Portrait of an Artist – Dickie Rock'. Some of the clips from that were used in Miriam's documentary to great effect. The reaction to 'Spit On Me, Dickie' was just wonderful. It was a highly personal account of not only my life but also my family's. Most of my kids, as well as Judy, were interviewed and came across extremely well. Some of the subjects touched on, such as Richard's drug problem and my one-off infidelity, must have been painful for my family to discuss in such a public manner but I was very proud of how they handled themselves.

I had told Judy beforehand that these issues were part of our life and were bound to come up in the context of the documentary. I feel sometimes it's better to talk candidly about sensitive issues than try to avoid them. I think my family were generally happy with how we were portrayed in the programme. The only negative offshoot was the fact that some elements of the media, namely the tabloids, used the documentary as an excuse to dig up old stories and repackage them. All the stuff about Adamstown was dragged up again, which was upsetting for Judy. The fact is, though, that even if this issue hadn't been discussed in the documentary, the tabloids probably would have still printed what they did anyway.

That said, I'm still glad I agreed to do the programme and was flattered and honoured to realise that there was still so much public interest in me after all those years. As had happened before, my profile was boosted by the documentary and the bookings started to pick up again. Not for the first time, the power of television had revitalised my career.

EIGHTEEN

Keeping Up Appearances

When my son Richard appeared on 'The Late Late Show' recently, it reminded me of the many occasions that I've been a guest on the programme. I've a good idea how nervous he must have felt waiting to come on before he was introduced by Pat Kenny. Performing in front of an audience is all well and good but it's another thing altogether when you have to do it watched by hundreds of thousands of viewers on live television. Throughout my career I've never liked doing interviews but I recognise that it's a necessity in my business. Any time I've been a guest on the Late Late, I've always made sure that they get the sound right when I sing. Quite often what the audience is hearing in the studio is nothing like what viewers are getting at home. The people who look after the sound in RTÉ are excellent. Before the show I always ask them to ensure that my vocal blends properly if I am singing live to a backing track. If it doesn't, it can sound like you're singing off key and there's nothing worse than that.

I've been on the Late Late a good few times down through the years, from the glory days of Gay Byrne to today's show under Pat Kenny's command.

I have great admiration for Pat Kenny and believe he's seriously under-rated as a light entertainment presenter. I think he has great feeling for his subject matter. His broadcasting style is completely different to Gay Bryne's so I feel it's unfair when the critics try to compare the two of them as hosts. Pat Kenny's extremely professional and looks great on television – he's a very handsome man. Most importantly, though, is that he has great empathy with his guests. If I were to sum up Pat Kenny in one sentence, I'd say that he's a serious broadcaster with great heart.

I remember I did a big interview with Pat on 'The Late Late Show' a few years ago and he was criticised for it afterwards because he asked me about wearing a wig – or as he put it, a "syrup of fig". I heard it said afterwards that Pat had offended me by asking such a personal question but he did nothing of the sort. He never warned me beforehand that he was going to bring up the subject of my hairpiece but I certainly wasn't embarrassed or offended about it when he did. As far as I'm concerned, if you put yourself up there to go on 'The Late Late Show' and be interviewed, then you're fair game, to some extent. I did ask Pat not to mention a specific subject on the show and he was good enough to respect my wishes on that. The wig comment was just a bit of harmless fun and the audience got a great laugh when I joked that nobody was interested in seeing a baldy old man up on stage.

I started wearing a hairpiece in my late 20s when I noticed I was getting a bit thin on top. It wasn't a question of vanity or anything like that. I wouldn't bother wearing one if I wasn't in showbusiness. To me, it's like putting on a suit before you go on stage. It's just part of the image. I can never understand people wearing hairpieces who are not in entertainment. It just doesn't make sense to me. The thing is, in my line of work you're always on stage, to an extent. Even if Judy sends me down to the shops to get milk and bread, I know that people will recognise me. If I'm wearing a pair of old tracksuit bottoms, there'll be comments about how shabby Dickie Rock was looking down at the local Spar. But when I hear people make those remarks, I always say to them: "I may look rough now but wait till you see me on stage tonight."

I was on 'The Late Late Show' many times during the Gay Byrne era as well, without the wig in those early days! It's incredible to think that he started presenting the show back in 1962, the same year I joined The Miami Showband. Gay's an extremely clever man and was up there with the best broadcasters in the world. I remember being a guest on his show in 1966 in or around the time I represented Ireland in the Eurovision. In fact, when I was over in Luxembourg rehearsing for the contest, my parents were asked to appear on the Late Late. RTÉ sent a taxi out to Cabra to bring them to Donnybrook. They were sitting with the rest of the studio audience but Gay came over to have a chat with them about my Eurovision hopes. Everyone they knew saw them that night and they told me later that they felt like movie stars.

People often talk about the cultural impact of 'The Late Late Show' and how it helped Ireland to grow up as a nation. I certainly feel it weakened the influence of the Catholic Church in Ireland and brought previously taboo subjects, such as contraception and divorce, into the public arena. I think this was a good thing. After all, this was the show credited with introducing sex to Ireland and in some ways it certainly did that. I'll never forget one particular night when Gay showed the nation what a condom looked like. There was quite often a deliberate shock element to the show. I think it was courageous of Gay Byrne to feature some of the more controversial items. I'm sure these topics were proposed in advance by his production team and he could easily have refused to agree to some of them. Since the beginning of the television era in Ireland, the Late Late has been the 'must see' show. Maybe its influence today is not as far reaching as it once was but it's still the most watched programme in Ireland.

I've always respected Gay, although he strikes me as a colder person than Pat Kenny. In fairness to him, though, he gave many celebrities their important breaks over the years. The amazing thing about Gay is that even though he hasn't hosted the show since 1999, he's still in the news and we're still talking about him. I've always been thankful that he doesn't sing because he'd probably have us all out of a job if he did – he seems to be able to do everything else!

While I have great time for both Gay Byrne and Pat Kenny, they did annoy me on one rare occasion. Back in 1995 I recorded a lovely album with the producer Tommy Ellis at Westland Studios called 'You Must Remember This – 42 Songs That Live Forever'. I was extremely proud of this album, which had cost Tommy and myself a lot of money to make. It featured some top class musicians, including legendary jazz guitarist, Louis Stewart, and acclaimed saxophone player, Ritchie Buckley, who has worked with Van Morrisson. The album was beautifully arranged by John Tate and Jim Doherty, who also played piano.

Initially, we were going to do an album of Irish songs but Tommy Ellis came up with this concept instead. His idea was to trawl through some of the most timeless songs ever and carefully select the ones that best suited my voice. Tommy and I share the view that a good song is always a good song, no matter when it was written. He sourced around 200 songs of mostly American origin and we whittled it down to 42 in the end. On some of the tracks, three songs were recorded at once so they all segue into each other. Songs featured on the album included 'It Happened in Monterey', 'All of Me', 'Red Sails in the Sunset', 'For Once In My Life', 'As Time Goes By' and 'Walkin' My Baby Back Home'. The album paid tribute to some of the most celebrated songwriters of all time, from George Gershwin and Cole Porter to Irving Berlin. Vocally, I was at a mature stage of my career and the songs that were handpicked by Tommy perfectly suited my singing range.

When the album was finished, I was very optimistic that it would be a hit due to the quality of the songs and the professionalism of the musical performances. An artist like me is heavily dependent on radio play to promote a new release. If my fans aren't aware that I've a record out, they'll hardly be inclined to walk into HMV or Golden Discs to go looking for it. Incredibly, however, the album got little or no support from RTÉ broadcasters. The notable exception was my old friend, Ronan Collins, who is always very fair to and supportive of all Irish artists. I couldn't believe it when Pat Kenny and Gay Byrne didn't give the album any airtime because they had always been good to me over the years. I was particularly surprised that Gay didn't plug it for me on his radio show because he knew Tommy Ellis well and had done some work in his studios. Gay Byrne's radio show had the perfect audience for the songs on that album and they would have appealed to all his listeners. Somebody made representations to Gay on my behalf and he eventually played a track off the album, but it was as a fade-out at the end of the show.

I was bitterly disappointed when the album didn't sell, as I believed it was among the best work I had ever recorded. At the time I attributed some of the blame to the lack of support it had received from people like Pat Kenny and Gay Byrne. Needless to say, the whole thing was blown out of proportion by the newspapers who ran stories along the lines of 'Dickie Slates Gaybo and Kenny!'. I didn't feel any way as strongly as that. I had just expressed regret that they hadn't given my album a fair shake. Cliff Richard has had a similar experience with radio stations in Britain refusing to play his new releases, to such an extent that he once said it was a waste of his time recording albums that no one would get to hear. I can certainly understand where he's coming from by saying that. However, in defence of Gay Byrne and Pat Kenny, they have both been extremely good to me on numerous other occasions throughout my career and I am more than happy to acknowledge that. All I'm saying is that it would have been great if they could have been more supportive of that particular album.

Being in the business for five decades naturally means that I'd know most of our top broadcasters at this stage and it also brings a high level of recognition from people out on the street. I think it's great that people still stop me and want to shake my hand or get an autograph. The warmth shown towards me by Irish people has been incredible down through the years. It's funny, because these days I notice that more and more young people are coming up to me and saying things like: "Dickie Rock – you're a bleedin' legend; it's great to meet you." Obviously they weren't around to see me in the early days when I had all the hit records and stuff but because I'm still out there doing it, nearly 50 years on, working hard and staying in the public eye, a whole new generation is aware of who I am and – more importantly – what I do. Others have come and gone in the business but here I am, despite all the changes in fashion and music, still showing up on the likes of 'The Late Late Show'. You wouldn't believe the reaction I get from all the young girls when I play at a wedding. They all seem to know the songs and always insist on telling me that their mothers love me.

In the midst of it all I've tried to lead as normal a life as possible. On a different scale, there were people like Elvis who couldn't leave his room without being surrounded by his managers, agents and all those hangers-on. He may have decided himself that he wanted to be treated in that way but that's no way to live your life, if you ask me. While my day-to-day life is fairly ordinary, I must admit that I love it when people stop me on the street. I'm often asked if it bothers me that I'm recognised everywhere I go and my answer is always the same – it will bother me when it stops.

Sometimes I'll be out walking with Judy and I'll see this couple nudging each other as they approach me. The more conservative ones are often too embarrassed to pretend they recognise me but I'm always tuned in to that and I'll go out of my way to wave and say hello to them, just for the laugh. Others will be less shy about approaching me and have no qualms stopping me to ask if I remember playing such and such a ballroom in Athy back in 1965 or whenever. I'm even recognised by Irish holidaymakers in Spain, which I always love. It's great too, when I'm flying out to Malaga and I'll know all the Aer Lingus staff from my various travels down through the years. Judy still doesn't mind the attention I attract and never gets jealous at all. She has always accepted it but it's been less easy on the kids, particularly when they were going through tough times.

These days I'm enjoying my role as a doting granddad. As my first grandchild – so far, anyway – Benjamin is a great source of joy to Judy and me and we love him to bits. Sarah stayed at home to look after him and be a full-time mother while her son was very young and I respect her for this. I believe that, whenever possible, it is important for at least one parent to be at home when you have young children. I have precious childhood memories of my mother bringing me to school and being there for me when I arrived home every single day. My own children had the benefit of Judy being a loving and dedicated full-time mother who was always there for them in every way. These days, however, the norm is for little children to be brought to crèches early in the morning and picked up by one or the other parent late in the evening. By the time they get home, the parents are in bits from working all day and haven't got the energy to give their child much time or affection. I can relate to that from when I was almost constantly touring and my kids were small. As I discovered then, there is no such thing as quality time in the evening. I've always believed that quality time can only happen during the day, when you're there to witness a child's developmental milestones as they occur: the first steps, the first words, the first tooth and so on.

I recognise, however, that life isn't perfect and sometimes you can become a parent when you are not expecting to. If that happens couples may have huge mortgages to pay and find themselves under a lot of financial pressure. I fully understand that, in these circumstances, both parents may feel pushed into working out of sheer economic necessity and I wouldn't be critical of them in the least. But if a couple consciously decide to have a baby, they need to stop and think about what will happen if both parents go back to work after the child is born. It may sound old-fashioned, but I believe that the woman should stay at home if the man is earning enough money to pay all the bills. And while feminists mightn't agree with me, man has historically hunted and provided for his family down through the ages. You don't generally see men flocking round a new-born baby in a pram. The girls will all be making a fuss wanting to pick the baby up and give it a cuddle – most girls are maternal by nature. The fella, on the other hand, doesn't want to hold the bloody baby – he might just say, "Oh, that's a lovely baby", or something along those lines, but that would be about it. Even on a practical, back-to-basics level, it doesn't make sense for a man to stay at home with the child. After all, a man can hardly breastfeed a baby every few hours or so, can he? The woman is the chief nurturer in every family – that's just the way the world is made.

I think it's very unfair on a child not to have the mother at home, particularly when a couple deliberately sets out to have a baby. It's easy to blame society for forcing both parents out into the workplace but in many cases it's because some women want to have it all – they want the baby and they want the successful career. On the surface it may seem like they can have it both ways but I believe they are taking a big risk in terms of the child's development and happiness. I had that type of happiness growing up because my mother was always there for me. We may not have had a lot of money, but I remember the sense of security that having my mother at home gave me. My father adored my mother for that – he loved her for it until the day he died.

Having said all that, my heart goes out to young couples starting out today, with or without children. They're under so much financial pressure, especially when it comes to desperately trying to get a leg up on the property ladder. It's hard to believe that Ireland has one of the highest percentages of home ownership in the EU. Unless you can completely afford to buy a house at today's prices, I'm not entirely sure that it's a good idea to put yourself in hock to a building society or a bank for the next 30 years. If I was in my 20s or 30s, I wouldn't relish the prospect of paying into a big mortgage until I was in my 50s and perhaps not earning as much money as I used to.

I think Irish people have developed something of an obsession with property in recent years. Everywhere I go they're talking about rising mortgage interest rates, the evils of stamp duty and how much their house has increased in value. I was very interested in property long before the Celtic Tiger turned it into the national talking point that it is today. My starting point was when I bought my first house on Leeson Park in the '60s shortly after I met Judy. Even on our first date, I dragged the poor girl all the way out to Sutton to see a building site, just because I wanted to show her the lovely houses that were going up in Offington Park. I used to change houses like people change cars. I might just be driving along and spot a house for sale and that would be it – I'd have to go and have a look around it. When I think back on it, my interest in property wasn't a good thing for my family and I definitely think that we moved house too often. We first lived in Leeson Park, followed by Sutton, Churchtown, Terenure, Rathgar, Knocklyon and then Rathmines. I loved living in Rathdown Park, which was a fabulous area and the boys were able to attend Terenure College.

Most of these houses would be worth an absolute fortune at today's prices. Regrettably, I always traded up and didn't keep any of them as investment properties. I couldn't afford to at the time anyway. I always hated the idea of borrowing or being tied down to a mortgage, particularly because of the unstable business I was in. If I had been in a profession, where I'd be guaranteed a good income for the rest of my life, then I wouldn't have minded taking out a mortgage. However, the way the entertainment industry went, I never knew whether or not I'd still have work in six months' time. The cabaret scene saved many of us from having to revert to day jobs but even then I knew that wouldn't last forever. The Christmas show places like Clontarf Caste and the Braemor Rooms used to put on every year, for five or six weeks, are all gone now. It's an incredibly insecure business to be in, even at my level where I'm perceived to be one of the most commercially successful performers on the scene.

My aversion to taking out a mortgage meant that I'd always wait for the property I was living in to increase in value. Then I'd cash in on the equity and trade up, time and time again. The last house we lived in as a family was in Temple Gardens in Rathmines. It was a superb property in a beautiful area but Judy didn't like it there. It was nothing to do with the house or the neighbourhood but more down to the fact that it was where we were living when we were having all that trouble with Richard. The house had bad memories for us so we decided to move. I'd be a rich man if I still had that house today – it must be worth about €10 million! At that stage, the kids were all doing their own thing so we decided we would downsize. We bought a lovely top floor apartment in Terenure around five years ago. This means that when we head over to our place in Spain, we can simply shut the door behind us and not have to worry about maintaining gardens or anything like that.

The price of houses is a big problem though. It doesn't affect me anymore because my days of buying property are over for good but as a father it certainly concerns me that none of my children have yet been in a position to buy a place of their own. It's okay for parents to give a dig out when you've one or two children, but it's very tough in a situation like ours when you have five kids and they all want to buy houses. The reality is that they're adults now and Judy and I have got to think of ourselves and our own future. I'd naturally like to do what I could to help them financially if they were trying to get a place but I wouldn't be in a position to just buy them all houses. Hard as it is to tell them that they're more or less on their own when it comes to buying a property, I think my kids respect where I'm coming from on this.

I've never lived to a very high standard from the point of view of spending money. I often see people doing well in their jobs and making good money. Then their salaries go up, which is great, but they go out and start buying bigger houses and bigger cars, completely negating the pay rise they've just been given. She may be driving a convertible Mercedes; he's driving the latest S-Class or BMW. To them, it's all about prestige and how high they can climb up the social ladder. Behind the flash lifestyle, they probably have to work harder than ever to sustain it. In reality, many of them can't afford to live like that in the first place and are up to their eyes in debt. In Ireland today, I imagine there's quite a lot of poverty behind the lace curtains and rich lifestyles.

I'm always bemused to see myself described in the newspapers as a "millionaire crooner" or something along those lines. When journalists ask me if I'm rich, I always respond that you're a millionaire if you have your health, if you can continue doing what you love best – in my case, singing and performing – and if you have the love of your wife and family. If you apply this criteria to assessing my wealth, then I consider myself to be rich. I don't like it when people speculate about how much I'm worth financially but that's just typical of what you have to put up with when you're in showbusiness. Now that I'm getting older, I worry that I may not always have my health in the future to allow me to continue performing, not just because it's how I make my money, but because I adore it so much.

Young people who've taken out 100 per cent mortgages must be doing a lot of worrying now as well. It looks like they could easily end up in negative equity. At least the Government has finally moved to abolish stamp duty for first-time buyers which should help my five out a bit. The powers that be should also change the stamp duty bands for people wanting to trade up. I don't see why the tax is on the entire price of the property. It should only be on the amount above the thresholds. There are other things that could be done, too. I think the practice of developers sitting on land banks for years is immoral and the Government should look at making it illegal. Of course I'm 100 per cent behind anything that makes it easier for my kids to get their own properties. As a father, I'd naturally love them all to be settled. Maybe Pat Kenny could dedicate a special 'Late Late Show' to the issue – I'd be happy to appear!

NINETEEN

The Importance of Being Irish

I recently confessed to a serious addiction, one that I have carried with me since the early '60s. My confession was made in a very public manner, from the stage of Vicar Street in Dublin, in front of a sold-out audience. Half-way through the show, I stood before my fans and declared: "I have something to confess to you all tonight: I'm on drugs and have been for over 45 years. As I stand here before you, I am high."

In case my remarks were misconstrued, I immediately added: "You are all my drug, playing in front of you tonight makes me high."

Joking aside, it's no exaggeration to say that I'm addicted to performing. There is nothing like the feeling you get playing in a fantastic venue like Vicar Street or the Gleneagle Hotel in Killarney, knowing that all these people have paid around €25 or €30 each to come and hear you sing. Some of them will have followed me faithfully since I started out with the Miami. I know many of them will have had to pay for babysitters and some of the women will have got themselves dolled up especially for the occasion. If my fans go to all of this trouble for me, then I always have to give them my best. I love the immediacy of the relationship you develop with an audience. Even though I just do it in the spirit of the show, I often look straight into the eyes of a woman when I'm singing a romantic ballad, as if the words were written especially for her. It's a lovely connection to have with people. There's one woman in particular who comes to mind. There was film footage of me shot in the mid-60s at the Olympia Ballroom in Waterford where I'm holding this young girl's hand as I sing to her. RTÉ managed to trace this same woman 20 years later when they were making a documentary about me and I was filmed once again holding her hand and singing to her. It was a great piece of television.

I never eat before a show and I'm always starving when I come off stage. If I'm playing in Dublin, I love to go for a good curry after a gig – it's my favourite dish. I've never needed alcohol to calm my nerves before a show or to wind down afterwards. While in the past I didn't drink at all, these days I might have the occasional glass of wine, but never if I'm driving. I don't believe in drinking and driving and that includes just having one drink. Can you imagine how you'd feel if you knocked someone down and killed them? Perhaps that one drink may have slowed you down just a fraction and affected your ability to react at that crucial moment. I was in favour of the introduction of mandatory breath testing and would welcome an outright ban on drinking and driving, full stop. Unlike the older generation who are stuck in their ways, I think young people today are less likely to take their car with them if they're drinking.

When I'm on my way home from a gig late at night, I can hardly recognise the Dublin I grew up in. Sometimes it's completely out of control. I was driving through the city centre one night a few years ago, after playing in Vicar Street, and I couldn't believe all the drunken young people I saw spilling out of the pubs and clubs and behaving in a disgraceful manner. It made me worry about the young women in particular. I wish they could see themselves in that state, not only the way they were dressed but also how they were carrying on. I saw them staggering out onto the road and wondered how they weren't killed by a car. As I mentioned earlier, I've always told my sons to respect women as they are all potential wives and mothers. I feel it's sad that many girls have to behave the way they do in order to have a good time. If they don't have respect for themselves, how can they expect others to respect them?

I'm always amazed when I hear young people say: "I'm going drinking tonight and I'm gonna get locked out of me head." I mean, my son, Joseph, was born with a mental handicap through no fault of his own, whereas these people are talking about drinking so much that they're virtually making themselves mentally handicapped. These youngsters are deliberately setting out to alter their state of mind. In the process, they're falling all over the place and getting sick everywhere. They are willingly and knowingly damaging their perfectly healthy brains.

When my own kids were growing up, I tried to warn them of the dangers of excessive drinking. I used to tell them that what you do to your body when you're young affects you in later life. I'd say things like: "If you start drinking and smoking when you're in your teens, what sort of physical state is your body going to be in when you're in your 40s or 50s? The bottom line is if you abuse your body when you're young, you're going to eventually pay a price for it."

In Judy's opinion, I probably went on too much about it. She felt that I might be planting ideas in their minds about alcohol that would have the opposite effect on them. Fortunately it didn't. I could see Judy's point though. I think all my children took my advice on board and drinking thankfully never became an issue in the family.

The drink culture has always been part of Ireland's social fabric, even back in the ballroom days when the men would go to the pubs before heading to a dance. While I witnessed many drunken fights in the '60s it was nothing like the violence you read about today in places like O'Connell Street or Dame Street. There was certainly no such thing as young people being attacked just for the sake of being attacked while they were on their way home late at night. I'm always concerned when I hear stories about some poor guy on the ground being kicked by a bunch of thugs for no reason because it makes me worry for the safety of my own children. From what I've heard, these type of incidents are generally alcohol related. Drink seems to drive some people wild.

I strongly believe it was a mistake to change our licensing laws, allowing pubs and night clubs to serve booze into the early hours of the morning. I've heard more stories about violent fights since the pub hours were extended. Even going on what my own kids tell me, there is plenty of anecdotal evidence to show that violent incidents have increased dramatically since then. I was a big supporter of Michael McDowell's proposals for café bars, as they have in continental Europe. Predictably, it was met with uproar from the publicans who wanted to protect their vested interests, but I thought it was a great plan. The idea that people can socialise in a place where drink is not the focal point has to be a good one. In other European countries you can go to a café bar and perhaps have a meal or a glass of wine. I've been living part-time in Spain for the past 26 years and there are bars everywhere but I've never seen the displays of public drunkenness that are so prevalent here. That's because the emphasis is on socialising and not simply getting drunk. I'd love to see our licensing laws completely liberalised to break the grip of the super-pubs and nightclubs.

Despite the worsening crime culture, I'm still proud to be a Dubliner and I passionately love my native city. You should never blame a city for its problems, which are generally caused by a minority of bad apples. I think the guards have started to do a good job now as well, even though they let the rise in crime catch them by surprise in the past. I'd love it if the police were given extra powers to deal with criminals but I know this will only be effective if they have the backing of the judiciary. I think we should adopt something like the 'three strikes and you're out' policy for jailing repeat offenders that they have in certain states in America. We need a 'get tough' approach to crime in cities like Dublin and Limerick and we must send out a clear message that if you're going to persist in breaking the law, you can't say you weren't warned. Even if my own children were in trouble with the law, I would expect them to face up to the consequences of their actions under the three strikes system.

The 'softly, softly' approach simply doesn't work, even on a more basic level when it comes to discipline in the home. If children misbehave, you need to issue them with a warning and then give them a second chance, but I think it's really important that parents follow up on a threat if the bad behaviour persists. I have to admit that it was left Judy to do most of the disciplining when my kids were small because I was away so much. I probably let them away with more than I should have because I didn't want to come down too heavy on them in the short periods of time we had together. I was definitely too soft on them and in hindsight I was far too giving. It wasn't a case that I gave them money all the time but my kids never wanted for anything materially, be it the latest trainers or designer jeans. I grew up in a working-class family so I think I wanted to give my children everything that I never had as a child. This was the wrong thing to do, of course, but that's the way I saw it at the time.

I believe there is an obvious solution to the twin dangers of anti-social behaviour and alcohol in modern Ireland – sport. I think that young people drink because, quite often there is nothing for them to do but hang around. If instead the Government were to offer young people an alternative lifestyle by providing state-of-the-art sporting facilities in every community in Ireland, I'm sure the results would speak for themselves. This country has been awash with money for over a decade and I can't for the life of me understand why no politician has pushed for massive spending on sport. The GAA is a fantastic organisation in terms of encouraging young people to participate in sport from an early age but its influence is not as widely felt in some urban areas and the Government needs to fill this gap. It's great to see young people joining sports clubs and taking part in competitions. My own kids used to play regularly in the badminton hall on Whitehall Road in Terenure and it was a fabulous outlet for them. The thing is, many of these sporting clubs have small bars and cafés in them. Wouldn't it be so much preferable to hear a young person saying: "I'm going up to the club tonight to take part in that competition and I'll meet you for a drink in the bar later." This is putting the emphasis on the sport rather than alcohol. Maybe if there were more publicly accessible golf courses, swimming pools and basketball facilities, it would lead to a noticeable reduction in public drunkenness. That's the way I see it, anyway.

I've always liked sport myself. When I started going to Spain after we got married, I tried water-skiing and instantly took to it. It's a great way to keep fit and once you master standing up for the first time, you'll never look back. Conditions in Ireland aren't always great for it of course because of our weather. These days, I still water-ski in Spain when the water is warm enough. I also became interested in karate when I was in my 20s and found it a fantastic form of exercise. I never joined a club or took part in competitions. I had a private instructor who'd come round to the house and put me through my paces. Karate is a brilliant skill to learn, although it can be dangerous in the wrong hands.

Outside of music, golf has always been my major passion. Being a non-drinker, it provides me with a great social outlet and helps keep me fit. Sometimes golf allows me to mix business with pleasure. In the past few years I've been invited to provide the entertainment on golf trips to Spain organised by Sean Skehan of Killester Travel. The main emphasis of the holiday is on golf but I get to perform maybe three or so gigs over there with the band during the week and all our expenses are looked after. It's always a great trip.

I feel so proud to be Irish every time I go on one of these golf trips as I meet wonderful people from all over the country, be it Cork, Limerick, Dublin, Kerry or Donegal. I get to have great chats with them about the showband era and they reminisce about the time they saw me play in such and such a ballroom during the Miami days or whenever. When I'm abroad, I always feel an instant connection with other Irish people. The camaraderie on those trips is just fantastic and it's great participating in any competitions that are organised as part of the holiday. Sil Fox and Finbar Furey take part as well. We're often put on separate teams and compete against each other. Finbar's definitely the best golfer out of the three of us although I'm well able to hold my own against Sil. I'm very competitive by nature and I always love it when our team wins. Sean Skehan jokes that he doesn't like it when that happens because he prefers it when his paying guests take the prize!

The thing I love about Ireland is that we are such a small country. No matter where we're from, we all pretty much look the same, listen to the same radio stations and watch programmes like the 'Late Late'. In order words, we have so much in common, whether we live in Sligo, Waterford or Kildare. You might have to drive 185 miles to go from Dublin to Killarney, but once you arrive you'll notice that the only discernable difference between the people is their accent. In a country the size of England you'll find that people up north in cities such as Liverpool and Manchester are very different to their counterparts down south in places like London – different attitudes, different ways of thinking and different ways of going on. America is even more diverse because of its size. I often feel that we're really lucky to be living in a small, intimate country like Ireland.

Golf keeps me sane when I'm not working. I hate it when I'm not busy because I have such a love of entertaining people. I think people know what to expect when they come to see a Dickie Rock show. Paul Harrington sang about the 'Rock 'n' Roll Kids' and that's exactly how I see myself – a Rock 'n' Roller at heart. These days I'm still recording albums. Unlike some artists of my generation who have reinvented themselves in recent years, I intend to simply keep recording the type of songs I have become associated with. Joe Dolan did an album of songs by all these modern singers – called, appropriately enough, 'Joe's Nineties' – and it went very well for him. Tom Jones did something similar a few years earlier. His record company probably thought that this would be a good way of reaching a new audience although Joe was doing great anyway.

Joe's a lovely guy and we always have a laugh about old times any time we meet up. We got to know each other through the showband scene and we go a long way back. I remember one time I went on a date with a girl that Joe had been out with a couple of times. I got his blessing first, of course, and he had no problem with it. He told me she was a lovely person and recommended that I should give her a call. I had to drive all the way down to Mullingar to go to the pictures with her. Her name was Carmel and she was a beautiful girl but that was the only time we ever went out. I think the distance would have been a problem. Mullingar was a long way to travel for a date in those days!

Carmel isn't the only woman that myself and Joe have in common. He often jokes that he could have ended up marrying Judy instead of me. The fact is that he did meet her first. By amazing coincidence he happened to be in the Ierne Ballroom on the same night I met Judy. I found out later that he had chatted to her earlier that evening, before I ever laid eyes on her. He's incredibly fond of Judy and has great time for her. These days when I talk to Joe he never fails to remind me that he saw my wife first. When he says that I always laugh and tell him: "That may be true, Dolan, but got I there first and I'm the one she married."

Sometimes, I suppose, when you're doing well, that's the time to give your career a kick. I love the fact that Joe's been in the business as long as I have and he's still phenomenally popular. He has chosen some great songs to perform down through the years and I still think he's one of the most unique sounding vocalists around today. While my style of music hasn't changed much over the years, I'm always amazed at my apparent ability to appeal to a younger audience. I recently performed a gig in aid of a cystic fibrosis charity in the Four Seasons Hotel and you'd want to see all these young, beautiful women flocking to the front of the stage. It just goes to prove that it's what comes from the stage that matters, not the age of the performer.

Although the days of playing six or seven nights a week are long gone for me I'd probably still be up for it. After regular cabaret work started to dry up in the '90s, I found myself with more time on my hands. In some ways this has been great and Judy and I can spend more time together in Spain, where we have a very nice lifestyle. But I rarely turn down the opportunity to come back to Ireland to do a gig, be it a summer festival in Killarney, a one-off special in Vicar Street, weddings or a corporate event.

In fact, corporate work accounts for the majority of my earnings these days and I've played at some lavish events in the past few years. Only recently myself and my band were flown to Italy to play at a birthday party for an Irish businessman. We were put up in a five star hotel in Venice and treated extremely well. There were around 80 guests at the party and we all had a terrific night. I also do a lot of charity work for causes that are close to my heart, such as the annual Dickie Rock Golf Classic. Weddings are another lucrative part of the business and I'm asked to perform at them from time to time. We played one in Wicklow recently and the speeches dragged on for so long that we didn't take to the stage until just before midnight. I was a bit worried about the lads in the band having to hang around for so long but what could we do? This was a very special day for the bride and groom and it wasn't the end of the world if we had to go on a few hours late.

Once we started playing I completely forgot about the wait and we put on a great show. As far as I am concerned, if doing weddings was good enough for Frank Sinatra and Tony Bennett, then it's certainly good enough for Dickie Rock. In fact, I heard that one time, when Sinatra played Dublin, after the show he flew straight to Connecticut where he was booked to do a birthday party – he was apparently getting a million dollars for it! People assume that I charge a fortune to take a wedding booking but I always judge every request on its individual merit. I love playing a good wedding and the challenge for me and the band is to keep everyone on the dance floor for the whole night, if possible. It's funny to think that I didn't even get to perform at my own wedding back in June 1966, as we had to leave the reception early to catch a flight.

There are certain places in Ireland where I seem to be more popular for bookings. My home turf of Dublin has always been good for me and I also continue to enjoy a loyal fan base in Belfast, Cork, Limerick and Kerry. Strangely enough, though, I haven't worked Galway in ages, even though we were regular visitors there during The Miami Showband years. I can't understand it. Maybe there are no suitable venues there for my type of show but Galway seems to have become a blackspot for me, career-wise. I suppose this business can be cyclical, to some extent. There are places in Dublin that I used to play regularly, like the Sallynoggin Inn and the Belgard in Tallaght, but I haven't performed either venue in a long time.

I've no regrets about choosing to remain in Ireland even though the opportunities can sometimes be limited here for a commercial artist. Many showband veterans went on to make a fortune under the bright lights of Vegas and beyond. For me, however, the grass was always greener on home soil. I think I was too much of a home bird at heart. While an international hit single and worldwide recognition would have been nice, I still feel justifiably proud of my contribution to the world of Irish entertainment.

TWENTY

The Rat Pack

During the recent general election campaign, it struck me that entertainers are a bit like politicians. As soon as the public get tired of you, you're finished. Thankfully, this hasn't happened to either myself or Bertie Ahern yet.

I couldn't believe the level of support that was out there for Bertie. The media had him written off but the voters obviously didn't see it that way. I can understand why people didn't go for Enda Kenny, even though I think he's a really nice guy. All his talk about a 'Contract for a Better Ireland' was a bit phoney, if you ask me. If I had been running Fianna Fáil's election campaign I would have come up with the slogan: "Everything is going great – is it worth taking a chance?" The majority of people obviously didn't think it was. I was over in Spain when the election was held and I was raging that I didn't get to vote.

I'm a Fianna Fáil supporter in the same way that I'm Roman Catholic – I simply inherited the tradition from my parents. That said, I've got a brain and a mind of my own and I wouldn't be one to vote out of sheer blind loyalty. If I ever felt that Fianna Fáil were becoming too smug and weren't listening to the people, then I would vote the other way. Otherwise, I'm happy to continue supporting the party in the same way that my parents did. When it comes to politics, I subscribe to the school of thought that says: "If it ain't broke, don't fix it."

I have huge admiration for Bertie Ahern and believe that his 'man of the people' image is genuine and sincere. His opponents often claim that it's all part of an act but I don't agree with them. I can't think of any other country in the world where you could walk into a pub and see the prime minister sitting there with his mates having a pint. It proves what I was saying about Ireland being a very intimate country. Say what you like about our politicians, they are certainly accessible to the public! I've met Bertie a few times in Drumcondra and have always found him to be a very approachable and sociable person. When my mother died, Bertie sent his aide-de-camp to represent him at her funeral, which meant a lot to me. He comes across as being a down-to-earth, ordinary guy but he's well educated and very clever, a fact even acknowledged by the late Charlie Haughey.

I knew Charlie, too, and met him a couple of times over the years. My son, Jason, used to go down to the stables at Abbeville to help out when he was young. People can say what they like about Charlie Haughey but one thing is for certain – his family are absolutely wonderful people, every single one of them. That sort of decency has to come from somewhere and children usually get it from their mother and father. I didn't know Charlie well enough to consider him a friend but it was always apparent to me that his children all loved and respected him. My impression of him was that he was a very charming, intelligent man. In my experience, brilliant people can sometimes do stupid things and instead of going down the correct route, they try to cut corners – that's what lands them in trouble.

I'm not just talking about Charlie Haughey here. Liam Lawlor was another brilliant man who I'd put into that category. In my view, Liam was a very clever individual who simply made some bad decisions. In terms of his ability, he could have been Taoiseach. I knew Liam pretty well and did a few fund raising gigs to support him. He was a big, imposing man, a lovely, decent fella and I liked him very much. Liam often played golf with us and Sil Fox nicknamed him 'Boom Boom Lawlor' because he had such a strong swing and used to hit the ball so far – but not always in the direction he wanted it to go.

There was a lot of stuff written about him in the papers but by the time of his death they still weren't able to nail him, that's how clever Liam was. There's no reason why he couldn't have been leader of the country if life had gone a different way for him. The media may well remember him for planning controversies but those of us who knew the real Liam Lawlor can tell a completely different story. He was the type of character that got things done. I approached him once on behalf of one of the guys in my band who was looking for help in getting a house transfer. Liam took his name and details and said he'd see what he could do. He later invited him to the Dáil to discuss his case and got the matter sorted for him in the end. What struck me at the time was the fact that Liam had nothing to gain by helping my colleague out – he wasn't even living in his constituency. After that, I was always happy to oblige Liam when he asked me to perform at any political fundraising events he was organising. If I could help him out in any way, I'd gladly do it, and vice-versa – that's the way it worked with Liam.

Liam was generally in good form when I met him, despite everything that was going on in his life. We were nearly always in a group so he never discussed the trouble he was in with me or talked about the times when he was sent to prison for not cooperating with the tribunal. I felt very sorry for him when he had to go to jail; the whole thing was very sad.

I played my final round of golf with Liam just a couple of weeks before his tragic death in Moscow. Like everybody else, I was deeply saddened to hear the news and shared the public's contempt for some of the inaccurate media coverage surrounding the circumstances of the accident. I was asked to sing at his funeral by his wife, Hazel, a lovely, decent woman. The newspapers often forget that the wives and children have done nothing wrong and they're the ones who suffer most as a result of irresponsible journalism.

* * * *

I love the fact that Ireland has had a run of great Presidents in recent years. I think we are blessed to have a person of the calibre of Mary McAleese in the Áras. She has a wonderful personality and is a great ambassador for our country. People respond instantly to her because she's such a genuine person. I admire the fact that she is so accomplished academically, yet very grounded when you meet her. I was absolutely flattered to learn from President McAleese herself that she was once a big fan of mine. I was playing golf up at City West and the President just happened to be attending a meeting there that day. I saw her coming down the stairs, dressed in a lovely coat, and I said to her: "Wow, you're looking terrific!"

With that, she smiled and exclaimed "Ah, Dickie – how are you?" Turning to the guard who was with her, she added: "I used to travel all over the North to see this man."

She came over to me and we had a great chat and a bit of banter. She's not only a nice person, she's a lovely looking woman, too.

I thought it was great when she was re-elected in 2004 as the only validly nominated candidate. The fact that there was cross-party support for her to remain on for a second term in office clearly demonstrates her appeal to people of all political persuasions. The only discordant note was sounded by Dana, which was a bit of a joke. Don't get me wrong, Dana's a lovely woman, absolutely gorgeous. I did a show recently with her and I think she's fantastic. We were performing on the same bill at the Helix in DCU. Her voice wasn't what it used to be but her performance was very entertaining. I remember she included an Irish dancing routine as part of her set, which was great. The thing about Dana is that people like her. I believe it's vital that your audience never forgets why they liked you in the first place. I'm sometimes asked if I get tired of playing my old hits, such as 'From the Candy Store on the Corner'. I always reply: "No, I get down on my knees every day and thank God for those songs because they helped make me the success I am today."

Good as Dana is, you can't compare her to President McAleese. Mary McAleese is from an academic background and can walk in any company and talk in any company and we should be very proud of her. I'm not saying we can't be proud of Dana; we can be proud of her for winning the Eurovision but that's as far as it goes for me. Being President of Ireland is another thing completely; it's a different job.

I think the profile of the presidency in Ireland has been boosted since the election of Mary Robinson in 1990 and people now attach more significance to it. I also admire Mary Robinson for how well she represented this country during her tenure, although I was annoyed by the fact that she left the job early to take up her position as United Nations High Commissioner for Human Rights. It left a bit of a bad taste in my mouth. That said, it has been fantastic for Ireland to have had two clever women in Áras an Uachtaráin. Many of our Presidents before them were pretty anonymous by comparison. I think the two Marys succeeded in elevating the position above mere figurehead status.

* * * *

When I think back on the showband era, I realise how hard we all had to work to earn our popularity. It meant being on the road constantly, away from our families and friends. When we weren't performing live, we were in a recording studio trying to produce a hit single. We may have had success but, unlike today, our success didn't come easily. Anyone, it seems, can have a hit record in the charts these days and it annoys me when I see mediocrity passing itself off as talent. I feel the same way about politicians who don't do their jobs properly. I can't understand how they still seem to get re-elected.

These days, you don't have to be able to sing to have success in the pop business. Boyzone were huge, even though most of them hadn't a note in their heads. The thing is, though, they could dance and they looked great and these seemed to be the only ingredients needed for stardom. If you're lucky enough to be good-looking and are able to get by with that type of setup, then fair enough. However, these boy bands and similar fabricated pop creations tend to have a fairly limited shelf life. Professional performers like Frank Sinatra were able to sustain their careers for decades because they were masters of their craft. Could you imagine a boy band lasting in the business as long as Joe Dolan, Red Hurley, Tony Kenny or myself? It just isn't going to happen. These guys are right to cash-in on their success while it's there because it certainly won't last for them the way it did for us. Some of them have gone for another bite of the cherry with groups like Take That and The Spice Girls reforming recently. There was even talk this year of Boyzone getting back together.

To me, singing and performing is a career. I have approached my chosen profession in the same way I would any other job. If I had continued on as a welder, I would have wanted to be the most skilled welder possible, the same as if I had chosen a career in law or accountancy. I don't just sing songs for the sake of singing them: I carefully choose the songs that suit my voice and try to put my individual interpretation or stamp on them. Anyone considering entering the music business today needs to look in the mirror and ask themselves some honest questions. For starters, do they have something to offer? Can they play their instrument well? If they don't believe it themselves, then they shouldn't listen when people tell them: "God, you're great, you can sing better than Dickie Rock or Joe Dolan." Unless they can convince themselves that they have something of worth to offer, they should do themselves a favour and consider another career path.

Some people say that the judges in shows like 'You're A Star' or the 'X-Factor' are hard on the kids and put them under a lot of pressure but you have to remember that the contestants are taking all that on themselves. In some ways the criticism can help them realise that they don't have what it takes to succeed in the music business and it will save them wasting their time and energy.

The Eurovision Song Contest is now a disaster area when it comes to sourcing new talent. No longer is it the prestigious event it once was. It seemed to lose its way during the 1990s. When I represented Ireland in the Eurovision in 1966, the competition was simply about the quality of the song and the strength of the performance. It launched the careers of fantastic groups like ABBA, as well as singers such as Celine Dion and closer to home, our own Johnny Logan, Linda Martin and Dana. Now the whole thing just looks like a circus with high production values – it's no longer a competition for songs.

The fact that we don't even have a proper National Song Contest anymore is a good indication of the way the Eurovision has gone. Ireland had great success in the Eurovision during its glory years. I was hugely surprised that Johnny Logan didn't go on to have a more successful career. I mean, you hear that he's popular in places like Germany and all of that, but I really felt that he could have been an Irish Elvis – he had a great look, fantastic voice and wrote good songs. For some reason, however, it didn't really happen for him, despite his genuine talent and natural star quality. I've met Johnny many times and have always found him to be a very personable fella. I think if he had been based in the UK with some hot shot agent behind him, he could have been huge. He missed the boat, really. He's had a comeback of sorts recently, with the remix of his 'Hold Me Now' single and the McDonald's commercials and I genuinely hope he does well out of it.

Most young people will be familiar with Linda Martin from her time as a judge on 'You're A Star' and won't remember her from her days as a singer with the popular group, Chips. It was fantastic when she won the Eurovision in 1992 in Malmo, Sweden, with the Johnny

Logan song, 'Why Me?' Linda is a great lady and I really like the fact that she has her feet firmly on the ground. She did a great job when she was involved with 'The Lyrics Board', which was a brilliant programme – I can't understand why RTÉ took it off. I was on the show with Linda many times and had a wonderful time doing it.

Another great girl in Irish entertainment is Twink, a very talented woman who I have a lot of time for. She has put an incredible amount of work and energy into those pantos over the years and they have all been very professional productions. Twink is such a showbizzy type character who really speaks her mind. Personally, I get on great with her but I think she can be her own worst enemy sometimes. That infamous phone message she left her ex-husband, which ended up on the internet, was an unfortunate incident, but in fairness to Twink, it didn't seem to bother her that much. I haven't seen her since that happened but I was sad to hear that her marriage had failed. Without wishing to know the rights and wrongs of the situation, it must have been a tough time for Twink and her daughters. I think it always hits the woman harder when a marriage breaks down.

The Irish entertainment world has certainly produced some great characters and talented performers. I'm proud to still be a part of it. I was recently discussing some future project ideas with my new manager Jackie Johnston, who I moved over to at the start of 2007. I told him that, as a lifelong fan of Frank Sinatra, I'd love to put my own version of the Rat Pack together. I could team up with Red Hurley and Joe Dolan and we could call ourselves something like The Three Amigos. Maybe we could expand it even further and bring people like Twink, Finbar Furey and Sil Fox on board. We'd take the production on the road and play all over the country. One thing is for certain – it would be one hell of a show!

TWENTY-ONE

It's Still Working

When I first started out in this business almost five decades ago, I remember trying to make sense of it all as I stood in front of the mirror, the sweat from that night's show still running down my face and creeping down the back of my shirt. I certainly didn't see Elvis Presley looking back at me, or Cliff Richard for that matter – just plain old Richard Rock from Cabra West, an average looking skinny kid with sticky-out ears.

Yet, just moments earlier, there had been scenes of near hysteria as hoards of beautiful women vied for my attention, packed in rows of ten, twenty, thirty deep in front of the stage. Every move I made seemed to set off a chain reaction of high-pitched screams, drowning out the sound of the music.

"We love ya, Dickie!" they'd shriek, much to the bemusement of my band mates. I even had to position my feet to make sure I wasn't pulled off the stage and into the sea of waving arms below. Getting that type of reaction from an audience was nothing short of exhilarating – but it was also inexplicable. I fully accept that the person you see photographed on the cover of this book is probably Ireland's most unlikely pin-up.

Writing this book has made me realise that I have had an extraordinary life, both personally and professionally. I still find it hard to believe that I've been singing and performing for the best part of 50 years. I'm often amused to see myself described in newspapers as a "showband legend", even though I'd like to think that my career has managed to transcend that glorious era of Irish entertainment. As flattering as it sounds, being elevated to legendary status in the eyes of the media brings its own problems. It can sometimes result in myth replacing fact and rumour replacing truth.

Above everything else, I consider my family to be my greatest personal achievement. I was extremely fortunate to marry a woman who gave everything of herself to her children and to me. We've had our share of heartache and tragedy – like any other family – but also have precious memories of countless happy occasions. Sometimes family life can drive you crazy and you get mad with your kids but you love them because they're part of you. Like everything else, you have to take the good with the bad. I can safely say that, despite everything we've been through together as a family, we're stronger and more united than ever – that has to count for something.

Most parents would like to see their children in successful careers but I genuinely don't care what mine do. As long as they are out there in the world, being responsible and making a life for themselves, I'm happy. I couldn't care less if they were sweeping the streets once they were doing an honest day's work. I'd be as proud of them doing that as I would be if they became doctors, surgeons, carpenters, lawyers, bricklayers.... It doesn't matter to me as long as they're happy and safe. Naturally, I'd love all my children to meet their perfect partners and end up in a marriage as happy and fulfilled as my own. My son, John, is the only one to get hitched so far. I'm extremely proud to say that he's married to Ruth Mulligan, a beautiful woman from Kilcock, County Kildare, and the pair of them are madly in love. I had the honour of playing at their wedding, something I hope to get to do for my other children in the future.

As it is, all my kids are doing great right now. Richard seems to have been bitten by the showbiz bug and is still riding high on the success of his starring role in 'Dancehall Q's and Hucklebuck Shoes'. John runs his own business and has a café/coffee shop in Dublin, which is going very well for him. Jason's involved in numerous different business ventures and is essentially working for himself as well. Sarah's doing a fantastic job as a full-time mother raising her son, Benjamin, who's turning into a great little fella altogether. My youngest son, Peter, is involved in the hospitality industry and is working in a restaurant. He would like to open his own place someday and I really think he has what it takes to realise this ambition.

It's great when I play a gig these days and the whole family comes along to see me. From an early age, all my kids would have been aware that their dad was famous and I remember them being there for some of the shows I did at the Gaiety and the Olympia during the '80s when they were that bit older. They still come to see me when I play Vicar Street and I'm always so pleased to see them there, this beautiful young woman and these fine young men I am proud to call my children.

* * * *

I always get nervous before a show but I think this is a good thing because it stops me from becoming complacent or taking my audience for granted. The way I see it is that this could be my 50th gig of any given year but it could be their first time seeing me. I mean, because I've been around so long, there is a certain expectation to be met. Sometimes I'll have mothers at my concerts who are bringing their daughters along to see me. The mother may well have been building me up beforehand, so it's important that I don't let her down in the eyes of her daughter. I need to make sure that the daughter will turn to her mother after a show and say: "You were right Ma, he is as good as you said he was." That puts me under constant pressure to perform at my best but it's the type of pressure that I thrive on. It doesn't matter if I'm in a bad mood that day or if there's something bothering me – the audience doesn't want to know about that. All they care about is being entertained and getting a value for money show. Being in the business for such a long time means nothing if you still can't produce the goods – you're only as good as your last show, as they say. Even though I had my first hit record in the charts 43 years ago, I always have to go out there, night after night, and prove myself, again and again.

I still experience that transformation from Dickie Rock, the introverted person, into Dickie Rock, the confident performer, every time I walk out on stage – we're still two completely separate entities. I did a gig recently and this woman came up to me afterwards and said: "Dickie, that was fantastic, you were terrific tonight. You looked like a 29-year-old man up there, all slim and looking great." Needless to say, I was flattered to hear that but in many ways I genuinely feel that young again when I'm performing. I enjoy it more than I ever did and I simply can't wait to get on stage. One of the biggest thrills for me is knowing that I am making people feel good when I sing and perform – getting paid for it as well is a bonus, of course!

When I took my first tentative steps as a singer in the local church choir, little did I realise back then that young Richard Rock, the boy soprano, would go on to tread the boards of the London Palladium, represent Ireland in the Eurovision and pack out ballrooms and dancehalls the length and breadth of Ireland. I consider myself privileged to still be doing what I love most – singing and performing. Don't think for a second that I am retiring from the business, simply because I'm taking stock of my life and career with this book – rest assured, I have no intention of stopping and thank God I still have the health to allow me to continue performing. The secret, I believe, is keeping fit, eating well and getting plenty of rest. Recently, I've taken up callinetics which, along with golf, helps keep me in shape. While I'm not as young as I used to be, I have no problem getting up on stage and giving it everything I've got for two hours solid. I've absolutely no intention of retiring from showbusiness. As long as I have my health, I won't be the one to decide when I should quit – my fans will. When people stop coming to my shows and no longer book me for corporate events or weddings, then I'll know the time is right to call it a day.

Nobody is more astonished at my longevity in the business than myself. I've never taken my success for granted and don't intend to in the future. The level of my success has been surreal. I often have to question if it really happened. Can it be possible that The Miami Showband were fêted with such overwhelming adulation back in the '60s? Did all those women proclaim themselves to be heartbroken the day I married Judy? Did I have all those Number One hits in the Irish charts? Am I one of the longest surviving performers of the showband era? The whole journey seems like an amazing dream sometimes. When I was training to be a welder, I could never have imagined the direction my life was going to take. And when I eventually got my break in music, who could have predicted that it would last for the best part of five decades?

When I eventually have to stop performing, for health reasons or otherwise, I will look back on a life full of extraordinary experiences. As a long serving member of Ireland's showbusiness establishment, I would like to be remembered for being professional at all times and as someone who never took his success or audience for granted. I will feel completely fulfilled as a performer if people say things like: "Dickie Rock, sure that fella was a class act, a pure pro." I simply couldn't ask for more than that.

More importantly, however, is how I will be judged as a father and a husband. At the beginning of this book, I wrote how I considered my own father to have been a complete success in his life, in that he had succeeded as a man, a father and a husband. While his were certainly big shoes to fill, I hope my children and wife will look at me in a similar way when I come to the end of my life. These days, I'm looking forward to happy times with my family and plan to make the best of the time I've left with Judy, with whom I've been through so much.

I like to think of myself as a positive person but sometimes it's hard not to dwell on the sad events that have occurred in my life: my youngest brother being killed; my first-born son being mentally disabled; the heartache I caused Judy; almost losing my son to heroin addiction; the death of my son, Joseph; the inevitable passing of my mother and father. Newspapers sometimes refer to all the tragedies in my life but I don't think that I've experienced any more or less than any other person of my age. The only difference is that you get to read about my personal life in the papers because that's part of the deal when you're in the public eye. For every negative incident in my life, there has been a corresponding positive one: my marriage to Judy; the birth of all my children; the successful career; the love of my friends and family – they're the things to stay focused on.

My mother came to one of my shows the Christmas before she died, accompanied by two nurses. She had a great time and I remember her telling me afterwards, with typical motherly concern: "God, Richard, you were working very hard up there tonight; look at you, you're all sweating and everything."

It was my mother who got me there in the first place. She's the one who tried to get me to learn a musical instrument and, when that failed, encouraged me to join the choir in Cabra West and later the amateur variety group. Without her influence I would probably be on the verge of retiring as a welder today, an honourable profession in its own right, I'm sure, and one I would have loved – but nowhere near as exciting as the world of showbusiness. I'm certain my mother got great pleasure out of my success given the huge part she played in it.

While my father wasn't musically inclined, my success was a tremendous source of pride to him. When I look back to 1966, at the height of my popularity, I was still living at home on Dingle Road in Cabra with my parents. My father used to come into the kitchen, with a bemused smile on his face, telling me that there was a crowd of young women hanging around our front gate. It never used to bother him and I think he found the whole experience very enjoyable. It's extremely gratifying for me to know that my parents were alive to witness all the various highlights of my career: my support slot with Cliff Richard in 1961; the number one hit records with the Miami; playing the London Palladium in 1964 with Petula Clarke; my appearances on 'The Late Late Show; my triumphant homecoming after the Eurovision in 1966; the packed-out concerts throughout my career; and, of course – the ultimate highlight – my marriage to Judy. It's such a powerful image for me to think back on my parents when they were still young, living through all of these exciting times in their eldest son's life.

My father and mother loved all their children equally but I'm sure my success as a singer and entertainer gave them a boost during some of the hard times in life. People were always coming up to my parents and telling them that they saw me on the telly the night before, or had heard one of my songs on the radio. They couldn't leave the house without someone enquiring of them: "How's Dickie doing?" This sort of attention was never a source of annoyance to either of them and I think they were proud of me, but in an understated and modest way. They wouldn't have been the type of people to go around bragging about how well any of their children was doing.

* * * *

I recently played a concert at Vicar Street, in Dublin's Liberties, a venue I love for its intimacy and atmosphere. It was one of those gigs when everything felt just right. I was singing well, the musicians in my band were sounding great and it seemed that we couldn't put a foot wrong with the audience. My fans were loving every single minute of it. As I belted out the old classics and perennial crowd favourites, it felt as if I was once again at the peak of my powers. The sense of goodwill emanating from the audience was palpable, with every song greeted with loud applause or cheers of recognition. I loved every minute of the show and could have stayed on stage all night. The feeling I got from performing in front of my home Dublin crowd that evening was every bit as exciting as it had been for me back in the days of The Miami Showband. There were people of all ages in the audience, including many of my diehard fans from the showband days and even earlier, when I first started out with The Melochords. Leaving the stage after my final encore, I was overwhelmed by the response I had received – the feeling was nothing short of euphoric.

I arrived home late that night, absolutely exhilarated from the evening's proceedings. Still on a high after the show, I didn't feel like falling asleep immediately. In my mind, I replayed the Vicar Street gig over and over in my head. I found myself sitting on my bed, suddenly transfixed by the photograph on my locker of my mother and father.

I picked it up and stared at it. God, they looked so well in that picture and I could almost feel their presence. I was thinking about all the good values they had instilled in me throughout my childhood; I was remembering the absolute love and devotion they had for each other throughout their married life and I found myself saying: "Well Mam, well Dad ... I'm still here, still doing it. It's still working for me, you know."